ORCHID SUMMER

JON DUNN

ORCHID SUMMER

In Search of the
Wildest Flowers of
the British Isles

BLOOMSBURY PUBLISHING
LONDON · OXFORD · NEW YORK · NEW DELHI · SYDNEY

BLOOMSBURY PUBLISHING
Bloomsbury Publishing Plc
50 Bedford Square, London, WC1B 3DP, UK

BLOOMSBURY, BLOOMSBURY PUBLISHING and the Diana logo are
trademarks of Bloomsbury Publishing Plc

First published in Great Britain 2018

Copyright © Jon Dunn, 2018
Illustrations by Holly Ovenden

Jon Dunn has asserted his right under the Copyright, Designs and Patents Act,
1988, to be identified as Author of this work

For legal purposes the Acknowledgements on pp. 335–6
constitute an extension of this copyright page

A catalogue record for this book is available from the British Library

Library of Congress Cataloguing-in-Publication data has been applied for

ISBN: HB: 978-1-4088-8088-3; eBook: 978-1-4088-8090-6

2 4 6 8 10 9 7 5 3 1

Typeset by Newgen KnowledgeWorks Pvt. Ltd., Chennai, India
Printed and bound in Great Britain by CPI Group (UK) Ltd, Croydon CR0 4YY

To find out more about our authors and books visit www.bloomsbury.com
and sign up for our newsletters

For Roberta and Ethan, with love

Contents

Orchid Summer locations

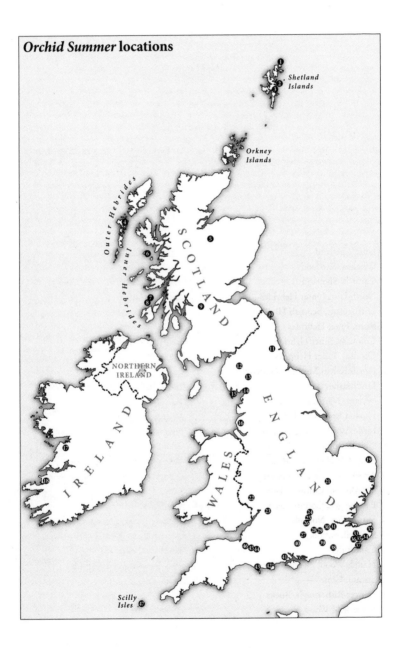

Map

The first orchid of them all

The hill in question was steep, and came at the end of our family walk out of Curry Rivel, across the sheep-pared field that surrounded the Monument, along the damp flank of the saturated Levels and thence back up to the village. It was early April, at the back of a wet and interminable winter, and the walk had been muddy. My dad was in a hurry to get back to the fireside, and my mum to our allotment, where there was digging and work to do. Red Hill was all that stood between us and an afternoon of predictable family life. I was lagging behind my parents as we tackled the incline, scraping thick wedges of Somerset mud onto the tarmac from the soles of my boots. I longed to stay down on the Levels, to see what wildlife I could find. The bubbling calls of curlews were receding as I headed reluctantly homewards.

It was at that moment when everything changed for ever. My mum was calling me from somewhere out of sight, and my head must have lifted in response to her impatient summons. There, high on the grassy bank that rose steeply above the lane, was a lone purple flower. Heedless of the brambles that laced the grass, I scrambled up to it – I knew what I thought it was or, rather, what I dearly wanted it to be. This, surely, was my first orchid.

Nobody shared my love of the natural world – certainly none of my peers, and definitely neither of my parents. I think they were always slightly bemused that it was all I cared about. I found people baffling and school relentless – endless weeks of petty restrictions, rules and incomprehensible lessons. Whatever I could discover in the countryside around our small house, I wanted to identify, to learn everything there was to know about it and, occasionally, to take home with me to marvel at some more. This was tolerated in some instances – half a blackbird eggshell on my bedroom windowsill was fine – and less so on other occasions: for example, my plans to keep slow-worms in my bedroom foundered in their infancy.

My reference materials in those early days were meagre – three volumes of the *Observer's* series, covering butterflies, birds and wildflowers. I devoured their pages, eager to see every species they contained. During our first summer in Curry Rivel, it was the butterflies first and foremost that caught my eye. I suddenly found butterflies wherever I looked. Our garden, so sterile and tame, at least had flaming small tortoiseshells and velvety peacocks on the buddleias, but once I started to explore beyond the village limits, I found countless treasures. I wandered hills shimmering with common blues like fragments of sky at my feet, sought chocolate-brown and burnt-orange gatekeepers defending stretches of hedgerows frosted with pink and white dog roses, and chased the fleet, saffron clouded yellows that eluded my every attempt to catch them racing through fields of red and white clover. In autumn, while I stole apples, pears and plums in abandoned orchards behind wooden gates lost in a choke of blackthorn and brambles, drunken red admirals feasted at my feet on fermenting windfalls carved hollow by drowsy wasps.

As autumn washed into winter, the water in the rhynes that bound the Levels rose inexorably. Soon vast silver sheets covered the fields below the village as far as the eye could see. I became more aware of birds – the Levels pulsed with wildfowl, while snipe exploded in front of my feet as I picked my way through sodden meadows. My usual routes through the fields were often rendered impassable by water, and more than once I relied on the kindness of farmers to lift me over swollen rhynes in the bucket of their diggers. Our garden, meanwhile, briefly hosted redwings, impossibly exotic thrushes for one who had only noticed blackbirds and song thrushes hitherto. School and the short winter daylight meant my wanderings were severely curtailed, and I returned to the *Observer's Book of Wildflowers* for inspiration on the dark evenings while my parents watched the news and I lay on the rug in front of our wood fire.

I yearned for summer and the return of the butterflies. Before they could come, there would be flowers as the world sparked into life once more. I had no idea how scant the coverage of Britain's wildflowers was in the poor little *Observer's* guide. These modest books were my bibles, and I took communion from their pages. My fervour was reserved for one family alone that winter – I read the descriptions of the orchids over and over again, and tried to find out more about them at our local library. I took what little I could glean home with me, like a special pebble brought back from the beach and set on a shelf to be admired daily. Now I knew what our orchids were: part of a vast plant family that ran into thousands of species, they had simple leaves but marvellously complex flowers comprised of three sepals and three petals, with one of those petals usually radically different from its fellows. Looking at illustrations in books, I found them utterly glamorous, so improbable and unlikely to be found in the waterlogged countryside around our little house. I longed to see one – nothing else would do.

When the moment came, on the sides of Red Hill, it had an intensity that I remember vividly to this day. Indeed, even now when I see a new species of orchid, I get a sense of the hypersaturated perception of reality that gripped me that afternoon when I knelt beside this keenly anticipated plant. The leaves were dark, glossy green, and heavily blotched with deep, bruised markings, like leopard spots that had run in the wash. But it was the flower that captured me – held proudly above the leaves by a thick, fleshy stem, the individual blooms were delicate, curving sculptures of a rich, royal purple with a clarity and intensity of colour quite unlike any flower I'd ever seen before. I felt breathless.

In the years to come, I would meet a woman who, in that first moment of our eyes locking, I would know with utter certainty was the one, the person I would love with all my soul, no matter what. I felt blessed and scared all at once. But I knew that feeling from a long time ago – I had felt that physical, visceral impact when I saw my first orchid on the side of a Somerset hill high above the Levels.

My parents had retraced their steps by that point, and were loudly demanding I stop looking at flowers and come back down to the lane to walk home with them. There was, of course, only one thing I could do under the circumstances, torn between the bonds of parental loyalty and the consuming beauty of my first orchid.

I picked it.

With hindsight, I'm not proud of that. At the time, however, it seemed like the sensible thing to do. I thrust the flower into my jacket pocket and scrambled back down to the lane. Now I couldn't wait to get home – I wanted to study my treasure in more detail before I consigned it to be pressed between some sheets of newspaper and a pile of my dad's Dick Francis hardbacks.

Today, sitting in my crofthouse in Shetland while the wind smears rain on the salt-encrusted windows and the day fades, I still have that first early purple orchid. It is a brittle, sad shadow of the beautiful flower it once was on a spring afternoon in Somerset. While the colour may have faded in the intervening years, the love that ignited that day never did. I had been lost to orchids, and this was going to be a lifelong affair.

Years passed. It was only when I was a student living in rural Kent at the foot of the North Downs that I at last found myself in something approaching orchid heaven. Within walking distance of my college were orchids I'd hitherto only dreamed of – in one field alone, interspersed with deep-blue chalk milkwort and the quivering globular heads of quaking grass, I found a plethora of species new to me. Common twayblades and man orchids flanked the way into the field – further uphill were green-winged and early spider orchids. Later there were bee, burnt and pyramidal orchids scattered across the hillside. All this in just one field... Hidden in woods and sheltered valleys were further orchidaceous treasures, rarer still.

I remained in Kent for a decade before heading to Shetland and orchid-studded pastures new. I had long since seen the paltry selection of orchids contained in the venerable *Observer's Book of Wildflowers* in their natural environment, and had graduated to a more comprehensive, colourful field guide – though once I'd settled in Shetland I soon stopped seeing new species. Fully a third of the species native to Britain and Ireland remained strangers to me, or at least in the British Isles themselves. Inevitably, on my travels through Europe I was always on the lookout for orchids.

I determined that something should be done about this, and the idea of a grand adventure coalesced. I would set out to see all of Britain and Ireland's orchid species in the course of one frantic, glorious, kaleidoscopic flowering season. My travels would take me from the very north of Scotland to Cornwall and Kent, out to the west coast of Ireland, deep into East Anglian fens, and to many points in between. I would visit new places, meet people as lost to these flowers as I was, and above all I would see orchids – thousands of them, of all intoxicating shapes, sizes and colours.

There are between fifty and sixty species to be found in Britain and Ireland – the precise number is fluid, depending on factors as mutable as the flowers themselves. Depending on the deliberations of taxonomists, valid species come and go as subspecies are elevated to the giddy heights of full species status in their own right, and what were previously considered good species are downgraded to mere subspecies. Occasionally new species crop up – orchids common on mainland Europe are suddenly discovered here, either colonists or deliberate introductions at the whim and behest of man. Very occasionally, we lose a species altogether – summer lady's-tresses, a delicate white-flowered orchid as alluring as the name suggests, was once found only in a few humid bogs in Hampshire's New Forest. It is there no longer, last seen in 1952, the victim of habitat change through drainage and, damningly, collection by botanists for their reference herbaria.

Mainland Europe can boast many more species than we can – but we do have species unique to our islands, oddities way out of their normal European ranges, and a host of intriguing stories attached to them. An average flowering season will run from late March through to September, but most of these species come and go relatively quickly. I would need to plan my route carefully to ensure I stood a chance of seeing every species. Furthermore, the actual dates on which each orchid flowers depend entirely on the seasons – the severity and rainfall of the preceding winter can dramatically hasten or delay when a given species comes into bloom. I would need to be quick on my feet, and I would need the cooperation of many of Britain's naturalists, my 'eyes on the ground', who would alert me when I needed to travel to see their local specialty.

As I was soon to discover, this was easier said than done. Unlike any other plant, bird, insect or mammal, orchids inspire an unparalleled level of secrecy amongst their observers. Quite why this should be is unclear – but I imagine it's another manifestation of the same orchid magic that has me under its spell. This obsession is part of a grand tradition. Back in the nineteenth century, the British upper and middle classes were gripped by a mania known as 'orchidelirium', when a global network of plant collectors was sending back spectacular tropical orchids to be cosseted in elaborate, purpose-built orchid houses. In the present, Professor Richard Bateman, Britain's preeminent orchid scientist, introduced me to a more contemporary expression for those of us obsessed with these entrancing flowers – he wryly referred to us all as 'orchidiots'.

I liked that. I could recognise the inherent silliness of obsessing over one particular family of plants, but that didn't make my feelings for them any less strong nor the urge to see them all any less compelling. Orchidiots had a self-deprecating tone that appealed to me. I could unashamedly be an orchidiot while

I sought to see all of our native species in the course of one flowering season.

I set about drawing up an itinerary for my travels. The commoner species were straightforward enough and I had plenty of sites for these. The scarcer species and some of the rarer flowers exist in a handful of places – some of these were public knowledge, but others were kept secret, known to the orchid cognoscenti and surprisingly difficult to discover without the right connections. And then there were the really difficult ones. None would be more trying than the mythical and aptly named ghost orchid, seen in Britain on just a handful of occasions since the middle of the nineteenth century. This elusive orchid was feared to be extinct for many years in the late twentieth century before returning from beyond the grave in the autumn of 2009. Seeing this phantom would be the hardest challenge of all; there are botanists who have devoted their lives simply to seeing, let alone finding for themselves, a ghost orchid in Britain.

My plans laid, I waited impatiently for the onset of spring. I felt that, if the orchid-hunting gods were to be appeased early on, I should return to the county of that very first early purple orchid. I would head back to Somerset, a place in which I had spent very little time botanising after those early, formative years. I returned at Easter 2016, making the most of the long weekend that fell in late March.

The early auguries were good – early purple orchid is usually, as the name suggests, one of the very first orchids to flower each year, and had flowered at two Somerset Wildlife Trust reserves on the same dates in 2015. With the preceding winter having been remarkably mild, I was confident I would find my first target with little trouble. I was to learn an early and important lesson in not being so presumptuous…

After a day of fruitlessly criss-crossing Great Breach Woods and Babcary Meadows, I was cold, wet and thoroughly disheartened. Spring was nowhere near as advanced in the south of England as I'd dared to hope from hundreds of miles away in my northerly Scottish home. Great Breach Woods were waterlogged, the paths sucking, ankle-deep churned mud, and the woodland floor choked with the spiky green clumps of stinking iris. Babcary Meadows oozed water underfoot with every step – only the very highest knolls, where a few optimistic cowslips were beginning to bloom, had any sign of incipient life. Most frustrating of all, at neither site had I been able to find so much as the leaf rosette of an early purple orchid, let alone a flower itself.

There would be plenty more opportunities to see this otherwise relatively common orchid as the spring progressed. I had simply wanted to begin my quest with an early sighting of this famously potent orchid. Shakespeare knew early purple orchids – in *Hamlet*, when describing Ophelia's garland, Gertrude refers to,

...long purples,
That liberal shepherds give a grosser name.

What this grosser name was remains unclear, though there are clues in the names used for early purple orchid at the time elsewhere in Europe. In Italy they were *testicolo di canne*, and in Spain *coyon de perro* – literally, dog's testicles. The Middle English term for orchids was ballockwort... Was this where the earthy English endorsement 'the dog's bollocks' came from? Early purple orchids would have had to do something quite remarkable in order to justify the epithet, and it appears as if they did just that.

Some two thousand years ago orchids had attained an enviable and potent reputation – both Petronius and Pliny the Elder reported their roots to be a powerful aphrodisiac. In AD 65 the Greek physician Dioscorides wrote a herbal, *De Materia Medica*, translated into Latin and Arabic and even until the late seventeenth century an influential guide to the use of medicinal plants. In it Dioscorides recommended the use of the orchid's roots as an aid to vigorous conception.

When she began to publish her self-illustrated *A Curious Herbal* in England in 1735, Elizabeth Blackwell featured the early purple orchid for the same purposes. Known in English medical circles as the Male Satyrion or Male Fools-Stones, the plant's roots were said to be 'a Stimulus to Venery, strengthening the Genital Parts'.

Satyrion was derived from the Latin *satyr*, the infamously lusty half-man half-goat of Roman mythology, while the very name, orchid, owed its origin to the Greek *orchis*, or testicle – a reference to the testicular appearance of many species' underground tubers. Elizabeth Blackwell would have been guided by Nicholas Culpeper's popular *Complete Herbal*, published towards the end of his life in 1653 – in it he warned of the Male Satyrion, 'the roots are to be used with discretion. They are hot and moist in operation, under the dominance of Venus, and provoke lust exceedingly.'

It seems likely that Shakespeare's shepherds would have been well aware of the aphrodisiac qualities ascribed to early purple orchids, and it is surely this reputation that led to the popular contemporaneous belief that witches used the orchid roots as a component in love potions. It was also contended that orchids could be used to counter malign witches' spells that had caused impotence or infertility. This vegetable Viagra may well have been known to the peasantry as the dog's bollocks if the physical effect was anywhere near as impressive as 1,600 years of hedge folklore and scholarly thinking alike believed them to be.

There is a parallel to be found further east to this day in Turkey. Here orchid roots are harvested from the wild, dried and ground into flour, to be used as an additive in the making of a traditional Turkish delicacy, salepi dondurma. *Dondurma* is the Turkish for ice cream – the *salep* is the flour milled from the orchid roots. The etymology of *salep* brings us back to the dog's testicles – the word comes from the Arabic *sahlab*, which translates as fox testicles. Hence salepi dondurma is fox-testicle ice cream.

Foxes, dogs … whatever specific testicles the orchid roots looked like, the effects ascribed to them were the same. Writing in 1751, the Swedish naturalist and father of binomial taxonomy Linnaeus continued to ascribe aphrodisiac qualities to salep. To this day salepi dondurma, and a hot drink derived from orchid roots also known in Turkey as salep, are believed to have potent effects on the male libido. (That and curing bronchitis, cholera and tuberculosis and, in a small nod to the female half of Turkey's population, facilitating childbirth – presumably a concession to the orchid-fuelled root cause of the pregnancy in the first place.)

Salep was a popular beverage across the Ottoman Empire at the height of its imperial power. When in 1570 Pope Pius V issued a papal bull declaring Queen Elizabeth I to be a heretic, swearing to excommunicate from the Catholic Church any that obeyed her orders, he was unwittingly the agent for the widespread consumption of orchids in England for hundreds of subsequent years. Elizabeth's advisors counselled that England should strengthen diplomatic relations with the Muslim world beyond Europe's immediate borders. With these growing diplomatic bonds came increased trade – in fine cloth, jewellery, spices, and a popular Moorish drink derived from orchid roots – salep.

Known in England as saloop, it proved a firm favourite throughout the seventeenth and eighteenth centuries, requiring that the orchid powder be added to hot water until thickened, sweetened with honey or sugar, and flavoured with orange blossom or rosewater. Cheaper than the latterly fashionable imports of coffee or tea, saloop's popularity here only waned when it came to be regarded as a useful remedy for venereal disease. At this point the drinking of it in public in the early nineteenth century came to be regarded as a damning, shameful activity.

Elizabeth Blackwell's *A Curious Herbal* was published to measured critical acclaim as a medical reference work, including an understated endorsement of her coloured illustrations of the plants from no less a luminary than the president of the Royal College of Physicians. Herbals were the field guides of their day, providing the reader with the means to identify a variety of useful plants one might encounter. Their emphasis was primarily of a practical nature – plants with useful qualities ascribed to them featured largely in their pages, and hence herbals were of particular interest to contemporary physicians.

Elizabeth was unusual at the time in being a talented and driven woman in a generally patriarchal society. She was the first British woman to produce a herbal, and the first to not only draw the plants but also to engrave them on copper plate for the printing process, after which she coloured them. Income from her *Herbal* was sufficient to allow Elizabeth to pay to release her ne'er-do-well husband Alexander from the debtors' prison in which he had been incarcerated. Such efforts on her part were poorly rewarded, as Alexander soon ran up further debts before fleeing to Sweden in 1742 to take up the post of court physician to the Swedish king. After becoming unwisely involved in political intrigue surrounding the royal succession, he was hanged for treason shortly afterwards, in 1748. History does not record whether he prescribed the Swedish king early purple orchid roots to strengthen the royal genital parts…

I reflected upon the orchid's colourful and varied history as I drove across Somerset on Easter Sunday – in the time remaining to me in the county I would try the same roadside bank on the flanks of Red Hill upon which I'd found that very first orchid some thirty years previously. There were myriad old English names for early purple orchids, though in the past two hundred years these had become coyer, with references to lusty satyrs and canine testicles wholly removed. In Cornwall, Hampshire and Somerset it was known as adder's flower, and in Devon and Dorset as adder's tongue – presumably a nod to the flowering time coinciding with the emergence of lately hibernating adders in the countryside. Similarly, its flowering also corresponded with the return of cuckoos to the hedgerows, so in Essex it was cuckoo-cock, and in Northamptonshire cuckoo-bud. The purple blotches on the leaves and the reddish-purple flowers may have been the origin of the use of bloody-man's fingers in Cheshire, Gloucestershire and Worcestershire, red butcher in Kent, and simply butcher in Herefordshire.

Perhaps the ultimate emasculation of the earthier names for early purple orchid came with the widespread old English country name for it of Adam-and-Eve – here we find a tame, biblical nod to the sexual potency allegedly locked inside those suggestively shaped roots. This shyness apparently extends to the present day – I had been promised a meeting with a local high priestess of Wicca in nearby Glastonbury that weekend to discuss the use of early purple orchid roots in past and contemporary magic. At the last minute she cancelled our appointment, apparently unwilling to share the finer points of current use of orchids as a sexual stimulant. If I wanted to try them for myself, I would need to go back to Dioscorides in AD 65 for my prescription and, according to Elizabeth Blackwell, I needed only to boil the roots before consumption. Saloop, with the inclusion of a sweetener and some additional flavours, was beginning to sound a lot more attractive.

Later English names for early purple orchid included Gethsemane, as the orchid was said to have been growing beneath the cross at the time of Christ's crucifixion – the spotted leaves we see to this day being the splashes of Christ's blood falling upon them. The irony of all this was not wasted on me. I was looking fruitlessly this Easter weekend for a plant with both Christian and eldritch connotations. Perhaps my quest had been hexed at the very beginning?

The taming of the early purple orchid's earthy reputation is nowhere better illustrated than in the *Unicorn Tapestries*, a series of richly coloured and highly detailed tapestries woven in Belgium at the start of the sixteenth century, recording the hunt for the legendary beast. The final tapestry, the *Unicorn in Captivity*, on display at the Metropolitan Museum of Art in New York, shows a white unicorn chained within a wooden corrall, surrounded by a cornucopia of garden and wildflowers. Chief amongst them, proudly erect in the centre of the corrall with its flower displayed in front of the unicorn's flank, is a recognisable early purple orchid. The unicorn, essence of pagan wildness, has been captured by a virgin. The triumph of Christian symbolism over pagan is an unsubtle metaphor, and it is surely no coincidence that the phallic, lusty orchid is so prominently displayed beside the unicorn.

The rejection of the sexual symbolism of orchids in art and literature continued over the years. The nineteenth-century writer and art critic John Ruskin regarded orchids with a scarcely concealed prudery, describing them as 'definitely degraded, and, in aspect, malicious'. In his *Proserpina: Studies of Wayside Flowers* he even expunged the testicular inference from their generic name – orchids became ophryds, from the Greek *ophrys* or eyebrow, while for everyday use he suggested they be known as wreathe-worts. The early purple orchid, for Ruskin, had completed a journey from the dog-testicle orchid of the Middle Ages to the sanitised purple wreathe-wort.

I crossed the saturated Somerset Levels back to Curry Rivel, where Red Hill rose like a shrugged shoulder from the body of the wet fields below. It seemed as good a place as any to try in the aftermath of the early disappointment of Great Breach Wood and Babcary Meadows. Both had been so waterlogged that perhaps I needed to look somewhere more free-draining, and I found myself retracing my childhood footsteps up the winding lane that scaled the side of the hill.

I had the curious sense that this was somehow preordained when, beneath a leafless bush at the very side of the road, I caught sight of those familiar purple-blotched leaves and above them, their flowers still tightly in bud but recognisable for what they were, early purple orchids. They were just a few yards from where I had found my first orchid decades ago and were, presumably, relatives of that very plant. In the coming weeks I would see many more of their kind flowering across the length and breadth of the British Isles. Yet here, on the exposed and wet side of the very same Somerset hill upon which I had discovered my first orchid decades previously, I had found the first orchid of my quest.

That it was not in flower added to the poignancy of the moment. My return to Red Hill was tinged with sadness. I had hoped to lay some ghosts to rest that weekend by sharing this first Somerset orchid hunt with my father. He had viewed my childhood interest in wildflowers with barely concealed suspicion – he hoped, I knew, for a son who played rugby and aspired to be a lawyer. I had achieved neither of those ambitions. I simply hoped that my dad would join me and, perhaps, at last realise that my interest in natural history and wildflowers was not entirely without worth. I remained haunted by a moment when he had angrily scorned my looking at the *Observer's Book of Wildflowers* as a young boy, telling me I should 'read a proper book, not one for girls'. There was, it appeared, something in the Somerset air that weekend – my father had not returned my calls, and I found myself orchid hunting alone.

However, unbeknown to me, at that very moment another orchid hunter was quartering another hillside in neighbouring Dorset. What he would find in full flower would change the course of my weekend and set my spirits soaring. While I returned to Glastonbury to fruitlessly search for a Wiccan priestess, he hurried to find a phone signal to release his news onto the orchid grapevine. A pithy text message was relayed to me by one of my orchid contacts: *Sawfly is out.*

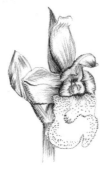

2

Sawfly and the early spiders

This was momentous and wholly unexpected news. Two years previously Mike Chalk, an orchid enthusiast from Hampshire with a particular interest in early spider orchids, had been searching a known colony of the latter with his wife, Lauraine, hoping to find unusual flower variations. This aspect of orchid obsession mirrors that of nineteenth- and early-twentieth-century butterfly collectors. Not content with possessing a standard example of a given species, collectors sought specimens with unusual markings on their wings – different colours and different shapes from those normally found. Butterfly collectors made annual pilgrimages to certain favoured locations that enjoyed a reputation for regularly throwing up these desirable aberrations.

When Lauraine Chalk spotted an unusual pink and yellow orchid standing proud on the short Dorset coastal turf, she would have surely have known immediately that this was no early spider orchid. Her husband knew exactly what it was, and the significance of her find: this was the first ever example of a sawfly orchid to be seen flowering in Britain. Sawfly orchids are normally found in southern Europe, particularly in coastal regions. Related to our bee and early spider orchids, they are perhaps the most spectacularly colourful examples of the *Ophrys* family of orchids, a lysergic concoction of sharp pink, sherbet-lemon yellow and cola-bottle brown.

At the time, Mike told only a small number of people about their spectacular find. The news was revealed more widely later that year with the publication of the Botanical Society of Britain and Ireland's periodical, *BSBI News*. The front cover of the September 2014 issue featured a sumptuous colour photograph of the sawfly orchid, and a short paper authored by Mike told the story of the orchid's discovery, speculating it may have come to be in Dorset by means of wind dispersal of seed from the Mediterranean. Orchid seed is dust tiny, and readily carried from the parent plant by gusts of wind.

The plant had failed to flower again in 2015. In the course of preparing for my quest to see all of Britain and Ireland's orchids I had tried, without success, to discover the plant's whereabouts for myself. Mike Chalk's paper was maddeningly vague on this subject, simply referring to the Purbeck coast. One clue helped narrow the search – I knew that Mike and Lauraine were searching for early spider orchid variations, and could therefore be sure that they were in one of Dorset's few colonies of the latter. My enquiries, however, had come to nothing. If anybody knew the location – and it was clear that amongst orchid enthusiasts very few, if any, did – they were not prepared to share it.

My breakthrough came in early 2016, when I read a local newspaper article written about the National Trust's concerns regarding public access to their land at Dancing Ledge. While the National Trust was worried about the numbers of visitors the site was attracting, and the potential for local damage and disturbance, it was a throwaway remark towards the end of the piece that changed everything for me: 'Dancing Ledge is ... the only known site [in the UK] for the sawfly orchid.'

I had already been planning on visiting Dancing Ledge to see early spider orchids that year, but now anticipated that I would also be scouring the slopes for something much rarer still – assuming it had not perished in the meantime. This orchid was, after all, hundreds of miles north of where it should be, growing in a climate that was generally cooler and wetter than that to which its kind were accustomed.

I had not anticipated that the sawfly orchid would bloom so early in the year – the main flowering season for early spider orchids was still some weeks away and, if the sawfly were to flower at all, I had assumed it would follow the pattern of 2014 and do so simultaneously with the early spiders. I looked with disbelief and a mounting sense of panic at the text message.

Sawfly is out.

Five minutes and some feverish phone calls later, all was much clearer. A photo of the orchid, taken earlier that day, had been posted online. Against all the odds, this Mediterranean orchid was still alive and flowering once more in Dorset. I had a few hours of daylight left to me, but trouble of a kind beyond my control was brewing nearby. Storm Katie had been gathering momentum in the Atlantic for some time and was already making landfall with scything winds and rain further west in Cornwall and the Isles of Scilly. There was a real chance that, were I not to find the orchid that day, there would be nothing left to see once the storm had passed through. Orchids, particularly delicate Mediterranean *Ophrys* orchids, are easily damaged by adverse weather conditions. I would need to act quickly.

My fruitless wait for Glastonbury's white witches to contact me was abandoned as I hurried to my car. I would have an hour, perhaps a little more, available to me by the time I had crossed Somerset and Dorset to Dancing Ledge. This was not long, but I had a sense that every minute would count.

By the time I parked the car as near to Dancing Ledge as Dorset's convoluted country lanes would allow, my emotions had been playfully toyed with by Katie. I had passed slowly through

Somerset in a grey blur of heavy rain. West Dorset had grown brighter and, with it, my passage a little faster. Arriving in sunshine, I shouldered my camera bag and prepared to run cross-country to Dancing Ledge. The wind was appreciably strengthening and, as I jogged past them, the branches of hawthorn trees were whipping at the curdling sky.

The scale of Dancing Ledge is daunting. Almost at the cliff edge, one enters a large, sloping field curved like an amphitheatre set above pale limestone cliffs. I could already see some early spider orchids emerging, still tightly in bud, from the short turf at my feet – but the prospect of finding a single rare orchid in the vastness before me was intimidating.

In the end I need not have worried. After a quarter of an hour of hurriedly walking back and forth, I spotted a bright daub of colour on the ground some distance before me. So lurid was it that my immediate impression was of a piece of litter, a discarded sweet wrapper perhaps. No reserved British flower could dare to be this gaudy. With hindsight, though, I knew exactly what it was – I simply did not dare to believe that it was true.

From above it looked like one of the saturated, colourful Rhodesian stamps I recalled from my childhood – the flower was almost at ground level, with barely any stalk whatsoever. It appeared to be two-dimensional and, had I not spotted it with the flower facing me across the hillside, I could easily have passed it by.

Looking west, immense towers of bruised cloud were boiling on the horizon. The last sunlight of the afternoon was stained by them, casting everything in a faded light like an old Polaroid image left carelessly on a windowsill for years. This only served to make the sawfly orchid look more otherworldly and surreal – if Salvador Dalí had designed an orchid, it would surely have looked something like this. Intense, acid-pink petals and sepals framed an indecently pubescent, bulging canary yellow labellum. At the very heart of this explosive statement of reproductive intent was a small, shiny, H-shaped speculum set in the centre of a conker-brown stained area. A single, yellow-pimpled pollinium dangled suggestively above from an arching column that thrust up and out from the flower. I had heard it said that orchids were the panting floozies of the flower world – this, my first *Ophrys* of the year, did little to dispel that notion. The sawfly orchid simply reeked of sex.

Unfortunately, once the initial euphoria of stumbling across it began to wane, I was uncomfortably reminded that there was also a whiff of something less palatable about this flower – the persistent, swirling rumours about its provenance.

Mike Chalk had speculated in his BSBI paper that it may have been blown here as seed from the Mediterranean. Robin Walls, the BSBI's Dorset representative and responsible for collating all rare plant records for the county, suggested to me that it might have been carried to Dancing Ledge as fertile seed in the treads of a visiting naturalist's walking boots, after that naturalist had spent time botanising in southern Europe. Both theories seemed plausible, though I innately felt the latter suggestion was rather far-fetched. I had heard a third theory mooted – that some person, for reasons best known to themselves, had deliberately planted the sawfly orchid here; Mike and Lauraine Chalk had then happened by chance across it, inadvertent victims of botanical foul play.

This last theory was at least as probable as the wind-borne or boot-carried seed origins. I had found Italian and Spanish vendors on eBay offering sawfly orchid tubers for sale for just a few pounds. When I shared my photographs of the Dorset sawfly orchid with Chris Thorogood, author of the *Field Guide to the Wild Flowers of the Western Mediterranean*, he commented that the extent of yellow on the labellum was unusual, reminiscent of the Italian populations of sawfly orchid. Chris also recounted finding signs of large numbers of wild orchids having been deliberately dug up in the Mediterranean, presumably for sale. This ready availability of sawfly orchid stock felt like sufficient evidence to cast at least some doubt on the provenance of this particular orchid in Dorset. Yet what possible motive would anyone have in introducing such an alien orchid to Britain?

I was rapidly learning that orchids exert an influence unlike any other plant upon those who fall under their spell. For some, that influence leads them to do things that other botanists would consider deeply questionable – such as introducing orchids into new areas in which they have not previously been recorded. In this regard, Dorset's coastal areas have a particularly rich history where unusual *Ophrys* orchids are concerned.

In April 1976 R.E. Webster discovered a Bertoloni's bee orchid growing on the Purbeck coast. With startling symmetry with what would happen almost forty years later, this was the first time this orchid, a native of southern Europe, had ever been seen in Britain. The discovery was reported at the time by the BSBI and also in the local newspaper. While the same theories of natural colonisation were advanced at the time, rumours also abounded that an ardent orchid enthusiast – suggested variously to have either been a local woman or none other than the highly respected botanist Francis Rose – had broadcast the seeds of several Mediterranean orchid species in the location in previous years. Rose had certainly adopted this technique beforehand with some success in the south east of England – the *Flora of Surrey* noted, disapprovingly, Rose's 'experiments' introducing early spider and lady orchids into the county, while Professor Richard Bateman recalled wryly, 'My first ever "accidental" find of lizard orchid proved to be the result of his machinations.'

The Bertoloni's bee orchid did not endure beyond that first flowering season in spring 1976. Visitors to the site the following month after its discovery found that it had gone – either grazed by cattle or, as some at the time suggested, destroyed by local botanists who regarded its presence as deeply offensive and an unwelcome addition to our native flora.

Francis Rose was not the only orchid enthusiast said to have deliberately introduced orchids to the area in the 1970s. The writer John Fowles had made his home in the elegant Georgian seaside villa of Belmont House in Lyme Regis since 1968, the year before the publication of *The French Lieutenant's Woman*. While it is for this book that Fowles is best remembered, there are clues in his other works that hint at his understanding of the nature of obsession, notably *The Collector* and, in *Daniel Martin*, his most autobiographical work of fiction, his own lifelong, consuming interest in orchids.

It is his journals that are most revealing of all, with decades of daily observations laced with references to hunting for orchids across

Europe – and to his penchant for collecting them, smuggling them back to Britain, and attempting to naturalise them in his garden. He had a particular fascination with the *Ophrys* family, those spectacular furry, colourful insect mimics – they emerge regularly from the fertile soil of his journals, growing in the French and Greek countryside, picked and in a jam jar of water on his desk, and flowering in his garden at Belmont House. In addition to other non-*Ophrys* orchid species growing in pots, three *Ophrys* species are recorded as growing in the grounds of Belmont – bee orchid, sombre bee orchid and woodcock orchid. Only the bee orchid is a British native – the other species naturally occur in southern Europe.

A holiday in France with Elizabeth, his wife, in May 1973, concludes with a diary entry on the day of their return to Britain that speaks volumes about how possessed by orchids he had become – and the extent to which he was collecting wild orchids to grow in the privacy of his garden: 'A moment of horror at the customs as I realise we are to be searched by a sharp-eyed lady officer – with four boxes full of orchid and other illicit roots to be found. But she seems content with charging duty (£15 on 36 bottles) on the wine.'

Fowles derived inordinate pleasure from his naturalised orchids, as can be heard in his heartfelt testimony that the woodcock orchids in his garden 'would make me cry, if I were the crying kind'. This was a sentiment I recognised – I had occasionally felt that sense of overwhelming emotion induced by a plant, a bird or an insect that was perfection simply by its very existence – but I found the revelation of Fowles' acquisitiveness faintly repellent. Simply seeing the orchids in the wild was not enough for him – he had to possess them, to control them.

Revisiting *The Collector*, knowing the extent of Fowles' behaviour where orchids were concerned, one is struck by the parallels between him and the novel's central character, the flawed and obsessive butterfly collector Frederick Clegg, who is driven to possess the things he desires, whatever the cost. Fowles publicly abhorred butterfly collecting, reflecting that he wrote *The Collector* to express his hatred of what he described as a lethal perversion. He went further in 1996, concluding, 'All natural history collectors in the end collect the same thing: the death of the living.'

Perhaps Fowles rationalised his own collection of wild orchids by telling himself that, as the orchids were for the most part still alive in his care, he had not extinguished the vital spark within them. He remembered saving bee orchids from a landslip near Lyme Regis in 1972, and the woodcock orchids in his garden certainly flourished in his care, as his journals note them still growing healthily there as lately as 1990.

In the later years of his life the gardens became overgrown. When local sculptor David West was asked by Fowles to create a sculpture for him, he instead persuaded Fowles to allow him to attempt to restore as much of the garden as possible and rescue what plants he could from encroaching dense vegetation. Fowles asked in particular that West try to rescue orchids and cyclamen that he had brought from Greece and France. West recalls that, despite clearing a great deal of invasive bamboo from the area of garden that Fowles thought he had planted them in, he could only find the cyclamen. Fowles' interest in orchids never waned – West recounts, 'When he was unable to walk far, he liked to be kept informed as to how well the various orchids were growing on Ware Cliff.'

Following Fowles' death in 2005, the gardens of Belmont House fell into disrepair, becoming choked and overgrown. The current custodians of Belmont House, the Landmark Trust, are in the process of gradually restoring the gardens to their former condition, but of the orchids Fowles removed from the wild and successfully incorporated in his garden, there is still no sign. It appears as if, without the intervening hand of man to maintain a suitable habitat for them, they were smothered by the encroaching vegetation of neglect.

Yet their legacy may live on elsewhere in the county. In April 2016 Robin Walls stopped to investigate a roadside verge in north Dorset and found thirteen intriguing orchids flowering there. He did not recognise them, but subsequent opinion from, amongst others, Professor Richard Bateman, considered them to be the hybrid offspring of woodcock orchid and fly orchid. Fly orchids are British natives, and found nearby – but woodcock orchids are unknown in Britain. Could these hybrid orchids be the descendants of John

Fowles' orchids at large in the Dorset countryside? It is tempting to think so. The site in question is less than twenty miles from Lyme Regis, so it is perhaps plausible that an insect could have borne a woodcock orchid pollinium from the garden of Belmont House to a receptive fly orchid in the north of the county. The resultant seed could have begat this remarkable colony of hybrids. One wonders what other orchid surprises may yet lurk undiscovered in Dorset...

Having seen the sawfly orchid and, in the light of Dorset's complicated history where unusual introduced orchids were concerned, I wanted to understand what the prevailing consensus was as to its origin. Which theory seemed most plausible? Were the sawfly orchid an unusual vagrant bird, its provenance would have been tested by what, in practice, amounts to a jury system: the British Birds Rarities Committee comprises twelve elected individuals who consider and vote upon the provenance of every rare bird found in Britain during the preceding calendar year. Only those birds that are correctly identified and for which there is considered to be an acceptable likelihood of natural occurrence are admitted to the official British list. Where reasonable doubt exists about provenance, a rare bird record is cast into a useful limbo – on the historical record as having occurred, but not officially accepted as being of wild origin. I wondered if such a 'not proven' mechanism existed for adjudicating upon rare orchid or other plant discoveries.

I posed this question to Robin Walls, the BSBI recorder for Dorset. His reply was helpful insofar as he confirmed that no such committee existed for plant records, but rather disappointing in that he made it clear that, in the absence of evidence to the contrary, the default position was to accept any unusual plant found in Dorset at face value. Reasonable doubt would not enter into the equation. The only BSBI involvement would be if there had been any doubt regarding the identification of the plant in question – in which case the BSBI's orchid referees would be asked for their informed opinion. BSBI referees are individuals considered to have the highest levels of experience and knowledge in their particular field of botany, and in this case they were Professor Richard Bateman and Dr Ian Denholm.

I had also written to Mike Chalk for, while it was his wife who found the sawfly orchid, Mike had authored the paper announcing the discovery. I sought his opinion on the rumours that the orchid might have been introduced by the hand of man. Mike replied to unequivocally reassure me that not only was Robin Walls, the Dorset county recorder, happy with the record, but also Professor Richard Bateman and Dr Ian Denholm: 'All the planted rumours have been officially squashed, as was the man–monkey hybrid I found in Hampshire.'

Mike's dedication as an orchid hunter shone through during his brief correspondence with me – he clearly devoted a considerable amount of time every year searching for unusual and rare orchids amongst their commoner brethren. This dedication had been rewarded only two years before the discovery of the sawfly orchid when, in 2012, just across the border in Hampshire at Alton Down, Mike had discovered the extraordinarily uncommon *Orchis x bergonii*, the hybrid offspring between man orchid and monkey orchid.

To put the scale of this discovery into context, this was a hybrid that had last been recorded in the late 1980s in Kent, in one of only three small monkey orchid colonies remaining in Britain. The man orchid was a rare plant in Hampshire – and monkey orchid was unknown anywhere near there. This was a once-in-a-lifetime find for an orchid enthusiast, and one nobody would have foreseen in Hampshire, of all places – but just two years later lightning had struck again with Mike and Lauraine's discovery of the sawfly orchid in Dorset.

Robin Walls had already made it clear that he considered the sawfly orchid likely to have been introduced via a visiting botanist's boot. His final thoughts on the origins of the plant sounded a more chastening note: 'In any case, the media, regulators and courts just want two states: foreign or native. None of this is conducive to a good understanding of ecology, population movement or management of a dwindling flora and diminishing areas for it to flourish. And it can waste a lot of time.'

While I did not want to waste anybody's time, I did want to understand what the British orchid world really thought about this pioneering plant. It seemed prudent to seek Professor Bateman's opinion on the origins of the sawfly orchid, confirmation that he and Dr Denholm had been consulted, and affirmation that they were indeed happy with the record. While waiting for the imminent flowering of the early spider orchids scattered along the English south coast, I eagerly awaited his response.

I saw my first early spider orchids in Kent over twenty-five years ago. I was a student at the time and, lured by the siren call of a hoopoe that had been spotted the previous day on the coast, I borrowed a bicycle and set out to pedal my way across Romney Marsh to birdwatch on the immense, jutting shingle peninsula that is Dungeness.

I had only the vaguest idea of how far away it actually was from my halls of residence, but reasoned that Romney Marsh was essentially flat and would not pose a significant challenge. I had taken into account neither the decrepitude of my friend's bicycle nor the potency of the early spring sunshine, so it was, by the time Dungeness nuclear power station drew near, an exhausted, sore and weather-beaten naturalist who threw himself down at the side of the road by Prospect Cottage.

Dungeness has a landscape like none other – the brooding Brutalist monolith of the power station finds its counterpoint on the horizon in the tall, slim, black and white lighthouse. Cream and tan shingle undulates as far as the eye can see, as if an immeasurably vast tide has just retreated but could, without warning, sweep back from the English Channel, obliterating all. The shingle is interspersed by flotsam and jetsam seemingly stranded by that receding tide – here and there are wooden fishing boats, while scattered amongst them are a handful of small, sun-bleached wooden houses, like beach huts that have aspired to greatness. There are a few stands of scrubby, wind-sculpted blackthorn bushes and a great many vigorous clumps of glaucous sea kale, with waxy leaves as wavy as the nearby sea itself. Discarded tools rust quietly to themselves, inadvertent burnt-sienna sculptures. *Abandoned Rotary Lawnmower. Lost Chisel. Seized Winch.*

Prospect Cottage, set a little way back from the road that curves across the flatness to the omnipotent power station, stops passers-by dead in their tracks. In a vista that abounds with striking visual moments it was, and still is to this day, a place apart. Home at the time to the film-maker Derek Jarman, it is compact, with black-painted weatherboards illuminated with buttery yellow windowframes. On one timber gable is a relief rendition of John Donne's 'The Sun Rising':

Busie old fool, unruly Sun,
Why dost thou thus,
Through windowes, and through curtaines, call on us?
Must to thy motions lovers' seasons run?
Sawcy pedantique wretch, goe chide
Late school boyes and sowre prentices,
Goe tell Court-huntsmen that the King will ride,
Call countrey ants to harvest offices,
Love, all alike, no season knows, nor clyme,
Nor houres, dayes, months, which are the rags of time.

While it was the 'sawcy pedantique wretch' who, combined with an ailing bicycle, had reduced me to a gasping heap at the roadside, it was the garden that bled from the cottage into the landscape that ultimately stopped me dead in my tracks. Jarman gardened without boundaries or restraint. Like his film-making, his garden was alternately challenging, avant garde, eccentric and playful. The garden merged seamlessly with its surroundings, mixing native plants with colourful ornamentals, and incorporating driftwood spars as deliberate sculptural accents. Apart from at Great Dixter, where Christopher Lloyd's orchid-studded wildflower meadows merged his exuberant garden into the countryside beyond, I had not seen the like of this before. In a landscape as surreal as Dungeness, this combination of garden and wilderness was even more arresting. I sat on the shingle somewhere in the hinterland between the cottage and the road and felt like Alice when she first set foot in Wonderland.

Like Alice, it took a moment for me to adjust my perception and to realise what I was seeing. Distracted by Prospect Cottage, I had unknowingly been looking straight past the orchids at my feet – three small, sturdy spikes with hairy chocolate-brown and lime-green flowers. I knew just what they were – I had been looking for them only days before on the Wye Downs – yet here they were at Dungeness, my first early spider orchids.

Their name suits them perfectly – they are one of the very first of all our native orchids to bloom, in a typical year peaking in late April. Their oval lip is a rich chocolate brown fringed with a luxuriant growth of fine, short hairs – this is the body of the 'spider'. On either side of the stigma above is a pair of beady, glossy black pseudo-eyes. While to us clumsy humans this may resemble a garden spider, it is airborne insects that this orchid hopes to attract as pollinators – in the centre of the hairy brown lip is a forked, shiny bluish-grey speculum. The illusion of a pair of shiny wings is surely deliberate. The petals and sepals are the chartreuse of an overripe lime. Though I did not know it at the time, Derek Jarman had a passion for native orchids – he and photographer Howard Sooley spent days searching for them in France – and he would surely have been aware of those on his doorstep. After these first plants at the coast, I found more in the coming weeks of that long-ago spring up on the downs above Wye. Inland colonies are atypical, for this is an orchid that seems happiest along the south coast of England, from Kent to Dorset.

Some weeks after my fortuitous encounter with the sawfly orchid I had an appointment with early spider orchids at the westerly extremity of their British range, back on the slopes of Dancing Ledge. The symmetry of this was deeply appealing – I had seen my very first early spider orchids on the interstice of Derek Jarman's garden, and now I would be seeing the first of the year on the site of the closing scenes of his punky, cult classic film *Jubilee*. As the film ends we see Queen Elizabeth I and John Dee, the court astrologer, walking together there with exactly the same portentous sky overhead that had provided the theatrical cyclorama to the sawfly orchid. I felt sure Jarman would have been aware of the resident orchid riches of Dancing Ledge – *Jubilee* was filmed in 1977, the year after the Bertolini's bee orchid had been found in Dorset. Would Jarman have known of this?

I had arranged to meet local orchid expert and ethnobotanist Susanne Masters at Dancing Ledge. Susanne's botanical knowledge is phenomenal, and put to the very best use – if you have enjoyed any of the delicious gins that are the fruits of the burgeoning micro-distillery scene, chances are Susanne has had a hand in their creation, advising on the sustainable and appropriate choices of local botanical ingredients for incorporation in the spirits. Above all, though, Susanne is passionate about orchids. While we would wander the Purbecks on a fine spring morning looking at early spider orchids, our conversation would range from orchid conferences in Japan to distilleries in Kentucky, via the mountains of Turkey, where orchid tubers are still harvested as a food additive.

We met late in the afternoon, too late to look for flowers but in ample time to spend an evening at Susanne's home near Lulworth Cove talking flowers. Having spent much of my adolescence exploring the area framed by Sherborne in the north of the county and, at the coast, Lyme Regis in the west and Lulworth in the east, this felt like a homecoming. I was back in the land that shaped me as a naturalist, the place that took the potent seed of my interest and nurtured it in the copses, commons and droves of Hardy country. I had lived and breathed Thomas Hardy as a teenager – his love of the county and its people had spoken to something deep inside me and, as I navigated the county by bicycle, I knew Dorset's towns and villages interchangeably by both the place names in his novels and those on the old white-painted signs at road junctions. This was Wessex, what Hardy referred to as his 'merely realistic dream country'.

Susanne and I left the area of Hardy's Lulwind Cove the following morning, passing the Weld Arms, a pub quietly famous as a Dorset locus for the Bloomsbury set. It was here that, during Easter in 1921, writer Sylvia Townsend Warner spent a weekend with, amongst others, sculptor Stephen Tomlin. This weekend led to Tomlin discovering Theodore Powys, the 'English Tolstoy', living a hermit-like writer's existence nearby, and was to inspire Warner herself to move to Dorset, where she spent much of her life, her writing greatly inspired by the countryside she loved so dearly.

Shortly after first light we had returned to Dancing Ledge – home a few weeks previously to the beautiful yet uncertain sawfly orchid. Of that, now, there was no sign whatsoever – Storm Katie had burned the struggling sawfly to a crisp, and there was nothing to be seen where once it had audaciously blossomed.

Instead, we walked across a hillside carpeted with early spider orchids. None were as tall as I remembered them having been in Kent, with even the highest barely scraping ten centimetres. What they lacked in stature they more than made up for in appearance. Each plant had one or two flowers in their prime, gorgeous confections of chocolate and lime. Newly arrived migrant whitethroats sang their scratchy, disjointed notes from the tops of scrubby hawthorns dotted around the edges of the main slope, which fell away to the greyish white cliffs below. I recounted the story of the sawfly orchid to Susanne as we slowly traversed the hillside, and we found ourselves discussing the nature of obsession in general and its manifestation in the orchid world.

'It's nearly always men who are the most badly afflicted,' she said and, after a thoughtful pause, added drily, 'I'll be interested to hear how many of the orchid people you meet this year are women...'

I had a feeling already that Susanne's veiled observation would prove prescient – if the intriguing story of Dorset's rare *Ophrys* orchids was anything to go by, the British orchid scene's most obsessive characters were every bit as colourful as the flowers they coveted the sight of.

The irony of this was not lost on me the following morning as I drove west out of Dover. The dual carriageway drags ponderously uphill from the busy Channel port before levelling out on the short drive to Folkestone. Halfway up that first long haul is a small junction – blink and you could miss it, though to the uninitiated it does not suggest that this is somewhere one would turn off to follow a public road. Stopping at an industrial stop/go traffic light, a round tunnel vanishes blackly down into the bowels of the steep hillside that rises to a precipitous cliff edge beyond. This access to the foot of Shakespeare Cliff was bored during a failed attempt to build an early iteration of the Channel Tunnel in the 1970s. The single-lane tunnel is unlit, dropping at a severe gradient as it descends sharply to almost sea level. Driving down it, with the car's headlights competing inadequately with the bright sunshine blazing at the far tunnel mouth, you have the feeling of trespass. This is surely not somewhere that the general public is welcome.

Emerging from the tunnel, the landscape beyond is largely man-made. When the Channel Tunnel was being carved far below the waters of the English Channel, this was where 5 million tonnes of chalk marl quarried from beneath the seabed emerged, blinking, into the sunlight. Far from being unwelcome here, this latest addition to the coastline of the British Isles has become a unique area of habitat, sporting a car park, a visitor centre, and even a small café. Dover residents come here to walk their dogs, for an ice cream and a little peace on a busy, sunny day, or to fish from the waterfront. Orchid hunters, meanwhile, come here for the burgeoning population of early spider orchids.

In 1998 there were sixty-one flowering plants on this virgin ground. Conservationists speculated that these were pioneers from the cliffs above Samphire Hoe, colonists that had drifted down as seed onto pastures new. Six years later there were over nine thousand plants to be seen flowering at the foot of Shakespeare Cliff. By 2016 numbers had plateaued and were no longer rising exponentially. The habitat itself had settled down – from the late 1990s to the present day, the chalk marl's vegetation has evolved and stabilised into, for the most part, rough pasture grazed by a combination of sheep and cattle. A handful of tracks and paths meander over the open ground, but one can wander freely here. I had come to do just that, tracing Derek Jarman's footsteps back from Dancing Ledge to Kent in search of more orchids. The early spider orchids found at Samphire Hoe are renowned both for their vigorous stature and their variability. I hoped to find for myself some of the unusual variations of colouration that so consume the avid orchid hunter.

Already I found myself wanting more than to see all of the British and Irish orchid species – now I wanted to find the freaks and the mutants amongst their number. This was why Susanne's acute observation about obsessive male orchid enthusiasts had chimed immediately with me: I was fast becoming one myself. Never mind simply seeing the rare species, I wanted to find the rarest of the rare and, who knows, maybe something nobody had ever seen before. It was, after all, while looking for these early spider orchid variations that Mike Chalk had discovered the sawfly orchid in Dorset two years previously.

I had been given a grid reference for one such variety, an early spider orchid that lacked all the usual chocolate-brown tones, its furry body instead a pale, mossy green. This was a well-known variety that botanists had accorded a Latin name all its own: var. (short for variation) *flavescens*. A Kentish orchid hunter had seen one three days previously at the side of the track that runs the length of the Samphire Hoe site, parallel to the railway line that links Folkestone and Dover. While I found the plant easily enough, it was by now beyond its best, the green flowers now turning faded ochre – early spider orchid flowers do not last for long. Though I was too late for this plant, I had high hopes I might find another.

I had allowed most of the day to search the area, so began to criss-cross the rolling grassland, starting at the very far end of the site and working my way back to the visitor centre and, I hoped, a celebratory ice cream. Almost immediately my eye was caught by something very different amongst the many hundreds of standard early spider orchids. Even from a distance I could see that this individual was very different indeed – at a glance it appeared to be pink and white. I found my heart beating faster as I drew close; my first impression was accurate but did this exceptional orchid scant justice. The furry lip was a glowing rufous, fringed with a deep-cerise border. Framing this were three snow-white sepals, veined towards their tips with a tracery of pale green; and two petals of a delicate coral pink. I had never seen an early spider orchid anything like this. While I busied myself trying to do this beguiling plant justice with my camera I found, despite the warmth of the sun on my arms, that I had goose pimples – this single orchid, unknowingly combining the rarity of the species with an utterly unique beauty all its own, had me spellbound.

'What are you looking at?'

The question, asked in a broad Eastern European accent, startled me – I was completely lost in the plant. Looking up, I found myself facing an inquisitive man perhaps a few years younger than myself. Beyond him were two companions, and a small rigid inflatable boat sitting upon a homemade trailer. At a time when the news was full of stories of desperate economic migrants trying to reach British shores from France, with rescues of small boatloads being made off the Kent and Sussex coastlines, I found myself shamefully wondering where this trio had come from. Perhaps my thoughts were writ large on my face, for before I could answer he had continued, 'We have been fishing. There are good fish here.'

Zoltan and his friends were originally from Hungary, and had been living and working in east Kent for some years now. I explained that I was here to see orchids. Zoltan knelt beside me and pointed at the plant.

'This is orchid? Nice. There are many of these here, yes?'

I was pleased that he had noticed them. He explained that they often came here to fish when the weather was fine. 'It is fresher than in the shops, yes? And it is free. We fished a lot, back home.' Home was a town near Budapest – I had lived there for a short while in 1995, and Zoltan was visibly delighted that I remembered the names of some of the nightclubs I had visited at the time. 'Yes, I know this one! Maybe we were there at the same time?'

We sat and chatted for a few minutes while his companions busied themselves packing fishing gear that, had I only noticed it sooner, would have stopped me from making those treacherous and ill-founded assumptions in the first place. I enjoyed our brief conversation and his interest in the orchids, and I sympathised with his eloquent fears about the impending EU referendum.

'Europe is not perfect. But it is better to be together. People forget how bad it is when countries grow apart.'

We wished one another well and, as Zoltan and his friends continued pulling their boat back towards the car park, I slipped back under my orchid's seductive spell, more contemplative than hitherto.

It was hard to pull myself away from it, but eventually the yearning to find a *flavescens* of my own proved too strong to ignore. I resumed my slow, orchid-hunter's walk – a posture that I would, in time, come to recognise in others from far away – slightly stooped, head bowed, the searcher's gradual progress interrupted time and again by pausing to squat down to closely examine a particularly intriguing or promising plant.

An hour passed in this way, interrupted only by my discovery of two further early spider variations – one a strange individual with canary-yellow petals and sepals, and the other a partially peloric plant – this being an individual where the brown tones and form of the orchid's lip are repeated on the petals. This particular plant had brown furry edges to the otherwise green petals, but was otherwise a typical example of the species. What I really craved, now the high of the pink and white plant had worn off a little, was a symphony in mossy green. Shortly afterwards, I found one.

There was a sense of anti-climax when I realised the orchid I had almost trodden upon unseen at my feet was, in fact, a pristine and delicate green version of the surrounding brown early spider orchids. My conversation with Zoltan had been playing on my mind and had brought my orchid hunt into some perspective. Still, there was no denying the subtle beauty of this latest iteration on the early spider theme, the clear green of the orchid's lip smothered with tiny silvery hairs. In the cool light at the foot of Samphire Hoe's looming white chalk cliffs, I began to take a series of portraits of this understated orchid. The lack of any strong colours made her – and somehow, this orchid felt wholly feminine in a way that, say, the swaggering machismo of the sawfly orchid did not – appear as aloof and unattainable as an *haute couture* model.

This time I saw my inquisitor before he startled me – and was pleasantly surprised to make my reacquaintance with a friend I'd not seen for some fifteen years since I had moved away from Kent to Shetland – Paul Holt, now the head ranger at Samphire Hoe. We recognised one another immediately and, once I'd shown him the orchid I'd been photographing, we relapsed into the easy conversation of two former birdwatching companions. As if on cue, a peregrine began calling noisily from the white cliffs above us – back then, this had been the only site in Kent at which we could reliably find these charismatic falcons.

Our conversation turned, naturally, to my orchid quest. Paul understandably assumed that early spider and early purple orchids would be all I had seen so far in this flowering season, so was surprised when I told him about the reappearance of the sawfly orchid in Dorset. To my surprise, he knew Mike Chalk.

'He comes here looking for early spider orchids. I like him – he's a nice guy. He gave a talk here all about orchids the other year. Some of his photos were brilliant. The strangest thing happened when he was showing us them, though…

'There was one picture; I think it was an early marsh orchid. When that came on the screen, I had the most incredible physical reaction. My mouth felt fizzy – it was as if I could taste – I don't know – pink lemonade or strawberry ice cream? I've never had a reaction like that before or since.'

I felt slightly jealous. While I derived enormous pleasure from seeing an orchid in the wild, and knew how good it felt to have taken a photo that did such a plant the justice it deserved, I had never experienced synaesthesia as a result of the interaction between me and plant. How amazing it would be to taste colours, if those colours were as clear and beautiful as those found on Britain and Ireland's orchids. I imagined early spider orchids might taste like chocolate-lime sweets, and early purple orchids like blackcurrant cordial – but what of the sawfly orchid? Perhaps rhubarb and custard. Sadly, unlike Paul, who had tasted an orchid's colours, I had only my imagination with which to paint my palate.

I finished my first Kentish sojourn of the year at Marden Meadow. This Kent Wildlife Trust nature reserve is a gem set deep in the countryside south of Maidstone, a green necklace of three small, ancient, damp meadows that are, in the spring, transformed into a rich purple carpet of green-winged orchids. Climbing from the roadside into the first of the meadows over a small wooden stile, I was greeted by the sight of hundreds of short, sturdy orchids studding the grass across the field before me. This was what much of our British farmland would have looked like in the days before the adoption of silage as animal fodder, the use of artificial fertilisers, and the development of sugar-rich grass strains spelt a death knell for traditional hay meadows. The intensification of agriculture came at a cost – now green-winged orchids are lost from half their former British and Irish range, being found only in unimproved fragments of the land where they once occurred.

First recorded in the seventeenth century, for a time green-winged orchids were believed to be the female equivalent of the 'male' early purple orchid. Authors of the time referred to them as *Cynosorchis morio foemina* or 'female Fool-stones', their supposed femininity established by the smaller size of their tubers compared with the masculine vigour and mass of those found beneath early purple orchids. Each flower rewarded close scrutiny, for they are startlingly attractive close to. While most are a rich royal purple, others are a delicate salmon pink, and some even appear in cool snow white – but all share the feature that lends this orchid its English name: bold parallel green lines on their curved lateral sepals, a feature unique to them amongst our native orchids. These are their green wings, said to resemble a jester's cap – hence the *morio*, or fool, in their Latin name *Anacamptis morio*. I had always assumed that Fool-stones was a reference to the ancient adage that men allowed themselves to be led by their genitals, putting lust before good sense and reason. Unable to see a jester's cap in any of these orchids, and well aware of orchids' prodigious history and connection with sexual potency, I continue to prefer my theory.

Returning home from this journey along the English south coast, I found a reply from Richard Bateman awaiting me. He shared Chris Thorogood's reservations about the colouration of the sawfly orchid but, more perplexingly, he confirmed that he and Ian Denholm alike had never corresponded in their capacity as BSBI orchid referees about the sawfly orchid, nor passed any judgements as to its likely provenance.

I now felt hollow and unsure what could be believed where the provenance of this strange orchid was concerned. The more I thought about the circumstances of the sawfly orchid, the more it left me with a bad taste in my mouth – and certainly not the rhubarb-and-custard flavour I had fancifully imagined for it. Sylvia Townsend Warner's poetry, written only a few miles from Dancing Ledge, sprang irresistibly to mind:

I, so wary of traps,
So skilful to outwit

Springes and pitfalls set,
Am caught now, perhaps.

I could count myself very lucky to have seen the plant in its brief twenty-four-hour flowering period – but could I really count the sawfly as a British orchid? This orchid of uncertain origins blurred the boundaries of what was actually wild and posed arch questions about other orchids I might encounter later in the course of the unfurling spring. If an orchid had been introduced by man, but was growing in a wild state without further intervention, should I nevertheless consider it a wild plant notwithstanding that initial human intervention? How long should such a plant persist before it was considered naturalised?

And, ultimately, did any of this really matter in the face of an undeniably exquisite orchid? John Fowles considered our relationship with nature to have diminished in the course of our desire to categorise and label it. In his searching essay *The Tree*, he explored our obsession with naming, categorising and collecting wild things, and concluded that in so doing we had stopped seeing nature. He described an encounter with a small colony of military orchids, an encounter in which he scrupulously documented, photographed and measured the plants, and then concluded: 'Yet five minutes after my wife had finally (other women are not the only form of adultery) torn me away, I suffered a strange feeling. I realised I had not actually seen the three plants in the little colony we had found. Despite all the identifying, measuring, photographing, I had managed to set the experience in a kind of present past, a having-looked, even as I was temporally and physically still looking.'

This rang uncomfortably true – I realised I was in danger of putting my desire to categorise and understand the sawfly orchid above the pleasure simply seeing it had initially engendered. That heart-thumping, euphoric moment when I dropped to my knees beside it and drank in the flower's alien beauty in the luminous, tobacco-stained light of Katie's gathering storm clouds – that was the feeling I should hold onto and take away from this encounter. Not doubts about whether someone had planted an orchid at

Dancing Ledge, not speculation about their motives – curiosity, mischief or attention-seeking? – and certainly not the uncomfortable feeling of uncertainty that my research had now created.

The last word on the sawfly orchid had to go to John Fowles, he to whom orchids had meant so much that, despite his condemnation of those who acquire and hoard wild things for their own gratification, he had quietly collected and naturalised Mediterranean orchids in his sheltered coastal Dorset garden. Ultimately, his love of orchids – and the sawfly orchid, *Ophrys tenthredinifera,* in particular – proved to be a rock he could hold fast to in his darkest hours. Towards the end of his life he recalled:

> For many years … I have pursued wild orchids all over Europe.
> When I was in a hospital bed just after having a stroke recently,
> I was near weeping with self-rage and self-pity, reciting a
> mantra to myself:
> *'Tenthredinifera,*
> *Tenthredinifera,*
> *Tenthredinifera...'*

3

The men, ladies and monkeys of Kent

To stand in Charles Darwin's study in Down House, his home in Kent for the last forty years of his life, feels like one is in the presence of the great man himself. The atmosphere is charged with the memory of the great pioneer of evolutionary theory. His handwritten notes jostle for space on his rectangular worktable with letters and postcards, a microscope, books, glasses and an inkwell. To the left of Darwin's worn, mahogany-framed armchair, the fabric shiny and frayed with use, is a deep-blue baize-topped drum table scattered with intriguing clear-glass bottles, faded red-card pillboxes used for storing insect and seed specimens, minerals, and bleached bones. Book-lined shelves fill the alcove to the right of a white marble fireplace. All that is missing is the man himself, poring over specimens or annotating the pages of one of the many books he was sent from around the world.

This was neither the first nor the last visit I would make to Kent in the course of my orchid quest, but this was the very first time I had made a pilgrimage to Down House. No sooner had the wholly unscientific thought that I was breathing the same air as Darwin occurred to me than I found myself feeling quite breathless. While I thought I knew the story of how Darwin arrived at his theory of evolution, little had I realised what a pivotal role Kentish orchids had played in defending it.

Darwin was surely well aware of just how momentous his *On the Origin of Species* would prove when it was rushed into print in November 1859. His evolutionary ideas and observations had been coalescing for decades by then, and were forming the backbone of a much larger planned work to be entitled *Natural Selection*. *On the Origin of Species* was, while substantial enough in its own right, but a summary of *Natural Selection* and, although its most strident critics were the theologians who objected to Darwin's thinking on religious grounds, *On the Origin of Species* was more widely criticised for an absence of facts to support the author's theories.

Darwin, a methodical and meticulous scientist, had found his hand forced when he learned the extent to which Alfred Russel Wallace, a contemporary naturalist, had independently arrived at similar conclusions to himself. In February 1858, while travelling in what was then known as the Malay Archipelago, Wallace sent Darwin an essay he had written – an essay in which he set out his theory of how species diverged over time, subject to environmental stimuli. While Wallace had not used the term natural selection and, unlike Darwin, did not ascribe divergence to competition between individuals of a species, in some significant regards his theory paralleled Darwin's own thinking, perhaps uncomfortably so. On sharing the essay with his friend, the geologist Charles Lyell, Darwin confided, 'he [Wallace] could not have made a better short abstract! Even his terms now stand as heads of my chapters ... all my originality, whatever it may amount to, will be smashed.'

Lyell, while harbouring personal religious qualms about the implications of all this radical evolutionary theory, was sufficiently dispassionate to wish to see Wallace's essay aired in public. He helped to arrange for it to be presented, in Wallace's absence, to the Linnean Society of London in July 1858, together with a paper by Darwin intended to demonstrate that Darwin had independently – and earlier than Wallace – come to similar conclusions.

The reading of both men's work did not, however, elicit the reaction one might have expected. In May 1859, the president of the Linnean Society remarked, with calculated understatement, that the preceding year had not been marked by any striking discoveries. In Wallace's continuing absence overseas, Darwin resolved to write an abstract of his entire work, and rushed to publish *On the Origin of Species* later that year.

To say the response to this publication was dramatic is to understate the case. Darwin, a more eminent and considerably better-connected society figure than Wallace, enjoyed a profile that ensured the contents of his theory would be heard far and wide outside the confines of the Linnean Society. They were not only heard – they reverberated, and nowhere louder than in the corridors and cloisters of the Church of England. Darwin had tilted the religious and scientific worlds on their axes with a publication that challenged the very tenets of accepted creationism.

Matters came to a memorable head just seven months later in the august surroundings of the Oxford University Museum. Following a presentation by John Draper of New York University, examining the intellectual development of Europe with relation to Darwin's theory, a heated and decidedly unholy debate erupted between a number of eminent scientists and theologians of the day.

It is easy to hear the withering sarcasm with which Bishop Samuel Wilberforce was said to have asked the biologist Thomas Huxley whether it was through his grandmother or his grandfather that he claimed his descent from a monkey. Huxley, known latterly as 'Darwin's bulldog', is reputed to have replied that he would not be ashamed to have a monkey for an ancestor, but he would be ashamed to be associated with a man who used his great gifts to obscure the truth. While Bishop Wilberforce revelled in the nickname of Soapy Sam on account of his boast that 'I am often in hot water, and always come out with clean hands', one imagines that the atmosphere at dinner in Oxford that evening was somewhat strained.

Wallace, meanwhile, appeared to harbour no ill feeling that Darwin had, effectively, taken the credit for airing the case for evolution, although they had independently arrived at similar conclusions. Instead, he complained to Darwin in a letter written in 1870 that, 'there are no opponents left who know anything of natural history, so that there are none of the good discussions we used to have.'

Indeed, following his return to Britain in 1862, Wallace went on to staunchly defend *On the Origin of Species* on several occasions. In the meantime, Darwin himself had marshalled his own robust defence of his theory. In 1860 he had returned to writing an expanded version of *Natural Selection*, but this was abandoned in the spring of that year. What had caused Darwin to abruptly change tack altogether? Nothing less than the orchids that were to be found in the countryside surrounding Down House.

I took enormous pleasure in learning that it was the humblest of them all, the commonplace early purple orchid, that provided Darwin with his moment of revelation. This was the mark of a man who found the extraordinary in the ordinary and humble. Darwin was studying cowslips at the time, observing how they were adapted to allow cross-fertilisation by insects. The rich purple flower spikes of early purple orchids would have contrasted in the meadows with the buttery yellow of the cowslips. Was Darwin looking for a diversion from the intricacies of the cowslips, or was he simply curious?

We will never know what prompted him to use the sharp tip of a pencil to imitate an insect probing an orchid flower for nectar. Upon withdrawing the pencil he was surprised to find the orchid's pollinia – tiny sacs of pollen set at the end of small stalks, like minute chicken drumsticks, with which orchids pollinate one another – stuck firmly on the tip of the pencil. In a matter of seconds, before his very eyes, the pollinia slowly bent forwards and splayed slightly apart. Intrigued, Darwin repeated the exercise with orchid flower after orchid flower. Each time he found the same thing happened – pollinia were stuck onto the pencil, and then bent and splayed seconds after their removal from the orchid.

What could this mean? Darwin realised that the movement positioned the pollinia in such a way that they were perfectly aligned to deposit pollen on the receptive stigma of another orchid flower. Away from the artificial vehicle of his pencil, an insect visiting an early purple orchid flower in search of nectar would find itself with an irritating pair of pollinia stuck on its head. Disturbed by this unexpected encumbrance, it would be more likely to fly to another flower and, if this was another early purple orchid, the pollinia would by now be positioned in just the right way to fertilise the flower. This was a revelation for Darwin and would prove to be pivotal.

At the time in Europe it was a commonly held belief that flowers fertilised themselves. That bees visited flowers was considered simply to partake of their nectar in the production of honey, just part of God's infinite bounty. Sexual reproduction was a controversial subject at the time, but it was at the pulsing heart of *On the Origin of Species* – Darwin had made a case for it being a crucial part of the shaping of natural selection.

From that moment, on his hands and knees probing early purple orchids with a pencil in a Kentish hay meadow, Darwin's research to provide the evidence to substantiate the claims made in *On the Origin of Species* took an entirely new direction. He studied orchids and their pollinators assiduously, convinced that each species was pollinated by insects that specialised in them. Though he rarely witnessed the actual moment of pollination itself, he was convinced that his orchid subjects had evolved a relationship with their insect pollinators as intimate and precise as that of a lock and key. He diplomatically – or was this with a sense of mischief at the expense of the outraged Church of England? – referred to bees as 'marriage priests', but in his snappily titled *On the Various Contrivances by which British and Foreign Orchids are Fertilised by Insects*, published in 1862, Darwin set out unequivocal examples and case studies of the mechanics and products of evolution.

Better known by its abbreviated title *Fertilisation of Orchids*, this was Darwin's first concrete defence of the case he had set out three years previously. Orchids had provided Darwin with a compelling body of evidence. Upon reading *Fertilisation of Orchids*, the American botanist and ardent Christian Asa Gray was moved to say, '[had] the Orchid-book (with a few trifling omissions) … appeared before *The Origin* the author would have been canonised rather than anathematised by the natural theologians.'

Gray represented a middle ground between staunch theology and evidence-based science – he perceived the natural world to be full of examples of intelligent design and that God himself was the source of all evolutionary change. One can sense Darwin's exasperation at this unswerving belief when he said, 'I feel most deeply that the whole subject is too profound for the human intellect. A dog might as well speculate on the mind of Newton.'

Darwin had a hothouse built in the gardens of Down House to provide a specialised environment in which to grow tropical plants, chief amongst them orchids sent to him by his close friend Joseph Hooker.

'You cannot imagine what pleasure your plants give me,' he wrote to Hooker. 'I go and gloat over them.'

The pleasure Darwin derived from these orchids would feel familiar to many current orchidophiles – as I was learning, no other family of plants inspires quite such an intense, proprietary sentiment amongst its admirers. Darwin's orchid observations could now expand to include species that occurred naturally from much further afield than the countryside surrounding his home. These included the foreign orchid with which he is most famously connected and, in his lifetime, most widely ridiculed.

The comet orchid is a native of the humid lowlands of Madagascar, an orchid with powerfully aromatic waxy white flowers characterised by an extraordinarily long spur at the back of each bloom. Darwin, upon receiving some of these star-like blooms from the distinguished horticulturalist James Bateman, experimented with the flowers, attempting to manually remove their pollinia using bristles and needles. It was only once he inserted an extremely narrow cylinder down the length of the spur that he was able to detach the pollinia from the flower. From this, Darwin postulated in *Fertilisation of Orchids* that there had to be a pollinator moth for the comet orchid with a proboscis sufficiently long to reach the flower's nectar at the far end of each spur. He calculated that this moth would have a proboscis 35 cm long.

While much of the orchid-related evidence Darwin had gathered in support of his theory of natural selection was seen as compelling, it was this claim of an unknown Madagascan moth with a preposterous proboscis that his critics seized upon. Many simply refused to believe such a moth could possibly exist. George Campbell, 8th Duke of Argyll, went so far as to publish a book in 1867 entitled *The Reign of Law*, in which he implied that any such complex species could only have been created knowingly by a supernatural being.

Alfred Russel Wallace, unsung champion of natural selection, responded later that year with a paper defending Darwin, in which he outlined the process by which such a relationship between orchid and pollinating moth could have evolved, noting that an African sphinx moth, *Xanthopan morganii* (known then as *Macrosila morganii*) had a proboscis that was almost long enough. He concluded, 'That such a moth exists in Madagascar may be safely predicted; and naturalists who visit that island should search for it with as much confidence as astronomers searched for the planet Neptune – and they will be equally successful!'

It was only in 1903, twenty-one years after Darwin's death, that news emerged of the discovery of a sphinx moth in Madagascar with a proboscis that was exactly the length required to fertilise the comet orchid. A subspecies of the sphinx moth Wallace had written about, it was named subspecies *praedicta* in honour of his prediction that the pollinator would be a sphinx moth rather than the more general moth Darwin had hypothesised.

I reluctantly left Down House, orchid laboratory and crucible of evolutionary theory, to make my way to the even more imposing surroundings of nearby Lullingstone Castle. Passing through a towering Tudor redbrick gatehouse, I wandered across the lawns of the manor house beyond in search of someone I'd been looking forward to meeting for years – gardener, plant hunter, explorer and self-confessed 'orchid nut', Tom Hart-Dyke.

Tom's obsession with orchids propelled him into the national consciousness back in 2000 when, while exploring the lush and magnificently biodiverse Darién Gap between Colombia and Panama, he and a friend were kidnapped by anti-government FARC guerillas and held hostage at gunpoint in the jungle for nine months. Having spent time birdwatching in Colombia myself, I could easily imagine what had lured Tom there in the first place – the astounding biodiversity of the neotropics is like a slap in the face for a European naturalist more used to our temperate fauna and flora. The potential for discovering new species hitherto unknown to science remains high in such places – a sphinx moth I photographed in the Colombian Santa Marta Mountains in 2015 turned out, to my thrilled surprise, to be entirely undescribed – and the opportunity to find new orchid species was at the forefront of Tom's mind as he left Panama.

Quite what his captors made of Tom's obsession is harder to say. He whiled away his time in captivity by creating gardens in the vicinity of his quarters, gathering tropical orchids from the surrounding forest to bedeck a small area of the jungle camp that was his prison. I am certain that FARC had never encountered anyone quite like him. Tom, in person, is enthusiasm personified – his sheer energy and the joy he derives from plants spills from him like the sprays of colourful blooms from one of his beloved orchids, irrepressible and impossible to dislike. Unless, of course, one is a Kalashnikov-toting, nervous young Colombian guerilla who considers the deep jungle a place in which to hold foreign travellers to ransom … in which case Tom's passion may have seemed a little misplaced and inappropriate, given the gravity of his situation. There were moments when the guerillas threatened to execute Tom and his companion. Mercifully that threat was never realised, but I had little difficulty in believing that Tom had found considerable solace in orchids.

'Jon! How great you could make it!'

Tom's greeting as we met on the lawns made me feel like we'd known one another for years. We both shared a love of plants, and orchids in particular, so this was enough common ground for us to bond immediately. We had plenty to discuss, but that would have to wait a while, as my visit coincided with the culmination of a dream for him – the grand opening of his very own tropical orchid house in the grounds of Lullingstone. A small crowd had assembled for this special occasion.

Passing through a greenhouse spilling over with thorny cacti of all shapes and sizes, some squat as barrels and others towering like extras from a spaghetti western, we entered a small greenhouse devoted to the family of plants that thrilled Tom above all others. An impressive array of tropical orchids awaited us. Tom had spared no cost in creating an environment in which they would be happy – hidden machinery created breezes that gently moved his charges' vegetation, while fine mists of moisture drifted through the air. Tom was justly proud of this latest development of his beloved World Garden. His visitors, meanwhile, were clearly impressed, judging by the appreciative comments I was overhearing. Tom stood outside, as proud as a new father, patiently fielding orchid-related questions from his guests, mostly centring upon how to care for the orchids they had bought at their local supermarkets to sit upon their kitchen windowsills.

These colourful additions to our homes are just the latest mani-festation of our desire to cultivate tropical orchids in Britain, a desire that dates back to the time of Darwin and further still. Tom's orchid house, measuring just a few square metres, is a modest affair compared to some built in the nineteenth century – vast affairs of glass heated by complicated boilers, tended ardently by their acquisitive owners, and stocked with orchids sent from overseas by a small army of collectors who scoured the jungles of Africa, Asia and the Americas in search of the new, the rare and the exotic.

This craze for orchids peaked during the Victorian 'orchide-lirium', similar to the 'tulipomania' that consumed the Dutch in the seventeenth century. Vast quantities of orchids were collected and dispatched from the tropics, bound for Britain. Their survival rate was dismal, and many perished in transit. Those that survived would command high prices for the people who craved them so badly, and new or rare species were known to fetch spectacular prices at auction. Their chances of survival thereafter depended largely on their new owners having sufficient wealth to afford a dedicated orchid house that could approximate the conditions of their native environments.

The most illustrious victim of orchidelirium was Queen Victoria herself – she was a passionate orchidophile and even created the position of royal orchid grower in support of her interest. Frederick Sander, the holder of this title, presented her with an orchid bouquet five feet wide and seven feet high in 1887 for her Golden Jubilee. Sander went on to become a baron of the Holy Russian Empire, ennobled by the Romanovs, who were grateful for his assistance in building their extensive orchid collection. He was subsequently awarded the Belgian Order of the Crown in 1913, an honour originally intended to recognise heroic deeds. Whether supplying orchids to a prestigious and wealthy clientele qualifies as such is moot – it was probably his collectors who deserved recognition for the privations they suffered on his behalf. At one point Sander had over twenty collectors scouring the jungles of Asia and South America to supply him with orchids and, it would seem, royal patronage.

These collectors shared a perilous existence – even now many of the locations in which they travelled remain remote, inaccessible and potentially dangerous environments in which to spend prolonged periods. Prey to tropical diseases, misadventure and foul play, many collectors died in the field. In 1901 eight orchid collectors entered the Phillipine jungle in search of orchids, but only one returned alive – five of his colleagues vanished without trace, one was burned alive, and one was eaten by a tiger. Our appetite for orchids was insatiable, as vividly recounted by Norman MacDonald in *The Orchid Hunters*, his thrilling 1939 account of collecting orchids in Colombia to supply the American corsage market: 'When a man falls in love with orchids, he'll do anything to possess the one he wants. It's like chasing a green-eyed woman or taking cocaine. A sort of madness…'

Nowadays we need not be nobility, nor rely on an overseas network of collectors to possess an orchid or two – we can pick one up while doing the weekly supermarket shop. Mostly *Phalaenopsis* orchids, they are reared in controlled environments on an industrial scale with, in some cases, a level of automation that would do a car assembly line credit. Keeping them alive once they're home is another matter, and it was largely advice against overwatering that Tom seemed to be dispensing at Lullingstone Castle.

A small collection of Tom's friends and family retreated to the potting shed to talk orchids over mugs of tea and homemade cake. It felt inspiring to be amongst people for whom an obsession with orchids was expressed in terms of sheer pleasure. The sour taste of subterfuge and secrecy I had experienced with the sawfly orchid was fading rapidly in the face of such unbridled enthusiasm, and good cake.

Tom's interest was first sparked by the orchids he found in the countryside around Lullingstone, and he shared directions to one such nearby colony of man orchids. Before heading there, we walked towards a meadow in the grounds of the castle where he has knocked back encroaching scrub and coarse grass, and now manages for the benefit of native orchid species. This management has included planting orchids raised by Jeff Hutchings of Laneside Hardy Orchid Nursery, and when we arrived at the meadow, Jeff was busy showing some of the castle's visitors the first of these orchids to flower. I soon spotted a lone fly orchid blooming in the grass, and drew Tom's attention to it. His reaction was startling, but summed up perfectly the extent of his passion.

'Hey! Everyone! You've got to come and see this! This is awesome! Jon's just found our first fly orchid!'

Tom was literally bouncing with excitement as he exhorted Jeff and the visitors to come to see this unassuming, subtle orchid. An *Ophrys* orchid, it was a relative of the sawfly and early spider orchids I had already seen, but had none of either species' showiness and flamboyance. Fly orchids are discreet, slim insect-mimics, their flowers dark chocolaty-brown with a small shiny, silvery-violet rectangular speculum, and their petals reduced to thin, dark filiforms. The speculum mimics the shine of a resting insect's wings, and the petals its antennae. The whole bloom is compellingly insect-like, far more so than any of the other *Ophrys* orchids. While digger wasps, their pollinators, clearly have no difficulty finding them, the same cannot be said for humankind – I had certainly struggled to spot them in the past, even at sites where I knew they were present. Finding one where I least expected would have been pleasure enough – but the experience was rendered so much more satisfying given Tom's evident happiness. I left Lullingstone feeling greatly buoyed by the experience.

Only a mile away I stopped at the side of the main road. Here, on a wide grassy verge with traffic speeding past out of the village of Eynsford, was the roadside colony of man orchids that Tom had assured me I 'absolutely have to see'. He was right – this was an impressive colony, with some individuals larger than I had ever seen before. Man orchids are justly named – each flower is uncannily humanoid, with a long straight labellum that is lobed to form two arms and a pair of rather short legs. The petals and sepals above this figure are closed, forming a cowl that shields the man's face. This anthropomorphic resemblance would be charming enough, but each flower is beautifully coloured too – most are a rich lemony yellow with delicate fringes of garnet red, but in some individuals the garnet is predominant on a peridot green background.

I lay down amongst them, careful to ensure I was not inadvertently crushing any unseen plants. While cars blurred mere feet away from me in a sickly sweet draft of exhaust fumes, I found myself face to face with the green men of Kent. I had barely had time to settle down to take some photographs before a van had pulled into the side of the road some way beyond where I lay. A man jumped out and began to walk purposefully towards me. While I was doing nothing wrong, I had been challenged enough times in the past to immediately feel trespass-related pangs of guilt, none of which was helped by the fluorescent-yellow high-visibility vest the man was wearing. By the time he reached me I had already decided that this was somebody who worked for the local council's roads department, somebody who was decidedly unamused to find an amateur botanist sprawling at the side of a busy road. On reflection, it probably was not the safest place in which to look at man orchids … Perhaps I had let Tom's passion for his local orchids blind me to common sense.

It transpired that the stranger, in fact, was neither from Kent County Council nor disgruntled to find me endangering passing traffic. Instead, David was a supermarket home-delivery driver, and had stopped as he was worried I had been hit by a car and left comatose at the roadside. His relief upon finding me conscious and unharmed gave way to piqued curiosity as I explained what I was looking at.

'Wild orchids? Here in Kent? God, my wife will love this. Hold on…'

David squatted beside me and took a photo with his phone.

'She'll never believe me otherwise. I might have to bring her to see them.'

David walked back to his van and his deliveries, evidently delighted at the strange turn his day had taken. I decided to take my leave of the roadside at this juncture too – I would see plenty more man orchids in due course, and in more salubrious surroundings. It had been heartening to see these individuals flowering in surroundings that, at first glance, seemed so inappropriate for them. While many, like David, might assume that orchids were the preserve of the tropics, still others would naturally think that these precious plants were found only in highly specialised habitats in Britain. For some orchids this is undoubtedly the case, but others are much less fussy than we imagine – given half a chance they will thrive.

I finished the day a few miles from my former home in Kent, in the heart of the peaceful and secluded Elham valley. Some twenty years ago, on a warm sunny evening just like this one, I had been walking down an ancient trackway off the chalk downs with a fellow student, Stephanie. We had spent the afternoon looking for wildflowers on the downs themselves and, as we returned home, my mind was probably clouded with my feelings for her rather than actively looking for orchids. In the golden light of the last hours of the day my first lady orchid was absolutely luminous at the side of the track.

My thoughts for Steph were forgotten – I knew in an instant what this orchid was, but was swept off my feet by the sheer scale and stature of this impressive plant. I had never seen an orchid like it – over a foot tall, with a thick core that was more trunk than mere stem. The flower spike that surmounted this was a proud, open pyramid. Each individual bloom was perfect – a blousy white dress peppered with tiny tufts of the richest cerise, surmounted by a deep burgundy bonnet formed by the petals and sepals. The flowers had the faintest aroma of vanilla – this was a lady enhancing herself with the subtlest perfume. I never did tell Steph how I felt at the time, for my heart was lost in an instant to an orchid.

This year it was important to me that I should see my first lady orchids in similar circumstances – that this would be in Kent was a foregone conclusion, as the county is the heartland for the species in Britain – but I wanted to immerse myself in their beauty in a wash of nostalgia and the fading sunlight that had bathed my very first lady. There are many woodlands in Kent graced by these dazzling orchids, and I chose one a stone's throw from my first lady orchid encounter: a site in the sprawling Denge Wood known to both orchid and butterfly enthusiasts alike as Bonsai Bank, due to the stunted conifers that had failed to prosper on its chalky soil. What had flourished, however, was a spectacular colony of lady orchids and a thriving population of equally rare Duke of Burgundy butterflies. I hoped to see both in the late afternoon, with the added incentive of confirmed news in recent days of an unusual pure white lady orchid in the midst of her already splendid counterparts.

The walk through Denge Woods from Penny Pot Lane follows a wide forestry track that gives little hint of what lies beyond. Here and there piles of recently cut logs tower sappily on the verges. The smell of fresh horse manure hung heavily in the warm afternoon air. It had been years since my last visit, and I found myself slightly uncertain how far into the woods I needed to walk before reaching Bonsai Bank. No sooner had doubt crept in than I spotted my first lady orchids at the side of the track and, beyond them in the opening glade, a host of further flowers.

I had never seen such a profusion of lady orchids, let alone such a variety of shapes, shades and forms of flowers – Bonsai Bank was an orchid catwalk. Many were the standard flower I remembered from all those years ago, but others were deeply flushed all over with a black-cherry-yoghurt wash, and others had bonnets the exact shade of pink lemonade. Some had wide, frilly skirts, while nearby flowers sported lips as bifurcated as culottes. Darwin would have delighted in this profusion of variety.

I slowly wandered amongst them, every few yards revealing yet another swathe of their number as the clearing unfolded around me. The ground was thick with a further orchid – my first flowering common twayblades of the year were common here. Did an orchid ever have such an underwhelming English name? While these orchids are both widespread and have paired oval leaves that form the 'twayblade', the flowers themselves have a subtle charm that is easily overlooked at first glance – they have green stems suffused with dark red tones, while the flowers are like small, lime-green angels. Each flower has a deeply lobed green labellum beneath a halo formed by their burgundy-fringed petals and sepals. Beloved of spiders, every common twayblade at Bonsai Bank had at least one small hunter lurking amongst its flowers, spinning a deadly mesh between the angelic hosts. The spiders were not the only surprise awaiting unwary insects landing on the twayblades – the flowers themselves pack an explosive punch for the unwitting.

Each flower has a poised hair trigger within it, the rostellum, waiting to be touched by a visiting insect. Upon contact with this part of the flower, a small explosion of sticky liquid violently fires the waiting pollinia onto the insect where they stick fast – the liquid sets in a matter of moments. The startled insect flies away, bearing the pollinia to be carried to the next twayblade flower it visits. This artillery approach to pollination occurs in orchids worldwide – Darwin, in the process of researching *Fertilisation of Orchids*, experimented with a South American orchid, the calloused catasetum *Catasetum callosum*, and noted, 'I touched the antennæ of *C. callosum* whilst holding the flower at about a yard's distance from the window, and the pollinium hit the pane of glass, and adhered to the smooth vertical surface by its adhesive disc.'

Long before their pollination techniques were unlocked, William Turner, a sixteenth-century English naturalist, described what is believed to be the common twayblade in *The Names of Herbes*, published in 1548 – he noted that it was to be found, 'in many places of Englande in watery middowes and woddes'.

By the time John Gerard's *Herball* was released in 1597 the name by which we know it today had been adopted – he referred to it as 'Twayblade' or 'Herbe Bifoile', and remarked that it had been seen at Southfleet in Kent. This would have been masterful understatement, as common twayblade is found widely across the whole of Britain and Ireland, being absent in very few places indeed. While it was satisfying to see my first common twayblades in Gerard's Kent, I could only be distracted momentarily – the lady orchids continued to exert their compelling allure. They were irresistible.

The rest of the afternoon passed in a delicious haze of photography in which I was distracted only by the occasional appearance of tawny Duke of Burgundies. Recently emerged from their pupae and as bright and fresh as a newly minted coin, they would appear suddenly, as if from nowhere, pausing to bask at ground level in pools of sunlight. With their chequered brown and orange wings spread wide open, it was easy to see why the old entomologists knew this as the Duke of Burgundy fritillary – the fritillary referring to the chequerboard pattern, in the same way that those graceful chequered-purple meadow flowers snake's-head fritillaries earned their name. With a host of *Nymphalidae* butterflies also known generically as fritillaries, the unrelated Duke of Burgundy fritillary only recently began to be referred to simply as Duke of Burgundy. Having grown up knowing it by the former name, I mourned the passing of the fritillary and, privately, still thought of it by the older and more beautiful title. Sometimes progress, while taxonomically accurate, seems needlessly ugly and dismissive of the past.

I had carefully transcribed directions to find the rarest of all the lady orchids, the wraith of the woods – a pearly white individual that had been seen flowering in a secluded corner of the clearing in recent days. In the end I need not have worried, for I found two further pallid flowers nearby. Their pure, bridal-white simplicity was captivating, but the real beauties here were the bridesmaids of Bonsai Bank, the masses of more typically marked lady orchids, glowing just as I recalled they did in the embers of May sunshine so many years previously.

With both genders of anthropomorphic orchid safely seen, there just remained their simian counterpart elsewhere in the county, the considerably rarer monkey orchid. First discovered near Faversham in Kent in 1777, the species has always maintained the most precarious of toeholds in Britain. Here it is at the very most northerly extreme of its European range, being more commonly found in southern Europe, north Africa, and east into the Crimea. Once more widespread in Britain, in common with many plants it underwent a dramatic decline during the nineteenth century and, by the 1920s, was restricted to just one site on a hillside at Hartslock in Oxfordshire. So shrouded in secrecy was this site that the general consensus amongst botanists of the time was that the monkey orchid had been, by this point, lost altogether as a British plant.

Nevertheless, in the years leading up to the Second World War this colony numbered some two hundred flowering plants. Unfortunately, in the aftermath of the war, in 1949 and 1950 the field in question was ploughed, a victim of the post-war intensification and mechanisation of agriculture. This act of wanton botanical vandalism meant that between 1950 and 1952 just one monkey orchid was to be found in bloom at Hartslock. The mistaken belief that the species was extinct had drawn perilously close to becoming true.

The colony recovered painfully slowly on the upper slopes of the hillside and, even in the late 1970s there were still fewer than ten flowering plants to be found there. Meanwhile in 1955, almost two centuries after the first example had been discovered near Faversham, a single flowering plant was found by botanist Hector Wilks in Kent in the Faversham area. Monkey orchids seem to love flirting with imminent extinction, as this single plant was no sooner found than it was gone, thought to have been eaten by a horse. Happily, more bloomed at this site in the following years and, from 1958 to the mid-1980s these plants were hand-pollinated to ensure that they set seed. This hand pollination was believed to be responsible for the inadvertent creation of one of the rarest orchid hybrids to have occurred in Britain – *Orchis x bergonii*, the hybrid offspring of man and monkey orchid parents. One such plant flowered amongst its parents briefly in the mid-1980s, though it was seen by very few people: to protect the precious monkey orchids, the site's exact location was kept secret, and remains so to this day.

Meanwhile, from 1958 monkey orchid seed from the site was taken by Wilks to be scattered at several likely looking locations elsewhere in Kent. This initiative, though well intentioned, was not notably successful, as in all but one site the seed failed to result in new satellite colonies. Fortunately, though, at one location a short distance from Denge Woods, a new colony was born in a sheltered, dry shallow valley known as Park Gate Down.

Nowadays the small valley is managed by the Kent Wildlife Trust and has lately been renamed the Hector Wilks Reserve in honour of the man who rediscovered and went to such lengths to conserve the monkey orchids of Kent. It is a remarkable site to visit in the early summer, and offers a glimpse of what many calcareous meadows may once have looked like: a botanical smorgasbord of orchids and more flowering plants besides. When I lived in Kent it was an easy cycle from home to Park Gate Down, and I visited it often.

A new day had barely dawned when I found myself back in one of my favourite orchid sites in Britain. Hidden in a myriad of narrow country lanes, entirely unsignposted until one is actually there, the small wooden gate that forms the entrance to the reserve prepares one little for what lies beyond. A chain of three grassy meadows unfolds the length of the valley, flanked on either side by thick deciduous woodland. The grass is studded with orchids, and the eye is immediately drawn to the rich cerise and white blobs that are monkey orchids peeping above the sward. Cowslips are thick underfoot as one explores the meadows. I walked into the first of the fields with a sense of a homecoming – this was my Kent, the place in which I had enjoyed so many happy hours and days. The monkey orchids had never failed to delight, and today was no exception. With the dawn chorus of birdsong stuttering to a faltering conclusion, I knelt in the dew-wet grass and renewed my acquaintance with them.

Each flower is dominated at first glance by large, pink-flecked white sepals and petals, but it is the capering figure of the monkey beneath that lends the orchid its name. The lip of the flower is deeply lobed, with pairs of twisty, curved arms and legs, while between the legs is a short further protuberance – this is the tail, and the illusion of a small, animated simian is complete. But what monkey ever looked like these small apes? The body is white, with the torso heavily spattered with deep-rose tufts of fur, and the arms and legs are suffused towards their extremities with further purplish-pink tones. Inside the hood formed by the petals and sepals, the suffusion intensifies still more, and it is not difficult to see a small face peeping back at one. My mind naturally fills in the missing links in the monkey's form.

Missing links drew me to one more orchid site that morning in Kent. News had emerged online a week beforehand of something I simply could not miss – Mark Sewell, a local orchid enthusiast, had found an *Orchis x bergonii* hybrid at the original monkey orchid site in north Kent. While the site's location was still a well-kept secret, and Mark was not publicly sharing precisely where he had found the plant, my immediate assumption upon hearing the news had been to assume that it would be at one location in particular. I knew it of old, as the site in question was within walking distance of the house in which I had lived briefly at the time.

If Park Gate Down was well hidden and heralded with little fanfare then this, the original monkey orchid site in north Kent, is the Area 51 of British orchids. In common with the notoriously secretive US Air Force base buried in the depths of the Nevada desert, there are no signs announcing its presence, and the perimeter of the site is kept extraordinarily secure. Set back from a busy road, the site is first guarded by a slumped low wire fence beside an unassuming gate. A small, shaded, ivy-choked former quarry beyond looks like the sort of place a fly-tipper would discard old fridges, mattresses and black bags of garden refuse. Anxious not to draw attention to where I was going, I had parked half a mile further down the road in a similarly dark, muddy gateway – this one sporting an abandoned pornographic magazine. There was little to suggest anything special was hidden nearby.

Once beyond the old quarry, the extent of the site's security becomes clearer, though what it is meant to keep out is not entirely certain. The purpose of the rabbit wire on the high-tension fence is plain enough, but the additional barbed wire and strand of thick electrified fencing wire above the fence posts suggest that larger mammals – deer and, it would appear, people too – are to be excluded. The obvious stile to access the small field beyond seems insurmountable, as the electric fence above it is too high to cross, and packs a charge like a punch to the chest for anyone foolish enough to touch it. The real entrance to the field is hidden in the woods beyond. If one did not know it was there, and if one was not focused on orchid hunting, it would be easy to be discouraged from persisting any further to enter this seemingly empty meadow. I knew better.

As I picked my way around the perimeter to the hidden entrance I caught sight of what had drawn me here – an orchid of a colour quite unlike any I had ever seen before, an unusual confection of deep magenta and yellow. I had spent the early morning mesmerised by the candyfloss colours of one parent, monkey orchid, but was unprepared for how strikingly these tones would have combined with the lemony yellow and claret hues of the man orchid parent.

I was also unprepared for how poorly the monkey orchid colony here was faring compared to those at Park Gate Down. There I had given up counting once I passed one hundred flower spikes, but here I found just a handful. I had heard that this site had been grazed in previous years by goats. If true, this struck me as an unusual choice of animal to use on such a delicate site – goats are notoriously indiscriminate and hard grazers, the Agent Orange of ungulates.

The poor fortunes of the monkey orchids notwithstanding, I found myself smiling broadly as I knelt on the short turf beside the hybrid – here it was, the missing-link orchid. Given the long intervening time since one flowered here last, it seemed unlikely that this was the same individual last seen in the late 1980s, though some monkey orchids have been known to flower for almost twenty consecutive years. If it was indeed a different plant, there was, in the absence of any rumours to the contrary, nothing to suggest that this was not a naturally occurring hybrid – both man and monkey orchids were present there, albeit neither now in any great numbers.

Sharing characters of both parents, the hybrid was more handsome than either man or monkey orchid. It was more colourful

than a man orchid, yet more elegant and less contorted than a monkey orchid. The humanoid figure that comprised each flower had
the length and straight limbs of a man orchid, and the sulphurous
shade of the torso and hood it owed to that parent too. Meanwhile,
the delicious raspberry-sorbet limbs and highlights on the hood
were clearly from the monkey orchid genes. This was a plant that
was even better than the sum of its already excellent parts.

I knew Charles Darwin would have enjoyed this unusual hybrid
orchid, vivid example as it was of his hypothesis that from, 'an
entangled bank, clothed with many plants of many kinds … endless forms most beautiful and most wonderful have been, and are
being, evolved'.

I was less sure what Bishop 'Soapy Sam' Wilberforce would have
made of it, given his firmly held and eloquently expressed views
on the immutability of God's creations. I had a shrewd feeling he
would not have approved, and I loved this curious plant all the
more for that.

Later, I found myself on consecrated ground that Soapy Sam
would, perhaps, have felt more comfortable upon. Standing in the
graveyard of St Mary's, at Headley in Surrey, I was in the company of Steve Gale, accomplished local naturalist and wildlife blog-
ger. Steve had brought me here so I could pay homage to one of
my childhood heroes, Frederick Frohawk. An entomologist and
natural-history artist who died in 1946 might seem like an unusual
idol for a boy in the 1980s, but the scientifically accurate text of
his skilfully illustrated butterfly books were, for years, my bedtime
reading. Steve, aware of my admiration for Frohawk, had brought
me to his grave after we had spent several hours orchid hunting in
the woods around Headley. As culminations of days went, this took
a lot of beating for me – a simple wooden cross marks Frohawk's
resting place with, on closer inspection, a Camberwell beauty
butterfly carved into the shaft. I patted the cross as we said our
goodbyes – I had a lot to thank Frohawk for.

I also owed a debt of gratitude to Steve, as I had asked him
to show me his local bird's-nest orchids, and he had more than
risen to the challenge. We had walked that sunny afternoon into a
beech wood that lightly covers a chalky ridge of the Surrey hills at

Ranmore. Steve had seen a profusion of bird's-nest orchids here in the past, and we hoped to find them here again. Our time together had already been blessed with a crowd of 125 man orchids and, in an omen Frohawk would have approved of, an iridescence of electric Adonis blue butterflies on the grassy flanks of Box Hill. As Steve parted the low curtains of beech boughs, I was not prepared for what lay beyond, but perhaps I should have expected a spectacular grand finale to a day that was already one of the finest so far this summer.

Steve proudly gestured to the ground beneath the widely spaced beech trees, their new leaves painting the sky overhead a mosaic of zingy, glowing green. Somewhere nearby a drowsy tawny owl hooted, but my attention was riveted on what Steve had saved for last.

'There they are, Jon. They're some show, aren't they?'

This was an incredible understatement. Before us were at least 250 bird's-nest orchids, most of them in fresh, newly emerged flower, but with still more nosing their way up through the beech-leaf litter that carpeted the ground. Each fully formed flower spike was tall, as long as my forearm and entirely the colour of horn – these orchids, while not totally lacking chlorophyll, have no hint of green about them and do not photosynthesise. Their pale-ochre stems were surmounted by thick assemblages of con-colourous flowers – each plant's uniformity of colour made them look as if they had been carved from a single block of solid, aged tallow by some unseen sylvan sculptor. The pointed, unopened younger emerging plants were faintly unsettling, appearing like the honey-coloured hooves of young goats reaching up from beneath our feet.

Bird's-nest orchids are entirely dependent on underground, mycorrhizal fungi for their nutrition – their roots are heavily infected with subterranean *Sebacina* fungi. The fungi have a reciprocal relationship with the surrounding beech trees, whereby they take carbohydrates from the trees and, in return, provide the trees with mineral nutrients. The bird's-nest orchid hacks the wood-wide web – it takes nutrients from the fungi, but gives nothing in return. I had never seen such a graphic demonstration of this relationship as that which Steve had set before me – that the orchids were following an underground fungal partner was astonishingly clear, for they grew in a large, perfect circle some four metres in diameter. Inside the circumference of flowering plants was another perfect circle, a little smaller, formed of the dead, dried husks of the previous year's flower spikes. The orchids were following a fairy ring of woodland fungus as it slowly spread outwards. There was something utterly magical about these strange, pallid orchids, more at home in a Grimms' fairy tale than a tame Surrey beech wood.

4

Sex, lies and orchid pollination

While Charles Darwin had his initial eureka moment probing an early purple orchid with the tip of a pencil in the fields near his home at Down House, there were other, more visually intriguing, orchids to be found nearby that provided further material in support of his hypothesis that orchids had evolved intimate relationships with their insect pollinators.

Fly orchids would have been the perfect case study for creationists and proponents of evolution alike – found in the woodlands and meadow fringes across Kent and further afield throughout much of the British Isles, these unassuming orchids' flowers bear an uncanny resemblance to an insect. The flower is approximately one centimetre in length, shaped and coloured like a child's drawing of a long-bodied fly or wasp. The body is a rich rufous brown, and there is a pale silvery-blue area that hints at the shiny wings on the back of the insect. Two black glossy knobs towards the head resemble beady eyes, while the petals are thin and antenna-like.

That each flower looks like an insect is clearly not accidental – but, depending on one's religious or scientific persuasion, quite how this had come to pass would have been a matter of heated conjecture. To the creationist, the deliberate hand of God would have been at work – how could an unthinking, dumb plant have created such a compelling simulacrum all by itself? The intervention of a superior power would have been no more evident than in a flower that resembled the very insects that came to drink the nectar God had provided within it.

Darwin, meanwhile, had discerned something more wonderful and remarkable still. Fly orchids were attracting one type of pollinator in particular to their insect-like charms – male digger wasps. These are not the fat-bodied wasps of picnic disruption and lancing sting. The digger wasps in question, *Argogorytes mystaceus*, have long, slender black bodies with thin golden hoops encircling their abdomens. Their antennae are long too, and their eyes are black and lustrous. They are elegant, delicate creatures.

Attracted to the fly orchids, the digger wasps are the key in the orchids' pollination lock – pollinia from one flower adhere to the wasps' heads and move, just as Darwin observed on his pencil tip, into a different position ready to fit exactly into the next receptive orchid flower the wasp visits. This much Darwin could see for himself, but it would be much later, during the twentieth century, that we came to understand the full, impressive extent of how the fly orchids had evolved a pollination mechanism of quite startling complexity and duplicity.

The wasps are not attracted by nectar – *Ophrys* orchids are nectarless deceivers, and the deception in question is purely sexual. It is no coincidence that the digger wasps visiting fly orchids are exclusively male: they attempt to mate with the flower itself, a process known as pseudocopulation – a term as dry as the act itself is unsatisfactory for the wasp. While the superficial insect-like appearance of each flower may catch a passing wasp's attention – the silvery-blue speculum on the insect's 'body' even reflects ultraviolet light, imitating the play of light on a resting wasp's folded wings – the fly orchids have an additional attraction that is as irresistible, and false, as the song of the Sirens of Greek and Roman mythology. Each flower produces a scent that, while indiscernible to humankind, is a potent and intoxicating promise for a male wasp – a floral bouquet that imitates with devastating accuracy the sex pheromones of a receptive female wasp. Ironically, while the Sirens are mostly associated with luring sailors to their inevitable doom on rocky seashores, the Greeks referred to them as inhabiting flowery meadows.

This matters not to a passing digger wasp. All he can know is that what appears to be a virgin female of his kind is nearby – the potency of this chemical bait proves irresistible, and it is not unknown for more than one male wasp to be seen attempting to mate with a particularly fresh and presumably enticingly odoriferous bloom. Scientists have discovered that the composition of each floral bouquet varies between populations of fly orchids, individual plants and even the flowers on a single orchid itself. It is as if the plants are mixologists in a bar, making endless variations on a theme in an attempt to create the perfect, intoxicating cocktail. Each flower's approximate resemblance to an insect is, it would seem, not so much to attract a digger wasp in the first place as it is to ensure that, once at the flower, the wasp assumes the correct position upon it for pollinia to either stick to the wasp's head and be removed from the flower's anther, or be deposited from the wasp to the receptive stigma of the flower – while the unsuspecting wasp, meanwhile, gamely attempts to mate with his unreceptive partner.

This sexual deception is, at first glance, a curious pollination strategy – by appealing strictly to male digger wasps, the fly orchids are limiting the number of potential pollinators that could provide that vital reproductive service. Yet the fly orchids are not alone in relying on sexual deception – orchids all around the world are known to have evolved similarly duplicitous pollination mechanisms. This can be no accident – something about this strategy clearly works for it to be repeated. Researchers in Australia and Italy have closely observed these particular orchids and their pollinators – and realised that those species of orchids with highly evolved, sexually deceitful strategies were more effectively pollinated than those orchid species that offered nectar to attract a wide variety of pollinators. A higher percentage of the pollen taken from the sexually deceptive orchids is deposited in the flowers of the same species. Orchids with multiple pollinators had more pollen taken from their flowers – but more of it was lost, either deposited in the flowers of other species or simply dropped on the ground altogether. As one of the researchers, Giovanni Scopece of the University of Naples concluded, 'Sexy orchids do it better!'

Darwin was blissfully unaware of this devastatingly effective chemical warfare on the part of orchids as a whole and, in particular, the fly orchids he saw near his home in Kent. Meanwhile I, while familiar with the duplicity involved in fly orchid reproduction, had never actually seen the act of pseudocopulation for myself. If I was honest with myself, I could not recall actually ever noticing a digger wasp before. Despite having seen my first fly orchid of the year in Tom Hart-Dyke's newly planted orchid meadow, I had not yet seen a truly wild plant this year, so it seemed fitting that I should not only see my first wild fly orchids of 2016 while treading in Darwin's footsteps, but that I should also attempt to see a male digger wasp caught in the act of inadvertently pollinating one. It was time to do some orchid dogging at Downe Bank.

When Darwin referred to 'an entangled bank, clothed with many plants of many kinds' it is thought that the bank in question was one not far from his home at Down House – Downe Bank is less than a mile away on foot from Down House. The bank itself comprises two sloping areas in a woodland clearing. I was armed with valuable advice from Grant Hazlehurst, a Kentish local who had made a particular study of the pseudocopulating digger wasps and had taken a remarkable series of photos, including a veritable orgy with no fewer than three horny wasps attempting simultaneously, stacked upon one another, to copulate with a single flower.

Grant had advised me to visit before 11 a.m. on a warm morning. In this regard, my dogging activities would be considerably less surreptitious than those reputedly conducted in Kent's car parks and laybys after dark. Nevertheless, this would be the first time I had ventured into the countryside, camera in hand, hoping to photograph sexual congress of any kind. I felt a little furtive and seedy as I walked into what is now a Kent Wildlife Trust reserve, but was known at the time to Darwin and his family as Orchis Bank.

My first challenge was to find some fly orchids amongst the hundreds of common twayblades that carpeted the clearing floor. There was no shortage of the latter, but finding the former was a little more difficult. Before I found a fly orchid I began to see digger wasps resting on vegetation, and then in flight too. Grant had told me that, rather than trying to follow a wasp to an orchid, I would be better to position myself near some likely looking fly orchids and wait for the wasps to come to me. Before too long I had found my first fly orchid of the day and, technically, the year. Even though I could not summon the kind of unbridled enthusiasm Tom Hart-Dyke had exhibited when I discovered the first flowering fly orchid in his newly planted meadow, I was nevertheless pleased with myself. I was in with a chance now of seeing a digger wasp in action.

In truth though, I felt it would have had to be a fairly desperate digger wasp that attempted to copulate with this particular orchid. As fly orchids went, this individual was particularly depauperate, a sorry and rather enfeebled plant with a weedy, thin stem and just two faded flowers. While, like Darwin, I could not discern the floral bouquet these flowers were emitting and hence could not say whether, looks aside, this plant was broadcasting particularly alluring come-hither signals, deep down I instinctively felt that if I was a wasp this wouldn't be the flower for me. I cast my net a little wider and, in due course, found myself a good patch of the clearing in which I could see almost a dozen fresh, crisp, flowering fly orchids. The stage was set – now all I needed were the players.

As orchid hunting goes, this was all extremely pleasant. I could sit in the sun and simply enjoy the fly orchids in their own right while I waited for the arrival of an amorous wasp. A song thrush emerged from the woods behind me and, wasting little time, began to batter furiously a hapless snail on an anvil stone at the side of the narrow chalky path upon which I sat. I sentimentally moved a large Roman snail traversing the path beside me into the short undergrowth, hoping this small act of random kindness might be rewarded by the appearance of a frisky digger wasp.

It wasn't. An hour passed, in which time I saw a lot more of the woods' birdlife as various species came and went about their business. My song thrush worked his way through several snails in short order and, frustratingly, I saw a number of small flying insects pass me that were recognisably digger wasps. I tried to keep track of where they were going, heedless of Grant's advice that it was better to wait for them to come to me. Their fast flight and inconspicuous colouration soon taught me the error of my ways and the wisdom of Grant's experience as I quickly lost sight of them against the varied green background of the clearing floor.

When, finally, a digger wasp deigned to settle on an orchid nearby it was, unfortunately, not on a fly orchid. This wasp had not read the script, for he landed on a common twayblade a foot away from me. Now, at least, I could enjoy an uninterrupted and close look at the fly orchid's pollinating agent. He was close enough for me to make out even the individual segments of his long black antennae and the reddish-bronze cast on his translucent wings – exactly, I now realised, the same tone as the rufous-brown lip of the nearby fly orchids. The golden hoops on his abdomen were glowing in the sunlight and, at this short range, I could see further yellow highlights on his body – each black leg had a golden section and a small further spot was present on the side of his thorax. That was not all – there was a small yellow area on his head... and I realised, suddenly, that this was an orchid pollinium stuck firmly on my wasp. I had not seen the act of pseudocopulation that had put it there, but it was indisputably present – the lipstick on my wasp's collar, evidence of his dalliance with a fly orchid rather than a female of his own kind.

Any hopes I entertained of seeing the final act of this sexual drama, the transfer of the pollinium to a new flower, were dashed when the wasp leapt back into flight and purposefully headed away down the slope and out of sight. Our shared moment had been relatively brief, but it had been significant. I had seen more than I might have dared hope I would. While I found the effectiveness of the fly orchid's sexual deception deeply impressive, I could not help but feel a little sorry for the hapless wasp in question. I hoped that the next time my wasp smelt a virgin female digger wasp's scent in the air of Orchis Bank, it might emanate from an actual wasp and not a coy, sly orchid bloom.

This insect and orchid relationship is given further complexity in the jungles of South and Central America. Here a particularly colourful family of *Euglossine,* or orchid bees, use orchids to enhance their own sexual attractiveness. Male orchid bees visit particularly fragrant orchids where, once they have found a scent that takes their fancy, they employ a technique like the enfleurage method once used by perfumers. Smearing a fatty substance on the orchid using special brushes on their forelegs, they extract the volatile oils from the orchid that provide the orchid's scent. These chemicals are transferred into a sponge-like storage cavity inside the bees' hindlegs where, added to over time by the bees, they blend to form what Thomas Eltz, an ecologist from the University of Düsseldorf, described as a 'rich and sexy bouquet'. Naturally, the orchids in question deposit pollinia on the orchid bees and use them as vehicles for their own sexual activity, but in this particular relationship there is something in it for the insects.

Male orchid bees gather in clearings formed by treefalls, where they form leks – territories at which they display to attract female bees, flying back and forth from perches on the trunks of trees – and here, as if their jewel-like metallic bodies were not attractive enough, they are believed to release their individually blended perfumes as an inducement to mating. I remembered getting ready to go out on a Friday night as a student in Kent after a day of orchid hunting – donning my best clothes and a splash of aftershave were my optimistic preparation for a spot of lekking of my own. Little had I known that I was simply mimicking the behaviour of Neotropical orchid bees.

Kent is home to two further British species of *Ophrys* orchids, one relatively common and widespread across the county and further afield, but the other restricted to Kent alone. It was the latter, late spider orchid, which I now hoped to see before leaving the county. When I was a student in Kent I had searched in vain for these on the Wye Downs – I knew they were reputed to be present there, but my searches had been fruitless. Because they formed small, discrete colonies on the chalk downs, I would have needed good fortune, or more free time in which to search than I had available to me, if I was to find them back then. A few years later, while looking for chalkhill blue butterflies on the downs near my house, I stumbled across a small host of heavy wire cages set firmly in the grass on the sides of a small concavity in a hillside. Within each cage was the remains of an *Ophrys* orchid, past their best by that stage in the late summer, so not readily identifiable as a particular species – but I had my suspicions. What other *Ophrys* would warrant such special attention?

Late spider orchids are one of Britain's rarest orchid species. Found only in Kent, and there at only a handful of sites on the downs in a triangle formed between Dover, Folkestone and Wye, they are the most spectacular of all our *Ophrys*. Each flower is simply magnificent, a rich confection of pink, lime and chestnut brown, their beauty gilded further for the orchid hunter by their extreme rarity – at one point in the 1980s it was thought that only around fifty plants remained and, even now, after dedicated conservation efforts including hand-pollination in the absence of the plant's preferred species of bee pollinators, fewer than five hundred plants flower in any given year. Any year in which over three hundred flowering plants are found is considered a good year for the species in Britain. Our late spider orchids represent the very most northerly tip of their extensive European range – they cling on to Britain's flora by their very fingertips, separated from their kith and kin by the narrow blue ribbon of the Dover Straits.

Across their European range they are famously variable, with dozens of varieties and subspecies that provide taxonomists with fertile ground upon which to squabble, with some choosing to split the late spider orchid into many further individual species in their own right, and others opting to lump these myriad plants into one technicolor dreamcoat of a species. Even those found in Kent are immensely variable, with differences in shape and colouration to be found between plants just a few feet apart in one colony. Needless to say, British orchid hunters love these plants and revel in their beauty, variability, and the rarefied atmosphere that their scarcity generates about them.

The year after I had found those odd metal cages, I returned to see if my suspicions were well founded. The site in question was an easy twenty-minute walk from home, so I visited it regularly as the spring progressed. To begin with there was little to be seen – the cages had been removed during the winter and left abandoned in an untidy pile beneath a nearby bush. To the casual onlooker from the country lane that skirted the hillside there would have been nothing to suggest this field was anything out of the ordinary. As the spring progressed some unknown, benevolent hand was at work, placing the cages over developing orchid rosettes set in the short turf on the steep sides of the slope. I watched their progress with interest as, safe within their cages from the attentions of any passing rabbit, the orchids developed further, sending up budding stems until, finally, they began bursting into flower. These were my first late spider orchids, and they were soon followed by dozens more in the area. Once they were at the height of their flowering period I widened my search along the nearby downs and found more, some caged, but others out in the open and blooming freely.

I had already visited my former haunts earlier this year while in Kent looking for early spider orchids – and I was a little worried. One site near Wye had been completely abandoned, evidently ungrazed for some years and now choked by thick, smothering tor-grass with a scattering of pioneer shrub saplings, field maples, dog-roses and hawthorns. At another site, where late spider orchids had once bloomed at the very crest of a hill where the chalk grassland fell precipitously away to a wet valley bottom, the hilltop's thick spinneys had poured in a wave over the brow of the hill and threatened now to reach the hedgerows at the valley bottom itself. At my original site the heavy wire cages lay in their usual winter quarters, tucked away beneath what had progressed in the intervening years from large bush to modest tree. I was concerned that I might struggle to find late spider orchids readily by myself.

Help was at hand in the form of Alfie Gay, the warden for an area of the North Downs near Folkestone that supported a further scattered population of late spider orchids. We had agreed to meet on a hillside overlooking the Channel Tunnel rail terminus on the outskirts of the town. While I wandered aimlessly, nearby clouds of small moths rose from the grass at my feet – Britain was, at the time, in the midst of an invasion from the Continent of diamondback moths – heedless of man-made borders, these tiny insects had poured into the country, allowing some sections of the press to ominously, and inaccurately, predict British crops would be wiped out that summer. When Alfie arrived, he proved to be a charming guide with a wealth of information about the area, the history of the late spider orchids and their conservation. A young man with irrepressible curly brown hair and an easy-going manner, Alfie led me to two discrete colonies of my quarry – one a population that seemed to be in decline in recent years, and another that was flourishing.

This latter colony demonstrated perfectly the dilemma that confronts those who find themselves responsible for conserving the rarer and more endangered examples of our country's wildlife. On the one hand, the ideal scenario is one in which the rare wildlife is kept safely out of sight of the general public and out of harm's way. On the other hand, if the public is unaware of the beauty and the rarity of that wildlife, how can it possibly understand the value of it and, hence, be motivated to cherish it?

For the most part the exact locations of Britain's late spider orchid colonies are not public knowledge. Broad euphemisms such as 'the Wye Downs' are not sufficient to allow anyone easily to find a late spider orchid, as I of all people knew only too well, having discovered my first twenty years ago purely by chance.

In recent years, however, the particular colony that Alfie was showing me had become, if not public knowledge, then certainly an open secret. It sits in a field just a few feet from a public road and on the side of a public footpath that traverses that field. It is, as I soon discovered, easy to see the brightly coloured orchids both from the road and the footpath alike. In fact, it would be hard to miss them from the footpath, as some of the flowering plants were no more than a few inches from the well-trodden byway. To make matters worse, visiting photographers had already flattened small areas of grass and other wildflowers beside some of the more flamboyant flower spikes, drawing further attention to them from even the most focused of hikers. And there were hikers aplenty – in the hour or so that Alfie and I spent at this colony of fine orchids in their prime at least a dozen hikers and dog walkers passed by.

Some stopped to exchange a few words, and to ask what we were looking at. Alfie, who planned to spend the entire day there in his capacity as a warden protecting the plants from the further careless attentions of their admirers, was doing himself and his employers enormous credit as he explained what the orchids were and how important their conservation was. I, meanwhile, happily examined each plant in turn, marvelling at their plasticity. No two were quite the same, with variations in both the shape and markings of their large, hairy lips, and the precise shape and colouration of their triangular petals and oval sepals – these varied from almost white through to a dark, bruised magenta. These were orchids at least as fabulously coloured as their tropical counterparts, if not more so. Scattered amongst them for good measure were a handful of man orchids – subtle counterpoints to the late spider orchids' lascivious extravagance.

Alfie and I discussed the complexities of managing such a public site that hosts a rare flowering plant. The flattened areas of vegetation left by visiting photographers bore stark testament to the inadvertent damage that the orchids' admirers inflicted – amongst the crushed grass were more delicate victims, including some broken orchids that would not manage to flower this year. It was this sort of damage that Alfie hoped to prevent by his presence during the busy weekend, when more photographers were likely to visit.

'It's the orchid people who cause the most damage, rather than the general public,' he concluded. I worried whether my quest to see – and to tell the tale of – all Britain and Ireland's orchids could, inadvertently, contribute to the adverse pressure that this sort of keen interest in orchids seemed to generate. Reassuringly. Alfie felt that, on the whole, it was better to engender enthusiasm for natural history rather than keep it hidden from sight, where it could only be cared about by the few.

'After all,' he said, 'most of the late spider orchid sites aren't public knowledge. This one is probably the most sensitive. They're safe enough elsewhere.'

As we stood in the warm spring sunshine with Folkestone spread out at our feet and the lowlands of Kent stretching away to the peninsula of Dungeness on the very horizon, I wondered how many of the people living in the countless homes before us, in the cars streaming by on the motorway, or in the trains heading back and forth to France knew that here on the downs overlooking them was one of Britain's rarest orchids of all. I felt sad to realise that most of them neither knew nor cared.

Whether it was an informed orchidophile or a guileless member of the public who simply wanted the pretty flowers for their garden, someone breached Alfie's protection of Britain's most public late spider orchid site one night in mid-June. The thief dug up three orchids – one, with its root severed, was thrown aside, but the other plants were removed altogether. I felt desperately sorry for Alfie, as he clearly cared so much for his charges. He told me, 'It's a real shame that this happened. My guess is that someone took them, probably using a trowel, late on Friday evening, though for what purposes I have no idea.'

I would have willingly spent the remainder of the afternoon there on the roof of Kent with the late spider orchids, but available time that weekend was all too precious and I had a lot of ground to cover – and myriad bee orchids to look for. I had planned to see this, the commonest of the British *Ophrys* orchids, elsewhere on the Kentish downs this summer, but fate, and social media, had intervened earlier in the week. A blurry photo had been posted on Twitter two days previously by a walker on the Suffolk coast. She had found a clump of bee orchids near Sizewell that looked radically different from their nearby companions – instead of the riotous confection of chestnut, pink and yellow that forms a normal bee orchid, these were cool, crisp mossy green and white. Known as var. *chlorantha*, these were a rare variation, and of the several named varieties of bee orchid that I hoped to find in the course of the coming days, this was the one that I wanted to see the most.

By chance, I had a friend living nearby who could readily follow up this virtual report. Dave Fairhurst lives almost a stone's throw from Sizewell and, when not managing swathes of the Suffolk coastline on behalf of the RSPB or leading wildlife tours around the world, he could be called upon at short notice to help me in my quest. Responding to my cry for help, Dave had searched the area in question and found not one clump but many individual plants of both standard bee orchid and var. *chlorantha*. A hand-drawn map in his notebook, scanned and emailed to me, resembled a pirate's treasure map – X marked the spot. If Dave himself was unavailable when I reached Suffolk, I could rest assured that I knew where I would find my quarry.

Fortunately, on arriving in Suffolk in the late afternoon, I found Dave at home playing football in his cottage garden with his young daughters. Although the orchids were relatively nearby, I did not want to waste a moment of precious daylight, so we drove the short way to park my car in the shadow of the nuclear power station that dominates the area. Dave had shared the news of the variant bee orchid colony with other interested local naturalists, and it seemed that, despite being on their collective doorstep, these hitherto overlooked orchids had been known in this location long ago, and had simply been forgotten about.

'One of the local old boys was telling us about white orchids being here years ago,' Dave confided. 'You'd have to imagine these are the same plants. There's dozens of the things here – maybe more of them than the normal bees.'

The nuclear power station is set just a few hundred yards from the shore, separated from the sea by a relatively narrow strip of shingle. A wide track runs alongside the site's perimeter fence, leading north along the coast in the direction of the RSPB's Minsmere nature reserve. Within just a few minutes we had found the first patch of bee orchids and, glowing an ethereal white amongst them, three flowering spikes of var. *chlorantha*. I fell to my knees. This was one of those happy moments when, upon seeing a new flower, the reality exceeded even the heightened sense of anticipation I had built up around it.

A normal bee orchid is a lovely thing – like a more subtle version of the late spider orchids I had seen earlier in the day, it has three rose-pink sepals, and a rich chestnut-brown, velvety labellum. This lip is dramatically accented by a lighter, burnt-orange area in the centre, bordered by alternate bands of pale yellow and dull purple, and, beneath this, two startling pale yellow spots. Hairy, pubescent lobes on the sides of the labellum erupt from further bands of purple and yellow.

While their name and, indeed, their appearance suggests an association with a pollinating insect, bee orchids have evolved to a more satisfactory – and effective – arrangement altogether. Within hours of each flower opening, two pendulous yellow pollinia have dropped downwards from the arching green anther above – they dangle, testicularly, only so long as it takes for a light breeze to waft them back to the sticky surface of the receptive stigma. Here they lodge firmly. This pollination mechanism is as efficient as it is simple and, as a result, bee orchids are the most commonplace and widespread of Britain's *Ophrys* orchids. They have an endearing habit of popping up in unexpected places – on the verges of industrial estates, in school playing fields and, given half a chance, even in the lawns of lucky householders.

For all their innate loveliness, they are also prone to variation, sometimes spectacularly so. Botanists have given a number of these Latin names all their own, names as pleasingly complex and suggestive as the flowers themselves: *atrofuscus, belgarum, bicolor, chlorantha, flavescens, friburgensis, trollii* … I wanted to see as many of these varieties as I could – all would be new to me – and the unexpected emergence of these var. *chlorantha* in Suffolk marked the beginning of my bee orchid adventure.

Punctuated by calls from Dave that announced he'd found further examples in the low vegetation that carpeted the area around me, I looked closely at my first var. *chlorantha*. They were, although lacking gaudy colouration, spectacular. The normal bee orchid's pink sepals were instead icy snow white on these flowers, each with a central delicate green vein, surrounding a labellum that was an intense, luminous moss green. The side lobes were swathed with myriad fine white hairs, and the dangling yellow pollina provided vibrant golden contrasts. We stayed in the area as the light faded from the sky – I was unwilling to leave these gorgeous flowers while I could still enjoy their beauty. A quick departure would have felt peremptory and, somehow, sacrilegious.

If the fringes of a nuclear power station seem, at first glance, an unlikely setting in which to find orchids, then the sides of busy main roads would perhaps be unlikelier still. Trapped in the bubble of a speeding car, we barely give the blurring verges a second glance yet, in some places at least, these unprepossessing strips of land provide fertile ground for the more adaptable and hardy orchids, and orchid hunters alike. The following morning brought me to a sloping embankment on the side of the Fosse Way in Gloucestershire. While this was an ancient road, this embankment was a relatively modern addition – the ground was sparsely vegetated, with patches of sticky, wet bare earth in places. Even this early in the day traffic drummed past, drivers heedless of the orchid hunter slowly traversing the embankment beside them.

I was hoping to find two varieties of bee orchid here – var. *belgarum* and var. *bicolor* – but my immediate attention was consumed with another orchid altogether, one that was flowering in a profusion I had never seen before in their kind. Pyramidal orchids shrouded the upper slopes in swathes of vivid acid pink. Each flower spike was a dense cone formed of dozens of small individual flowers, each dominated by three large, deeply divided lobes. It was easy to see how this orchid had earned its English name – the conical flower spike was perfectly pyramidal, with the flowers opening from the base of the pyramid and working their way up towards the apex in the course of the following days. This early in their flowering season only the first few rows of flowers were open – above them the unopened pointy buds formed a tight, darker pink pyramidion.

The flowers are scented, but their perfume was lost to me on this cool, damp morning. The time of day did not help – their scent is strongest in the evenings, presumably to attract nocturnal insects to pollinate them – but even if they had retained a trace of their floral notes they would have been lost to the pervading odour of the exhaust fumes that drifted around me. I knew I would see more pyramidal orchids in more salubrious surroundings in the course of the coming weeks, so I concentrated on looking for bee orchids. They were few and far between, scattered loosely along the embankment. The first I found hinted at the variation that I sought – the rarer of the two at this site, and one of the rarest of all in Britain, var. *bicolor* – as they lacked the usual two yellow spots on the base of the chestnut-brown lip.

Then, suddenly, there was a particularly weedy bee orchid growing from a bare area of soil a little way ahead of me. My initial impression of the flowers was that this was a strangely bleached and muted bee orchid, as if it had been washed one too many times. Closer inspection revealed its true colours, or lack thereof – retaining the normal pale pink sepals of a bee orchid, the lip of this var. *bicolor* had lost all the usual rich complexity of markings one associated with its kind. Instead, as the Latin varietal name suggested, the lip was simply two-toned – the lower half comprising an unmarked, dark chocolate brown and the upper half a washed out, sickly greenish purple.

My initial joy at finding this rare variety was somewhat muted by the orchid's understated appearance. Whereas a normal bee orchid was a rich visual smorgasbord, and the previous day's var. *chlorantha* were a refreshing and delectable reinvention of the former, this var. *bicolor* left my orchid palette feeling jaded. I drew some consolation that this was at least proof that I was not judging the orchids I saw by their rarity alone – their beauty remained central to my enjoyment of them, and I was still no mere orchid-twitcher.

It was the latter, or the signs of their passing, that led me to find the other bee orchid variation I had been told this roadside harboured. Upon crossing the road to walk back to my car, I noticed a well-trodden path of flattened grass leading to a tell-tale circular area of crushed vegetation. Having seen the very same signs on the downs above Folkestone, I had a fair idea of what this portended even before I followed in the footsteps of those who had been here before me – this marked the place where photographers had carelessly laid themselves flat on the ground to take images of something special. Sure enough, at the centre of all this thought-lessness I found an orchid – a var. *belgarum* bee orchid.

This variation marks the breakdown of genetic order – the lip lacks the magnificent hairy side lobes so characteristic of bee orchids, and is instead a jumbled mass of yellow and brown markings. Confronted with this latest iteration on the standard bee orchid, I could appreciate anew the subtle charms of the var. *bicolor* on the opposite side of the road. That at least was symmetrical and broadly resembled a bee orchid – this strange flower looked like a crude facsimile of its parents, as if rendered by some clumsy hand in melted candle wax. I half-heartedly took some photos of it but chose not to linger. The nearby pyramidal orchids had far more allure for me than this sorry aberration, and it was via them that I returned to my onward journey.

The Fosse Way, when built by the Romans, formed the spine of their administration in this remote outpost of their Empire – this arrow-straight road enabled the rapid movement of troops, communications and commerce from Lincoln in the north-east to Exeter in the south-west. As the day progressed I planned to follow this diagonal axis down to Somerset and Dorset to search for further forms of bee orchid.

My next stop was only a few miles south – a small layby at the side of the road, depressingly scattered with discarded takeaway-coffee cups, plastic soft-drink bottles, and a heavily used nappy. The Roman legacy of the Fosse Way had been reduced to its very name, but the contemporary legacy of man's passage was sadly all too evident. Just a few paces into the long grass at the back of the layby brought me to six plants of a bee orchid variation that, not so very long ago, was considered a species all of its own. Known as the wasp orchid – a name that suited the thin, attenuated flower perfectly, for they are as much wasp as those fat, bumbling flowers of a bee orchid are bee – these flowers are now understood to be an extreme variation of the common or garden bee orchid. While their former English name persists colloquially amongst botanists, they are officially known as var. *trollii* – named after the eighteenth-century Swiss flower painter and copperplate engraver Johann Heinrich Troll.

This was another orchid that I had yearned to see as a young boy exploring the countryside on the edges of the Somerset Levels but, until today, this flower had remained the stuff of fantasy. While dimly conscious that the thick grass around the orchids might yet conceal further unpleasant evidence of recent human passage, I could not resist looking closely at these longed-for plants.

Each flower shared a normal bee orchid's pink sepals and petals, but the lip was radically and structurally different – instead of the rounded, friendly fat-bottomed bumblebee shape I was accustomed to seeing, these orchids had long, narrow and sharply pointed bodies. Each labellum was a broken and random motley of brownish blotches on a dull greenish-yellow base. The resemblance to a wasp was striking, not least in the sharp 'sting' at the base of the lip.

The plants were noticeably spindly, more grass-like than orchid, being tall, thin-stemmed, and willowy to a fault. I spotted a seventh individual further back in the grass, the stem broken in half, yet with no sign of any more sinister cause than the strong back-draft of passing traffic. Every time a lorry passed by on the nearside of the road the verge was swept with a powerful and sudden gust that receded as quickly as it came. Every other bee orchid I had seen had been sturdier and shorter than these strange plants.

By late afternoon, my bee orchid odyssey was drawing to a close. I had swapped the seething roadside of Gloucestershire for the more peaceful surroundings of the RSPB Radipole Lake reserve in the heart of Weymouth. This was a place with happy memories for me – I had spent countless hours birdwatching here as a teenager, sometimes with my father, but often when I should have been in school. Until I had a car of my own I had relied on hitchhiking, leaving Sherborne at lunchtime straight after lessons had finished, and returning to the school a few hours later. In this way I could see birds that were impossibly exotic in the north of the county – bearded tits clambering through the reedbeds like tiny parrots, and Cetti's warblers delivering their detonating songs from the bushes that dotted the reserve. In winter there were sometimes small flocks of scaup to be found out on the deeper water, and the possibility of a scarce Arctic gull or two. I even met my first girlfriend in the visitor centre there.

I had returned here this summer for the last of the bee orchid variations I could hope to see – one that made up in dark allure for what it lacked in markings. Var. *atrofuscus* was the rarest of the lot, known only from a mere handful of sightings in Britain. This was an orchid that looked as if it were wearing a dark velvet smoking jacket – the labellum of each flower was entirely brown, so deep in colour it appeared to absorb all light that struck it. This particular plant had been discovered at the side of one of the footpaths that loop around the reserve in 2008 and, unusually where rare orchids are concerned, had not been kept a closely guarded secret. News that it was flowering again this year had been announced by the RSPB themselves, and armed with precise directions kindly supplied by Lindsey Death at Radipole RSPB, I walked out onto the reserve to see it for myself.

It felt as if I had never left. The calls of Cetti's warblers assaulted me with every step. These drab warblers colonised the south coast of Britain from France in the early 1970s and, while hard winters had occasionally set them back, they continue to prosper in mild microclimates like that of Radipole Lake. When I first saw a Cetti's warbler there in the mid-1980s, it was one of the few reliable places one might hope to encounter one in Britain – but now, in the absence of regular prolonged cold spells of weather, they had expanded their range further and by 2006 were breeding north of the River Humber. Since I had left Kent for Shetland, however, they had been absent from my birdwatching life – I greeted these noisy birds as old friends.

The var. *atrofuscus* was just where Lindsey had said it would be, right on the very edge of the narrow pathway and only a few feet away from the water of Radipole Lake itself. The bushes that shielded the path from the water grew up to the path, so this orchid eked out a precarious existence on a knife edge between smothering vegetation and bare stony ground. The path at least meant that I could lie down nose to nose with the flower without worrying about damaging any surrounding flora. I assembled my camera and tripod, and set about taking a series of portraits, interrupted periodically by passing dog walkers. There seemed more of them than I remembered, and far fewer birders – in fact, in the entire time I was there I failed to see a single bird-watcher. The dog walkers meanwhile were unfailingly interested in the stranger blocking their thoroughfare, and I enjoyed showing them the orchid.

'I thought it was just birds here,' one remarked. 'Just goes to show. Always something new to see, isn't there?'

He was right, and there was one more novelty I was eagerly anticipating seeing before I left the south-west. Known from only three sites in England, I would find myself back on a roadside as the day drew to an end in order to see a colony of *Ophrys x pietzschii*, an unusual hybrid between bee and fly orchids. Given the specific pollination mechanisms of both parents – the fly orchids relying on digger wasps to pollinate them, while the bee orchids made do with self-pollination – the chances of a pollinium from one arriving on the stigma of another are vanishingly small. A thriving colony of the hybrid offspring of one such happy accident exists in Somerset, and I couldn't wait to see them – judging from photographs I had seen of them the previous year, they looked absolutely gorgeous, a wonderful combination of characteristics of both their parents.

The day finished as it had begun, with me scaling a bank at the side of a busy main road, this time near Sparkford. The hybrids were immediately obvious all around me – with classic hybrid vigour they were larger, taller plants than either parent, with flower spikes dripping with individual blooms. Superficially each flower had the shape and colour of a fly orchid about the labellum, but the surrounding sepals betrayed the bee orchid genes with dusky pinkish-grey tones, the bubblegum pink of bee orchid sepals being watered down by the green sepals from the fly orchid parents. These dirty pretty things were more than the sum of their parts – more extravagant and lush than a fly orchid, but less lurid than a bee orchid. I could see both parents nearby on the slopes of the bank – diminutive fly orchids in full bloom, and a handful of bee orchids just coming out of bud – but neither parent was a patch on their offspring. The aqueous light of early evening was perfect for photography, so I busied myself taking a long series of images of them, careful not to damage any surrounding vegetation.

As I finished, with the light fading fast, I was aware of a car pulling up nearby in the layby. I emerged from the bushes, camera and tripod in hand, to find the car's driver squatting at the foot of the bank. There was an awkward moment as we made eye contact, both of us shocked at the sight of the other.

'Evening!' I said brightly, hastening past him. His reply was a little more strained than my greeting – he seemed concerned that I was hiding in the bushes with a camera, and even I had to admit that my blithe reassurances that I was taking photos of rare orchids sounded implausible. This encounter was, if indeed I needed telling, the final straw – I had had enough of searching for orchids on roadsides, no matter how rare, unusual or beautiful they might be. It was time to return to the field.

5

An Irish interlude

Parliamentarian Edmund Ludlow is probably best known for his involvement in the execution of Charles I – he was one of the king's judges, and personally signed the warrant for Charles's execution. In Ireland he is remembered less fondly still, for here he persecuted the Irish vigorously at Oliver Cromwell's behest. He was said to have spared neither health nor money in his campaign against Irish guerrillas: besides hunting them down assiduously, he adopted a razed-earth approach to disrupting their activities, destroying crops and foodstores with equal vigour. It was when campaigning in the remote and challenging terrain of the Burren in County Clare during 1651–52 that he famously declared, 'It is a country where there is not enough water to drown a man, wood enough to hang one, nor earth enough to bury him.'

I had not had time enough to judge for myself the lack of water, trees or soil in the Burren before I almost killed a man. Having landed at Shannon in the late evening, I was hastening along narrow country lanes to my bed and breakfast near the small town of Ennistimon when it happened – I came around a sharp corner in the road to find an elderly man driving a green ride-on lawnmower in the lane before me, his progress dimly illuminated by a torch held unsteadily in one wavering hand. I had barely time enough to bring my car to a standstill inches behind him. He, apparently blissfully unaware of the drama in his wake, continued his erratic progress, weaving slowly down the road away from me. The lane was too narrow to pass him, so by the time he arrived on the outskirts of Ennistimon the shock of almost driving through him had abated. On this inauspicious note I began my short visit to Ireland, my targets two orchids that I could find nowhere else but here – the dense-flowered orchid and the Irish marsh orchid.

I had never visited the Burren before, but I could hardly fail to have heard about it. Botanists speak of it in hushed tones – it is a botanical wonderland, a landscape of extremes that is home to a flora unlike any other in Britain and Ireland. Here there are plants growing side by side that, by rights, have no place being anywhere near one another – alpine species grow almost at sea level alongside species usually found in the Mediterranean. When I mentioned to friends that I was visiting the Burren in search of dense-flowered orchids, their unfailing reaction was to tell me that I would love the place. Needless to say, with my expectations built up to such a high extent, it was with a certain degree of trepidation that I set out the following morning to explore the Burren's extensive limestone pavements.

If there is one feature that defines the Burren, it is these expanses of rock – slabs and sheets of stone that appear laid upon the landscape in fractured, sculpted planes by some mighty hand. John Betjeman, in his poem 'Ireland with Emily', was unflinchingly blunt about the Burren's dominant rocky nature:

Stony seaboard, far and foreign,
Stony hills poured over space,
Stony outcrop of the Burren,
Stones in every fertile place.[1]

Covering almost a hundred square miles, the Burren's karst land-scape is home to almost three quarters of all the species of flowering plant found in Ireland as a whole, and virtually all of the country's orchid species. While it was two species in particular that drew me to Ireland, I could reasonably hope that I would see some other orchid species besides, even this early in the summer.

The Burren hides many of its wonders where the casual onlooker cannot see them – the limestone pavement is riven with count-less cracks, fractures and crevices known collectively as grikes and clints. In these sheltered spots plants find a toehold. Areas of shat-tered gravel support still more greenery and, in the small sheltered meadows found in the vicinity of the Burren's freshwater loughs, there are further flourishes of wildflowers. This is a landscape that does not give up its secrets easily.

Signs of the ancient and prolonged presence of man are visible throughout the area. Drystone walls created from shattered slabs of limestone bleed seamlessly into the grey rocks whence they came. Scattered through the landscape are mightier statements of man's passage – immense ringforts squat on hilltops and cliff edges while, more ancient still, megalithic portal tombs like the Poulnabrone dolmen erupt ponderously from the ground.

I felt like a child on his way into a fairground on the sunny morning in late May that marked my Burren baptism. Passing houses with garden walls built of haphazard chunks of jagged lime-stone, I soon found myself, with mounting anticipation, enter-ing the limestone pavement habitat I had heard so much about. Immediately there were orchids – thousands of them – dotting every available tiny patch of grass, thrusting up from every shal-low crack in the rock, innumerable splashes of every conceivable spectrum shade between the palest of coral pinks and the deepest of royal purples.

These were early purple orchids as I had never seen them before – exuberant and unashamedly growing in the open in such profusion it would have been impossible not to crush some had I chosen to walk where they grew most densely. Here and there were impossibly blue counterpoints, a deep, clear cerulean blue that one encounters so rarely in nature – spring gentians, their blooms fragments of fallen sky. They are an alpine species widespread from the uplands of northern Spain east to the mountains of central Asia. I had last seen them high in the Alps, yet here, in Ireland, they grow almost at sea level. This was my first taste of the Burren's improbable flora, and it could not have been sweeter – a swathe of flowers like stepping into an Impressionist painting.

In one enclosed meadow near the foot of the imposing hill of Mullaghmore I found a stand of pure white early purple orchids – the first of their kind I had seen this year, an unusual and comparatively rare variety of the species known as var. *alba*. They were growing on their own in the corner of the meadow, two dozen snow-white spikes set apart from their pink and purple counterparts as if by aloof design. White butterflies stuttered like windblown cherry blossom along the shrubby edges of the field. I recognised this distinctive flight at once – they were surely wood whites? I followed one as it danced erratically along a pathway leading into a thicket and there, before I could confirm its identity – though I was quite certain – there were still more white orchids growing in the shade of the trees from a bed of bronzy moss. At first I thought they were more pure white var. *alba* early purple orchids but, as I set up my camera to capture this pleasing tableau, I realised to my delight that each flower had a small collection of tiny purple spots at the base of the white lip – a royal purple ermine effect. They were stunning, and it proved hard to tear myself away from them.

My main target would not be found in these spinneys, nor in the meadows they encircled. Dense-flowered orchids are found in the British Isles only in western Ireland, and there only sparingly. They are a Mediterranean species that thrives in the hot summers and mild winters of that region – one would not expect such a specialised orchid to be found in the cool, damp Atlantic coast of Ireland, yet it was here and here alone that I might hope to see them in flower in late May. The Burren's unusually temperate climate may explain why the orchids endure here – the soil temperature rarely drops to the point at which plant growth is inhibited, unlike much of the rest of Britain and Ireland – but it does not explain how the orchids came to be there in the first place.

On the one hand, colonisation of this habitat by wind-blown seed has been mooted as the origin of this far-flung outpost of dense-flowered orchids. Yet the peculiar and diverse assemblage of plants found in western Ireland and on the Burren in particular suggests that something more profound is responsible for this potent cocktail of alpine and Mediterranean species. The dense-flowered orchids were first found in Ireland in 1864, but are believed to be in decline nowadays. Whether theirs is a relatively temporary colonisation that is slowly concluding as our climate changes, or whether this marks a pattern of longer-term decline, we cannot be sure.

If I was to find dense-flowered orchids I would need to take myself back out onto the limestone pavement itself. Brendan Sayers, Ireland's foremost orchid expert and glasshouse foreman at the National Botanic Gardens in Dublin, had provided me with precise directions as to where I should find my target. So detailed were these instructions that I felt confident that seeing dense-flowered orchid was practically a formality and a foregone conclusion. Buoyed with this complacency, I was in no great hurry – the day was too perfect to be rushed. The sun was warm on my skin – hot, even – and I was happy to amble and explore the floriferous network of small sheltered fields and turloughs that skirted Mullaghmore's flanks.

Brendan had suggested that I might find a number of *Dactylorhiza* orchid species in the damper grassy areas of the Burren – I particularly hoped I might find one of my favourites, early marsh orchid. This orchid comes in a variety of flavours, with five generally acknowledged subspecies that vary from the creamy ivory of *ochraleuca* through to the rich, carmine red of *coccinea*, via the raspberry-ripple pink and white tones of *incarnata* and the pale purple shades of *pulchella*. In western Ireland I might hope to find subspecies *cruenta*, with flowers of a clear, dark rose pink marked with bold hoops and loops of darker red.

I walked the margins of turloughs, seasonal ponds and lakes that form in the autumn and dry up the following spring. These disappearing lakes are rich in plant life, with their high-water marks often demarcated in the summer months by a golden halo of shrubby cinquefoil flowers. It seemed as if I'd arrived a week or two before the early marsh orchids came into flower – many were still in tight bud, with only a handful beginning to show signs of opening, their buds swelling at the base and beginning to show colour as a butterfly's chrysalis does in the final hours of pupation.

One orchid, however, caught my eye amongst the heavily poached margins of an almost completely vanished turlough. This particular field had been grazed closely by cattle, and many emerging orchids had been crushed by the churning of their hooves at the edges of the dwindling body of water. This orchid had been spared, and was in full bloom – but this was no early marsh orchid.

The flower spike was, frankly, a little pathetic – a loose gathering of just five large-lipped, floppy and densely speckled pale purple blossoms. They were set, for the most part, off one side of a spindly stem that rose from a sparse rosette of three slender, unmarked green leaves. I was thrilled to see it – this unprepossessing plant was my first Pugsley's marsh orchid of the year. While Brendan had suggested that they might be seen in the area, I had hoped to find them later on the Scottish island of Rum. This solitary flowering plant was an unexpected bonus and, try as I might, I could find no others of its kind anywhere else in this turlough or its neighbours. The species was first found in Ireland by Herbert Pugsley, who initially described it as a subspecies in 1936. Four years later he underwent a change of heart and became more confident that it was, in fact, a wholly new species altogether.

This drew the unfortunate Pugsley into the orbit of Britain's most controversial and outspoken twentieth-century botanist, John Heslop-Harrison. Heslop-Harrison was vehement in his belief that Pugsley had overstepped the botanical mark in ascribing this orchid to a new species altogether. In 1953, Heslop-Harrison made the case that the orchids Pugsley had described were, in fact, British representatives of a different European orchid species entirely, the narrow-leaved marsh orchid, *Dactylorhiza traunsteineri*. There the matter appeared to rest until the late twentieth century, when advances in science allowed the genetic material of the orchids to be examined – and Pugsley's original description of a new, endemic species to be exonerated. His orchids were, after all, a species distinctive in their own right. The Latin name bestowed on them in 1940 by Pugsley, *traunsteinerioides*, means *traunsteineri*-like – he knew all along that they were similar to their Continental siblings.

Their distribution in Britain and Ireland is patchy, and this too is not without controversy and an element of confusion for the orchid hunter. Until very recently they were believed to be found at a few locations in England – primarily in Hampshire, Norfolk and Yorkshire – and in the very north of Wales, in western Scotland and at a few sites in Ireland. By the early twenty-first century, botanists observed that some of these English populations appeared to be in danger of being subsumed by hybridisation with closely related and considerably commoner southern marsh orchids – a population of pure Pugsley's marsh orchids in Norfolk at Beeston Common, for example, numbered several hundred in the 1980s but had all but vanished by the turn of the century.

This observation was to prove ironically prescient as, in a further genetic twist in the tail, in 2012 those English populations of Pugsley's marsh orchids found beneath a diagonal axis drawn from the Wash to the Bristol Channel were described, on the basis of further genetic analysis, to be merely a subspecies of southern marsh orchid known as *schoenophila*. This announcement was not universally welcomed by British botanists, particularly those who lived relatively near to sites that held what had formerly been the species known as Pugsley's. Henceforth anyone wishing to see a genuine Pugsley's marsh orchid would need to do so by travelling to one of the scattered populations in the north and west of Britain and Ireland. I had not counted on seeing my Pugsley's marsh orchid in Ireland, but was delighted to do so far away from the cloudy genetic waters of the controversial English populations.

As the morning wore on, I finally wandered back onto the Burren's limestone pavement. Following Brendan Sayer's detailed instructions to the letter, I began to search for my first dense-flowered orchid. This would be an entirely new orchid for me and, although they are far from the most ostentatiously beautiful of orchids, it was one I keenly looked forward to seeing. I knew that I was in the precise location in which they ought to be, and at the right time of year for them to be in bloom, but something was immediately awry – I simply could not find one. My mental search image for the plants was entirely based on looking at photos of the flowers in my field guides – I knew them to be small, the flower spikes typically around ten centimetres tall, and rather plain, with a column of some twenty densely packed small greenish-white flowers set on fat green ovaries larger than the individual flowers themselves. Having not seen one in real life, I was not sure quite what to expect, but what I rapidly came to realise was that, in spite of having Brendan's excellent description of where to look, I could not find a single orchid, no matter how hard I looked.

At first I doubted my interpretation of the directions I had been given. I retraced my steps over and over, but try as I might, I could not convince myself I had misinterpreted the instructions – they were too specific for that. My search area was a relatively narrow grassy strip running along the top of a tall rocky shelf that marked where the pavement stepped down a metre from one plane to another. I worked my way back and forth along it, starting where Brendan had indicated the plants should be, and gradually working my way outwards from that point.

Nothing.

I repeated the fruitless exercise again and again, with a mounting sense of panic. Looking around me, the pavement stretched away towards Mullaghmore in an almost unbroken, shimmering, pale grey expanse. In the bright sunlight the rocks were rendered almost white, and the glare from them made my search no easier as I began to walk randomly back and forth from grike to grike, looking hard for orchids in every small grassy area I found. The early purple orchids that had seemed so charming earlier in the morning were now, to my shame, simply annoying me. They were blousy, omnipresent and, it seemed, I could find nothing but them. Stumbling across a flowering saxifrage was a brief diversion during the ensuing two hours – I could not remember the field characteristics of Irish and mossy saxifrages and, in other circumstances, I would have enjoyed the challenge of trying to work out which species this was. Today, however, with the afternoon slipping by and no sign of my unexpectedly elusive quarry, I was in no mood to grapple with the leaf shape or tufting of saxifrages. I needed to find a dense-flowered orchid – just one would do.

Hours later I returned to my car hot, sweaty and uncomfortably thirsty. Walking across the pavement required considerable concentration in itself as the surface was endlessly uneven. Every rock edge was jaggedly sharp and I found myself stumbling more than once. Such a stumble could, potentially, have serious consequences. Some of the grikes in the rock were deep enough to stand in, and many of them were more than adequate to break a leg. Even a minor trip might end in a broken wrist or, worse, a shattered camera.

I finished the last of my water and steeled myself to resume my search. I reread, for what must surely have been the hundredth time, Brendan's instructions. It seemed inconceivable that I could be facing the possibility of not seeing a dense-flowered orchid today. Yet that remote possibility now felt distinctly likely and I found myself ruing the hours I had spent blithely meandering amongst the early purple orchids and spring gentians. Even the time spent with the Pugsley's marsh orchid seemed wasteful now that every minute counted. I walked the short distance back to where I had begun my search: on the narrow grassy strip where Brendan had assured me I would find my target.

How I had missed them previously I could not tell. As soon as I cast my eyes across the area he had indicated, there were two small but distinctive shapes side by side, nestling in the short grass. I knelt reverently beside them, hardly able to believe they were real. The sense of relief within me was overwhelmingly palpable, and I felt like crying with release. Never had a small, visually insignificant orchid assumed such a profound significance for me in such a short space of time.

I realised now that my quest had, hitherto, been relatively straightforward. I had, for the most part, visited sites I knew already from first-hand experience to see flowers I knew of old. This was the first time I had gone looking, on my own, for a plant I had never seen before in a location I had never visited before – a plant which, moreover, flowered only in a location far from home and did so for a relatively short period of time. The last few hours had been a taste of what it would be like to see my quest undone in an instant – the enormity of the practicalities inherent in my seeing every single British and Irish species this year was, suddenly, made starkly evident to me. I could afford to take nothing for granted. My complacency that morning had come close to costing me a species. Miss one species and my quest was over. I vowed I would not make that mistake again.

Neither of this pair of dense-flowered orchids was at its best – they had already begun to mature, their flowers crisping and browning on the fat green ovaries beneath. While in no mood to be overly fussy – I had seen them, at last – I still harboured a hope that I might find some in better, pristine flowering condition.

Having found them, it was now as if the scales had fallen from my eyes. Backtracking across the same areas of karst I had spent the past hours combing to no avail, I now found dense-flowered orchids in, if not profusion, then certainly their dozens. Amongst them were just a few in fine condition. Their flowers were, when examined closely, reminiscent of the anthropogenic man orchids I had seen in Kent – each individual flower lip formed a small white-legged body, set beneath a greenish-white cap formed by the tightly closed petals and sepals. From even a short distance away the flower spikes were unremarkable – but at close quarters each proved surprisingly attractive.

At last I could appreciate anew the stark beauty of this limestone landscape. It had been a favourite place of the late Raymond Piper, a botanical artist who became so inextricably linked with the Burren and its flora that, in time, he became known to some simply as 'the orchid man'. His orchid paintings have a luminosity and depth that are without parallel – they are like a window back to the Burren, if one could only step beyond the orchid itself. He explained that 'an artist can see things more clearly than a botanist'. His affection for the Burren was legendary, and now I too began to understand the magic of this outwardly bleak place – though I emphatically drew the line at removing any of the orchids I found there. Echoing the behaviour of John Fowles and Derek Jarman, this creative man was not above taking home an orchid root to grow for his own pleasure – in his eulogy to Piper, his great friend the Irish poet Michael Longley recounted how Piper had cherished, in his Belfast greenhouse, an autumn lady's-tresses he had brought home from County Mayo.

I tried half-heartedly to refind my mystery saxifrage but was drawn irresistibly time and again back to the dense-flowered orchids, distracted only when I found an Irish hare motionless in his form, his large ginger-furred body basking in the sun. He looked at me with impassive liquid amber eyes as I slowly backed away from him. I had no wish to disturb him, so withdrew cautiously until I was hidden from his line of sight.

This hare felt like a good omen. Hares have a powerful presence in north European mythology, often closely associated with a past disaster. Irish folklore, meanwhile, tells of the great warrior Oisin wounding a hare in the leg. Following the stricken animal into a thicket, he enters an underground hall and there finds a striking young woman sitting upon a throne, bleeding from her leg. I hoped my leaving this particular hare undisturbed went beyond mere good fieldcraft and would stand me in good stead with whatever gods looked over orchid hunters.

Leaving the limestone pavement, I felt as if a weight had been lifted from my shoulders. I could move on now to look for my remaining target, Irish marsh orchid, without hesitation – I had learned a valuable lesson today. My destination was the small town of Lisdoonvarna, where I had been told there was a damp meadow that supported a small colony of orchids.

My fine intentions of remaining steadfast and free of distraction took an early and unexpected turn for the worse as I rounded a corner and found myself confronted by a strangely familiar house. This was the isolated Georgian dwelling made famous as the Parochial House in the quirky and much-missed Irish comedy *Father Ted*, a television series populated by a cast of eccentric and incredible local characters. Now the previous night's nearby encounter with an elderly drunk riding his lawnmower to the pub made complete sense. Truth may be said to be stranger than fiction, but sometimes the two collide.

The sense of being somewhere surreally different from home only grew stronger as I drove into Lisdoonvarna. A large, colourful billboard at the side of the road proclaimed, *Lisdoonvarna, home of matchmaking festival, all September. Europe's biggest singles event*, with a quotation designed to entice: '*We're here for the craic, the women, and the beer...!*'

I was here for the orchids, although they were not featuring largely in Lisdoonvarna's marketing spiel. The previous evening my landlady had told me, knowingly, all about Lisdoonvarna's matchmaking festival.

'You're here months too early to meet a fine Irish girl! You'll be needing to come back here in September...'

She went on to describe the legendary matchmaker Willie Daly, who was said to hold court every year in The Matchmaker Bar in town. 'People queue for hours to get their name in his book of love,' she confided.

Meeting a fine Irish girl was the least of my concerns, and I sincerely hoped I would not need the intervention of the improbably named Willie Daly to help me to find the object of my desire in Lisdoonvarna. Abandoning the car in the town square, I followed a footpath that led me from the street to a meadow studded promisingly with dark green tufts of sedge. This looked like prime *Dactylorhiza* habitat. Sure enough, I began to find orchids – my first heath spotted orchids of the year, with their characteristic white flowers sporting hoops, loops and squiggles of brightest cerise. Beyond them were much taller, sturdier plants, with darker purple flowers. These, I hoped, would prove to be Irish marsh orchids.

What I found, on closer inspection, was a considerable variety of colouration and shape in the flowers. Most were somewhere between the images I had seen of Irish marsh orchids and my experience of heath spotted orchids. While one or two were approaching the uniform darkness of flower I would have expected to find in Irish marsh, they were the pale purple of blackcurrant ice cream. Irish marsh orchid should have a rounded central lobe on its lip, but not one of these plants had flowers with that feature – they were all sharply pointed, like the neighbouring heath spotted orchid flowers. I knew in my heart what I was seeing – this appeared to be a hybrid swarm between heath spotted and Irish marsh orchids. If there had been Irish marsh orchids here, they were nowhere to be seen now – their hybrid young had taken over the field.

Brendan Sayers had provided me with details of what he considered to be the best site in western Ireland for Irish marsh orchid, at the coastal village of Ballyheigue in nearby County Kerry. While this description ought to have been reassuring, on the basis of my travails with the dense-flowered orchids I was far from confident. By the time I had driven south through County Clare, caught the car ferry across to County Kerry, and driven to Ballyheigue, it would be almost nightfall. I would have the morning of the following day to find my orchids. Brendan had sounded so confident about this particular site that I decided I would place my faith in him once again, rather than cast around in Lisdoonvarna's damp places any more than I had already.

There is nowhere to park on the side of the narrow road that runs out of Ballyheigue's seafront car park to the large marshy area that hosts Ireland's best Irish marsh orchid site. Instead, one must walk down the road, flanked on one side by tall, grassy dunes and, on the other, past the Ballyheigue hurling club followed by a chain of fields given over to static caravans. After a while the road narrows further still, becoming sandier and with a central grassy strip. The fences that border the caravans become higher and more personalised. By the time one reaches the end of the road, one has passed from benevolent seaside charm to something a little more intimidating. The sounds of televisions, children squabbling and dogs vehemently barking had marked my passage by the caravans. I felt self-conscious, acutely aware that I was a stranger here on this grey early morning.

Ballyheigue has a reputation for startling violence – on 24 June 1834 one of the largest recorded faction fights in Irish history took place on the Strand, involving in excess of three thousand fighters armed with shillelaghs, heavy staffs cut from blackthorn trees. The wake of this explosion of tribal violence left as many as two hundred dead. These faction fights were, happily, now just a memory. I quickened my pace along the road, accompanied for a while by a territorial male stonechat who, judging by his litany of pebble-striking alarm calls, resented my temporary presence in his space.

The stonechat's calls and the dogs' barking soon faded behind me. I was relieved to reach the end of the road, where the remains of an electric fence encircled a small pasture and the marsh beyond it. There were orchids everywhere here – dark, rich purple orchids pushing through the lush grass, exactly what I had hoped to find. I stooped to examine the first of them, comparing the markings and structure to those in my field guide; these were indisputably pure Irish marsh orchids, their blooms a clear deep purple unsullied by any taint of hybridisation, as immediately right as the Lisdoonvarna specimens had been terribly wrong. Now I had found the real thing, I could enjoy having seen the latter and appreciate them in their own, hybrid right – but that was for later. All thoughts of the Lisdoonvarna orchids and my initial unease were now set aside.

I wandered from the field into the marsh itself, following no path but instinct alone, letting myself be drawn to open areas where further orchids abounded. The ground was wet underfoot, sometimes threatening to overspill my walking boots. I gave up counting the Irish marsh orchids, for there were hundreds, probably thousands in this large area that stretched away along the coast to the near horizon. Here and there were pale, flesh-pink orchids – my first flowering early marsh orchids of the year. I knew the subspecies at a glance – these were my firm favourites, *incarnata*.

Lurking snipe exploded into jinking, angular flight as I cut through a wetter area still, the promise of wet feet a reality now. I was heedless to them, lost in the magnificence of the Irish marsh orchids – some stood almost a foot tall, sturdy thick green stems surmounted by long, tightly packed purple flower spikes. Then, as I wended my soggy way back to the roadside field, I found two white orchids – visible from a distance away, they glowed amongst their many purple, with a handful of pink, counterparts. I hoped they might prove to be Irish marsh orchids, for very rarely they can throw up a white sport, but instead they were early marshes of the white variety known as var. *leucantha* – still a good plant to unexpectedly stumble across; they felt like the icing upon a particularly rich *Dactylorhiza* cake.

With skylarks stitching the sky overhead with their cascading song, and orchids abounding all around me, I was reminded of the words of the ill-fated Roger Casement, hanged in Pentonville prison in 1916 for attempting to bring arms and ammunition into Ireland from Germany. A statue to his memory stands to this day in Ballyheigue. He recalled:

> When I landed in Ireland that morning … Swamped and swimming ashore on an unknown strand, I was happy for the first time in over a year. Although I knew that this fate waited on me, I was, for one brief spell, happy and smiling once more. I cannot tell you what I felt. The sandhills were full of skylarks rising in the dawn, the first I had heard for years … and all around were primroses and wild violets and the singing of the skylarks in the air, and I was back in Ireland again.

Ireland had been good to me – my struggles with dense-flowered orchids had, if I was honest with myself, been self-inflicted and borne of complacency and, in the end, I had seen them and countless Irish marsh orchids better than I might have dared hope. I could leave Ireland happy and smiling. There were more *Dactylorhiza* orchids to hunt for, and to see these I would need to travel north into the islands off Scotland's west coast.

6

The trouble with marsh orchids

If I was drawn to Rum to look for Pugsley's marsh orchids, it was John Heslop-Harrison who drew me there. I had, of course, already seen one flowering plant on the Burren and there were many, far easier, places in which to see Pugsley's marsh orchids in the Hebrides. The last record for the species on Rum dated back almost twenty years before my visit. Yet it was Heslop-Harrison who compelled me to look for them here – his association with the orchid and the island as a whole was irresistible to me.

Back in the mid-1930s, Heslop-Harrison, Professor of Botany at Newcastle University, began leading annual field trips to the Hebrides and, in particular, the island of Rum. At the time access to the island was strictly by invitation only. The island was owned by Sir George Bullough and his glamorous society wife, Lady Monica – the latter rumoured to have been the mistress of Edward VII. Sir George had lavished his immense inheritance on a dream of building the perfect Edwardian aristocratic retreat on the island once he had inherited Rum from his father, a wealthy Lancastrian industrialist, in 1891. He had red sandstone imported at vast cost to build a castle to match the scale of his ambition.

Inside Kinloch Castle no expense was spared in furnishing Edwardian partygoers with the very height of contemporary luxury – Sir George even installed an immense steam organ originally commissioned by Queen Victoria, capable of simulating a forty-piece orchestra. This epic instrument was only the tip of the iceberg of Sir George's extravagance – in the castle grounds he had heated pools created to house alligators and turtles, while a heated aviary was created to house birds of paradise from Papua New Guinea and hummingbirds from the Americas. This astonishing playground was tended by a team of fourteen under-gardeners who, in order to complete the Edwardian vision of a Highlands and Islands estate, were paid extra to wear kilts while undertaking their duties. Access to this wonderland was strictly by invitation only – guns were said to have been fired at approaching, unauthorised boats – and Rum was known as the Forbidden Island.

By the time Heslop-Harrison began visiting the island, the Bulloughs' flamboyant, hard-partying days were behind them, though access to Rum was still problematic. In August 1938 three young friends set out to emulate John Buchan's fictional anti-hero John Macnab by landing illicitly on Rum and, while there, poaching a stag from under the laird's nose. Robert Atkinson's account – *A Stag From Rum* – of this ultimately successful escapade makes for thrilling, Buchanesque reading, and stresses how restricted access was to this forbidden isle: 'You can buy a steamer ticket to Rum but you must stay aboard the steamer. I have heard, but don't know if it has any truth, that once a shipwrecked crew was turned away from Rum.'

The Bullough family fortunes were in decline by the 1920s, and after Sir George died in 1939, visiting the island was at the discretion of his widow and occasional summertime Rum inhabitant, Lady

Bullough. Lady Bullough duly granted permission for Heslop-Harrison and his students to visit the island in the interests of furthering botanical knowledge. The professor was to guard this honour zealously while, for his students, this must have felt both a privilege and a chance to be involved with some pioneering field-work. Who knew what floral riches unexplored Rum might yield to a careful and discerning botanical eye?

It must have been more exciting still for those students when the discoveries began. A handful of new plants would, perhaps, have been just reward for their efforts surveying a hitherto *terra incognita* from a botanical perspective. But the discoveries kept on coming, year after year, and what discoveries they were. Nothing large or ostentatious – no shrubs or colourful orchids – they were instead, for the most part, a succession of sedges and similarly diffident and unassuming small plants that were many hundreds of miles away from where contemporary wisdom said they ought to be.

Plants that were normally found in the mountains of mainland Europe were growing on Rum, unseen to all until Heslop-Harrison's expeditions stumbled across them. This was groundbreaking stuff and it seemed as if Heslop-Harrison was, literally, rewriting the record books as his discoveries were announced in a succession of academic papers penned by himself and his students.

After a while, with the pace and extent of the discoveries show-ing little sign of abating, some of Heslop-Harrison's peers began to feel uneasy about the likelihood of Rum harbouring montane spe-cies usually associated with central Europe. Heslop-Harrison was a firm believer in a theory known as periglacial survival – a theory that suggested some forms of life, in particular hardy alpine plants, had survived the 1.7 million years of the last Ice Age, when much of Scotland and England were swathed in deep ice. His particular contention was that the Hebrides had been more or less ice-free during that period, providing conditions that, while certainly cold enough to inhibit many species, allowed the toughest to endure. Such ice-free areas are known to geologists as *nunataks*, a word of Inuit origin but in common use by the time Heslop-Harrison was championing his theory. In a paper published in defence of peri-glacial survival in 1951 he proclaimed, 'Thus on scattered nunataks, and on cliff ledges, it is pictured that most of the Alpine plants, exemplified by the sedge *Carex capitata*, *C. bicolor*, and *C. glacialis* … survived the rigours of the Ice Age.'

The examples he provided were pertinent – amongst the sedges he discovered on Rum, *Carex bicolor* figured prominently, both in providing supportive evidence of his theory and in the eventual unravelling of his reputation. Heslop-Harrison consistently presented the plants he found on Rum as evidence of periglacial survival – and in 1941 he published a paper in the *Journal of Botany* announcing the discovery of *Carex bicolor* on Rum. Many other botanists considered there was inadequate evidence to support his theory, and preferred the theory that plants gradually recolonised land in the wake of the retreat of an Ice Age's glaciers. But the discovery of *Carex bicolor* hundreds of miles from its known range conveniently supported Heslop-Harrison's belief, which he held and defended with a vehemence typical of his character.

'It seems incredible,' he wrote, 'that anyone should appeal to postglacial and recent dispersal of an accidental nature to account for [these unusual species'] present British distributions.'

Amongst those who intimately knew the flora of the Hebrides, not least the marvellously named botanist Maybud Campbell, whispers of suspicion were mounting into a clamour. Rumours of foul play swirled amidst the botanical establishment – that persons unknown, perhaps even Heslop-Harrison himself, were deliberately planting these unusual plants on Rum. But given Heslop-Harrison's well-deserved reputation for being a vitriolic correspondent and master of the scathing public put-down, who would dare openly challenge him?

With the announcement of the discovery of *Carex bicolor*, John Raven, a young classics don at Cambridge University and a keen amateur botanist, decided that the time had come to, in his words, 'make a determined effort' to find the truth out for himself. It seems likely that Raven was not acting solely on his own initiative – the botanical establishment was perplexed by the records coming out of Rum, and Heslop-Harrison's abrasive manner had caused offence to a number of influential men and women of the day. Time and again Heslop-Harrison had used papers published in scientific journals as vessels to deliver personal attacks on his peers' abilities and characters – for example, in a paper published in the botanical journal *The Vasculum*, Heslop-Harrison unleashed a broadside against Alfred Wilmott, an accomplished botanist and the keeper of the British Herbarium. Wilmott had suggested that an orchid found in the Hebrides, hitherto considered to be the common spotted orchid, *Orchis fuchsii*, might in fact be a new species unique to the islands, *Orchis hebridensis*.

Heslop-Harrison was not the sort of man to readily accept the principle of another finding a new species beneath his very nose on 'his' turf. His paper roundly derided Wilmott's claims, citing his own 'much more extensive' experience of the plant in question, and concluding witheringly, 'the publication of the alleged species was quite premature. The whole episode simply confirms the logical view that armchair botany, spiced with a modicum of field work, is hopelessly inadequate.'

The potential unlikelihood of the species Heslop-Harrison was finding in Rum notwithstanding, it seems clear that he would have made sufficient enemies in the botanical establishment that a groundswell of opinion would have built against him by the late 1940s. A plan was formulated that an expedition would be mounted to the Hebrides to find the plants that Heslop-Harrison claimed were growing there and, in so doing, to attempt to ascertain whether there were any signs of foul play or human interference.

At first this expedition was to include a number of botanical luminaries: Maybud Campbell, a good friend of Alfred Wilmott and expert on Hebridean flora, and Arthur Clapham, Thomas Tutin and Edmund Warburg, professors of botany at Sheffield, Leicester and Oxford respectively. In the months preceding the expedition, for one reason or another, these participants all dropped out, leaving John Raven to organise the expedition for himself. He successfully applied to the council of Trinity College, Cambridge, for a grant of £50 to fund the expedition in the late summer of 1948.

Obtaining funding was one thing, but gaining access to Rum was quite another. Access was nominally negotiable only with the permission of Lady Bullough but, where botanising was concerned, in practice this was further controlled by Heslop-Harrison himself. Having gained Lady Bullough's permission to visit annually, Heslop-Harrison jealously guarded his domain and its secrets. Dr John Lorne Campbell, the owner of neighbouring island Canna, writing to John Raven about access to Rum, impressed upon him the need to gain Lady Bullough's permission but cautioned, 'There is no certainty that your request will be granted; I am under the impression that the party who usually goes there considers it something of a closed field, or monopoly, and outsiders may not have much chance.'

Raven was to be accompanied on Rum by just one close friend, Tom Creighton. Heslop-Harrison was aware that Raven planned to spend a short while botanising on Rum while he himself was on the island, and had innocently promised that he would show Raven some of the island's rare plants – unaware, of course, of Raven's ulterior motives. When their paths crossed at Mallaig, Raven told Heslop-Harrison that Creighton would be accompanying him to Rum; the professor brusquely told Raven that he would need to send Lady Bullough a reply-paid telegram seeking her permission.

While waiting for her reply, Raven and Creighton went to stay on Canna, where they met Dr John Lorne Campbell, and acted upon his suggestion that they might land unseen and without permission on the west coast of Rum. On 4 August 1948, conveyed from Canna in the small boat of a local crofter, they made a secretive landfall at Harris Bay. From here Raven was to climb the steep flanks of Ruinsival in search of an alpine flowering plant, Norwegian sandwort. This species, while rare in the UK, is found scattered across Scotland in suitable habitat, and was not out of place on Rum. The objects of Raven's particular interest, the controversial plants discovered by Heslop-Harrison, would have to wait.

On returning to Canna that evening, Raven found a telegram from Lady Bullough waiting for him:

NO ACCOMMODATION AVAILABLE. MUST BRING
TENTS, FOOD AND ALL EQUIPMENT.

With access arranged, the friends travelled by steamer early on 5 August. Unfortunately, in their haste to disembark, they managed to leave behind on the boat all of their food and cooking equipment. This was an inauspicious beginning to their two-day stay on the island, and their misfortune was compounded later that evening when, while misguidedly attempting to fumigate their tent and rid it of the numerous midges that were making their lives unbearable, they managed to set fire to the tent's fabric with a Primus stove. The next two nights were to be spent sleeping rough on the island.

Their days, meanwhile, were filled with botanising. On the first day, Raven accompanied Heslop-Harrison and his colleagues onto Fionchra, a hill east of Rum's small township of Kinloch. Creighton, meanwhile, spent much of the day on the lower slopes socialising with a female member of the professor's party. Raven was shown a small selection of rare plants, noting that they were invariably either weak and in poor condition, or growing in vulnerable and atypical habitat, or both. Nevertheless, retiring to the smouldering remains of his tent at the end of the day, Raven must have felt he had yet to find the smoking gun he sought.

On 6 August Heslop-Harrison announced that his party would spend the day on Ruinsival, above Harris Bay on the far side of the island. This must have been both awkward and a wonderful opportunity for Raven. On the one hand, he had already been to Ruinsival during his secretive day on Rum two days previously, but could hardly admit as such to Heslop-Harrison. On the other hand, a day to himself allowed him the opportunity to attempt to find evidence of the botanical foul play he suspected. He politely declined to accompany Heslop-Harrison, saying that he planned instead to look for other of the professor's rare plant discoveries on the mountain of Barkeval. To his delight, Heslop-Harrison provided him with detailed instructions as to where these plants might be found.

Thus armed, Raven and Creighton spent the day methodically searching for Heslop-Harrison's plants. When they found them, Raven carefully studied them – their location, their general condition, and the other plants growing close by. What he found amounted to a damning catalogue of suspicion: some plants looked to have been only recently introduced, and were ailing where they appeared to have been planted by some unseen hand. Some grew with none of the other species one might have expected to find in close association with them elsewhere in their native range. Most damningly of all, some grew with plants in their midst that were, in their own right, strikingly alien.

Carex bicolor, the unassuming sedge that Heslop-Harrison had announced as a new addition to the British flora, provided a circumstantially compelling body of evidence. Raven followed Heslop-Harrison's directions and found, on the gravelly banks of a small stream, a colony of nine plants. Of these, one ailing specimen appeared to have been recently dug into the gravel with a trowel. No fewer than five plants had, growing in their midst, other plants more usually found as garden weeds in the British lowlands: annual meadow grass and annual pearlwort. Neither was a likely species to be found at this altitude on Rum – and when Raven searched the surrounding area he could find no trace of either species anywhere but growing in the midst of the *Carex bicolor*. It was beginning to look very much as if the sedges had been cultivated elsewhere and transplanted to Rum – bringing with them the seeds of common garden weeds that had, latterly, germinated incriminatingly in their midst.

Raven struggled to locate other species, finding Heslop-Harrison's directions maddeningly vague with which to locate plants that numbered just a handful of individual specimens in total. This scarcity in itself concerned him and he noted, 'no genuinely British alpine is quite as scarce as that'. Eager to make the most of his time unfettered by Heslop-Harrison's presence, Raven finished his day's botanising and evidence-gathering by examining a colony of four-leaved allseed near to their base at Kinloch.

This was another of Heslop-Harrison's startling discoveries, a plant known elsewhere in the United Kingdom only from the Channel Islands and a handful of locations in Cornwall and Devon. Arthur Wilmott, Raven's confidant and co-planner of the current expedition, had seen a specimen of four-leaved allseed collected in Rum and had noted that it was of a form completely unlike those found elsewhere in the country. Raven's suspicions, naturally, were aroused and he felt the colony deserved close inspection.

There, growing from the very midst of one of the four-leaved allseed specimens, Raven noticed a tiny flowering plant he was unfamiliar with. This, given the breadth of his knowledge of the British flora, was notable enough in itself. What this plant proved to be, and the implications of its identity, was remarkable – this was *Wahlenbergia lobelioides* subspecies *nutabunda*, a native of the Canaries, quite unknown in the wild in Britain, but occasionally found in botanic gardens. It seemed certain that, like the *Carex bicolor*, whoever had planted the four-leaved allseed had done so oblivious to the seeds that lurked in the soil transplanted with the donor plant.

Raven left Rum the following day having amassed a body of evidence that seemed to corroborate the feeling at large in the British botanical world that something was awry on the island. He returned to Cambridge and wrote a report for the Council of Trinity College, which had helped to fund his expedition. He concluded that there were three possible explanations that might account for the evidence he had gathered:

1 That the Professor himself is the victim of a practical joke.
2 That as Dr Jekyll he [Heslop-Harrison] plants the specimens which as Mr Hyde he later discovers.
3 That the Professor is deliberately indulging in the most culpable dishonesty in order to secure for himself an immediate reputation and an immortal place in the annals of British botany.

Raven was in no doubt whatsoever that it was the latter hypothesis that explained what he had found on Rum. His conclusions were excoriating and explicit. Noting that Heslop-Harrison was 'the type of which dictators are made' – perhaps a reference to Heslop-Harrison's unfortunate penchant for sporting a moustache of the kind favoured by Adolf Hitler, even during the dark days of the Second World War – Raven speculated that Rum had, by virtue of its inaccessibility and lack of previous botanical exploration, provided Heslop-Harrison with the ideal stage upon which to exercise 'his peculiar psychology', either completely fabricating or deliberately introducing rare plant records on Rum in pursuit of personal botanical fame and an enhanced reputation.

The implications of this were twofold – Raven felt that a number of Heslop-Harrison's botanical discoveries on Rum, including *Carex bicolor* and four-leaved allseed, should be struck off the scientific record. As to whether Heslop-Harrison should be publicly exposed and disgraced for his misdoings, Raven was more circumspect. Displaying a sensitivity that would have been as alien to Heslop-Harrison as *Carex bicolor* was to Rum, Raven remarked, 'I cannot help hoping not, since, for all his eccentricity, he treated me throughout with a rather touching, if usually gruff and peremptory generosity.'

Raven's sentiment was to be respected, insofar as his report was never published. Instead it was lodged in the library at King's College, Cambridge, held in a plain manila folder with the intriguing injunction: *Not to be looked at in the life of J. Heslop-Harrison (Jnr)* written on it. (Heslop-Harrison's son, also John was, like his father before him, a botanist – he went on to become the director of Kew, a preeminent position in British botany).

Word of the report's contents, however, could not have failed to spread. This was helped in no small part by Raven himself. His scrupulous sense of honesty and scientific accuracy meant that, although he did not feel comfortable with the idea of publicly exposing Heslop-Harrison, he could not allow the matter of the plants at the root of the scandal to go unchallenged. In January 1949 a letter from Raven was published in the journal *Nature*. The title alone left little doubt about the flavour of what was to follow: 'Alien Plant Introductions on the Isle of Rhum'.

Raven's letter was characteristically carefully constructed, with a scholarly portrayal of the facts that would have done a barrister justice. While he made it clear why he considered both *Carex bicolor* and four-leaved allseed to have been deliberately introduced to Rum, he did not go so far as to openly accuse Heslop-Harrison of having been the agent of that introduction. He did, however, make explicit reference to the announcement of the discovery of both plants being made in papers authored by Heslop-Harrison – and the implication, if not an outright accusation, was plain enough for all to see.

Given how long it took Heslop-Harrison to respond, one must assume that Raven's letter was not brought to his attention at the time of publication. Certainly, given Heslop-Harrison's usual readiness to respond to any implied criticism of himself or his work, one would have expected him to react sooner had he known about it. In early 1951 he prepared a letter for *Nature*, provisionally entitled 'Alien and Relict Plants in the Hebrides', which would make the case that *Wahlenbergia nutabanda* and four-leaved allseed had escaped into the wilds of Rum from the disused greenhouses of Kinloch Castle. In the end Heslop-Harrison chose not to see this published, and instead set out the case for the integrity of his records – and himself – in his own newsletter, *Occasional Notes*.

In the years that passed, Heslop-Harrison's unusual records from Rum were systematically reappraised in publications that might, had the records been considered credible, have featured them unequivocally. If mentioned at all, the likes of *Carex bicolor* were heavily caveated. Botanists made it clear that they considered these extremely extralimital species to have occurred on Rum unnaturally. While never explicitly stated in public, the twentieth century's greatest British botanical fraud had been uncovered, and the records in question censored.

Raven corresponded by letter with Heslop-Harrison in the days following his short visit to Rum. This correspondence helped him to refine his report for Trinity College. It began civilly and cordially enough on both sides, but shortly afterwards deteriorated on the part of Heslop-Harrison, who seasoned his penultimate letter to Raven in 1948 with choice drops of vitriol. Raven's letters to him 'verge upon impertinence' and contain 'crude attempts' to discredit Heslop-Harrison's botanical discoveries on Rum. Heslop-Harrison closed the correspondence saying, 'I have come to the conclusion that you came to Rhum prepared to find fault, and therefore, quite naturally, but without the slightest justification, managed to do so.'

A little more than a year after Heslop-Harrison considered publishing a response to Raven's letter in *Nature*, he wrote one final letter to Raven in the spring of 1952. It followed the death of Heslop-Harrison's wife, and his anguish is tangible. Unfortunately, he chose squarely to blame Raven's presence on Rum in 1948 and the publication of his letter in *Nature* in 1949 for the deterioration of Christian Heslop-Harrison's health. This must have made appalling reading for one as principled as John Raven. Heslop-Harrison went on to state that Raven's letter in *Nature* was 'a complete fabrication cemented together by a few facts, often distorted' – given the weight of evidence that Raven had dispassionately gathered, this assertion would have been as water off a duck's back to him, but the personal attack on his integrity and the accusation that he had caused Heslop-Harrison's wife's suffering would have been extraordinarily hard to bear.

This remarkable story of alleged botanical fraud, subterfuge and detective work was very much in my mind as I stood on the deck of the ferry pulling into the pier that serves Kinloch on Rum. The parallels with the mystery that surrounded the occurrence of the sawfly orchid in Dorset were striking – if it had not occurred there through natural causes, I wondered anew at the motivation that might have driven an unknown hand to plant an alien orchid at Dancing Ledge.

Rum itself was shrouded with cloud – all I could see were the trees that lined the shore around a small bay beside the pier. Above them was a grey nothingness from which a heavy drizzle emanated. If I was any judge of island weather, this felt like the sort of drizzle that was settled in for the day. At least getting onto the island had been simplicity itself – I had not needed to apply for permission from a belligerent botanist or a Scottish aristocrat with a colourful past. Nowadays anyone so inclined can visit Rum on a regular ferry service running from Mallaig on the Scottish mainland.

There were further parallels between my expedition to Rum and that of John Raven nearly seventy years before me. Accommodation on the island remains fairly limited and, with only a day to spend on Rum before I had to leave on the next passing ferry, I too would need to camp for the night. Just like Raven, I would also be looking for rare plants – although in my case there was no taint of fraud surrounding them, simply an absence of reports, which suggested they might no longer be found on the island. The last records from Rum of Pugsley's marsh orchid – the orchid that Heslop-Harrison had derided as 'not a species' in the aftermath of Pugsley describing it as such – were in 1998.

I loved the delicious irony of the situation – these orchids had surely been present on Rum in the 1930s and 1940s when Heslop-Harrison was conducting his wayward botanical exploits there, a new and undescribed British orchid species under his very nose. Yet when another botanist dared to announce it a new species, Heslop-Harrison not only could not agree with him, he had to go to the lengths of publishing a paper to prove that the claim was factually incorrect. Only the passage of time and advances in technology had allowed a definitive rebuttal of Heslop-Harrison and a vindication of Pugsley. While I had already seen Pugsley's marsh orchid in Ireland, I wanted to look for the species where Heslop-Harrison had failed to recognise it.

The grid reference for the last record of Pugsley's marsh orchid on Rum placed the plants near the old pony track that traversed the coast from Kinloch to the glen at Dibidil, some six miles away. As I needed to spend the night on Rum, I planned to hike to Dibidil, where I could stay at a camping bothy – a two-roomed stone building that, while lacking electricity or running water, would at least be dry and better overnight quarters than a tent. Never had the prospect of such basic accommodation seemed more enticing as I began the uphill trek out of Kinloch, climbing a rough stone track that led up into the cloud layer shrouding the island. The drizzle had collapsed into steady rain, leaving the uneven path running with water while my backpack, heavily laden with camping gear, firewood, food and my camera equipment, rendered me dangerously top heavy. My walking boots skidded time after time beneath me, and more than once I stumbled before regaining my balance.

At first this was merely inconvenient, but as the path finally breasted the hill that overshadowed Kinloch and began crawling along the hillside and, below, the brink of the tall cliffs that bordered the island, I realised that the situation was, potentially, more dangerous than I had given it credit for. A slip here could result in a broken ankle, or worse. I was forewarned by the salutary story of a hiker who had been swept to his death crossing a burn at spate on this very section of the pony track some years previously.

Somewhere, unseen above me, were the peaks of Hallival, Askival and Barkeval – the latter the scene of John Raven's discovery that *Carex bicolor* had been deliberately planted on the island. The sedges did not survive long on Rum – I wished I could see Barkeval, but I had more pressing demands on my attention. The pathway crossed a number of burns as it made its way to the glen at Dibidil. All of these were swollen with rainwater coming off the mountains and hillsides above me. Crossing even the smallest of their number presented a challenge I had not anticipated as, at the very least, they were deeper than my walking boots, and too wide to jump. Where possible, I crossed them on rocks protruding from the rushing water, leaping gingerly from one to another, the tragically killed hiker never far from my mind.

After an hour, I stopped briefly to shelter beneath a rocky overhang beside the now increasingly boggy path. This was not quite a cave, but was adequate to provide a brief respite from the relentless downpour. I had been concentrating on where I was putting my feet and had not really appreciated the view that was now before me – the island of Eigg, glowing in sunlight across the water from Rum. Sunbathed Eigg was to be my constant companion for the coming day, always in my peripheral vision, and always enjoying considerably finer weather than Rum. My light summer waterproofs had, by now, proved themselves hopelessly inadequate for the task at hand: I found myself soaked to the skin, unpleasantly chilled, and feeling rather sorry for the exotic reptiles and birds that Sir George Bullough had brought to live out their days in this cool and uninviting climate.

Resuming my trek, I pressed on towards Dibidil. I planned to shed most of my backpack's contents at the bothy there, change into dry clothes, and then head out anew to search for Puglsey's marsh orchid. Despite my best efforts to concentrate on the path, I could not help myself as I drew closer to Dibidil and the location at which my quarry had last been reported – my questing eyes sought out familiar shapes on either side of the path. Here and there were pink and white louseworts hugging the ground, but I could find no orchids of any description. The same could not be said for acid-bog-loving carnivorous plants – ruby-red, glistening great and round-leaved sundews grew side by side with sickly yellow butterworts in mottled carpets of insect peril. Such a profusion of insectivorous plants suggested that Rum's reputation as a stronghold for biting midges was probably well founded. Luckily for me, the heavy rain was keeping the midges at ground level.

The sense of relief was profound when, breasting a final summit, I saw the green glen at Dibidil opening up before me and, nestling in the very foot of it, the small stone bothy that would be my home for the next day. Nothing was dry any more, with the exception of the contents of my backpack. I was cold, soaking wet, hungry and shivering. The final water body that needed crossing was a small river that flowed swiftly down the glen before disgorging into the sea below. The river was significantly wider than the burns that had gone before it but now, with boots oozing water at every step, I was past caring about trying to keep my feet out of the water – I picked the widest and shallowest spot I could find and simply waded across, the ice cold, knee-deep water tugging at my legs.

The bothy's freshly painted wooden door was a welcome sight. What I found inside was basic but felt like the height of luxury – two bare, stone-walled rooms, each with a spartan wooden sleeping platform, a table and a bench, and a fireplace. Nobody else was staying there, though there were signs of previous occupants – a tin of ham, some candle nubs, and some abandoned paperbacks. I gratefully shed my heavy backpack, stripped off and enjoyed the luxury of a dry towel and change of clothes from within it. I was glad that I had brought firewood with me, for there was no fuel to be had in the bothy and, on later inspection, no driftwood to be found on the shore. As it was, I got a fire burning in the smaller of the rooms, rigged up a clothes line above it to dry my wet clothes, and made myself a mug of hot, sweet tea. My boots were saturated but, with the simple expedient of plastic bags worn over my socks, were considerably more comfortable than hitherto. Outside the window the rain had stopped at last. It was time to retrace my steps and look properly for Pugsley's marsh orchid.

The river proved a little more troublesome than it had half an hour previously, as I had no wish to soak my only remaining dry pair of trousers. Freed of the heavy rucksack and carrying just a camera bag, I managed to leap from boulder to boulder at a narrow point and so to the far bank. This minor victory made me feel a little better.

Armed with a grid reference, a map and a GPS, I walked back uphill towards Kinloch. The supplied coordinates brought me to a rough grassy area surrounding a seep emanating from high above on the hillside. This looked like the most promising habitat I had yet seen on the island for *Dactylorhiza* orchids. My GPS promised accuracy to within six square metres so, with no obvious sign of any orchids, I began carefully looking in the long grass, systematically working my way back and forth across the breadth of the marshy area. In a short while I had covered the area and had found three orchids deep in the grass, growing within a foot of one another. Quite what species they were was another matter, for they had already flowered and their green, glossy ovaries were swelling with seeds.

That they were *Dactylorhiza* orchids was beyond doubt – and their few leaves were unspotted. They looked weedy and felt, somehow, like they should be Pugsley's marsh orchids. The few ovaries on each flower stem suggested this might be the case, as Pugsley's often has rather sparse, lopsided flower heads. Yet I could not be certain with non-flowering examples of this most contentious of orchid families. That single, indisputable Pugsley's marsh orchid in Ireland suddenly felt a lot more precious than it had at the time – perhaps it would prove, in its way, to be every bit as important to me as the Irish marsh and dense-flowered orchids that had been the original objects of my Irish sojourn.

I cast my search wider, working my way up the seep and examining every promising area of grass I found. I reasoned that if there had been Pugsley's marsh orchids at my starting coordinates in 1998, and the plants I had just found there were possibly the descendants of those original orchids, there may well be further examples in the area. What I found on the hillside above were more *Dactylorhizha* orchids, but no further clarity – a scattering of early marsh orchids were just finishing blooming, their flowers for the most part browned and frazzled but with a few florets still recognisable for what they had been in their prime.

Appropriately on this island of all islands, I found myself confronting a minor botanical mystery. Were the fruiting orchids Pugsley's marsh orchids that had finished flowering? Or could they be early marsh orchids like those a few hundred metres away, which had also almost finished flowering? The leaves of both small colonies' orchids appeared identical, and offered me no helpful clues. The first orchids' sparsely packed ovaries were indicative of Pugsley's marsh orchid, but provided no certainty. The indisputable early marsh orchids were far from the most substantial representatives of their kind I had ever seen – perhaps all orchids on this nutrient-poor, rain-washed hillside were impoverished and insubstantial?

As I walked back to the bothy at Dibidil, its chimney issuing a thin trickle of blue smoke that promised a warm place for the night, I dwelt on Professor Heslop-Harrison and John Raven's botanical exploits on Rum. The one appeared to have attempted fraudulently to embellish his professional reputation as a botanist, while the other used his amateur botanical skills to undo the tangled web of deceit that spanned the island's corries, hills and nunataks. While it was frustrating, I appreciated the symmetry that found me struggling to identify my target orchid on this strange and mysterious island. With my quest in mind, and having seen a Pugsley's marsh orchid already in Ireland, I could afford myself the small luxury of being thwarted on Rum. As John Raven had found before me, the truth was an elusive and slippery thing here.

My troubles on Rum were to prove more complicated than simple plant identification. The following morning I found the river that flowed through the glen had swollen overnight. The large boulders that had studded the water the previous day were nowhere to be seen beneath the surging water that flowed swiftly to the sea. Time was an issue here – I had to be back in Kinloch in time to catch my ferry back to the Scottish mainland. I felt I could ill afford to head inland – and uphill – to find somewhere I could cross the river easily. With a dry change of clothes in my backpack, I decided to ford the river once more. I eyed the rushing water nervously – I knew it would be fairly deep, as it had been up to my knees the day before, and the speed with which it flowed was worrying me.

I shrugged my backpack off – if I went over, I didn't want it to be dragging me down – and put my mobile phone inside a Ziploc bag in my pocket. What Rum lacked in dry weather it made up for, unusually in rural Scotland, in mobile phone coverage. If I had an accident I might at least call for help. With my backpack held over my head, I gingerly slid from the riverbank into the water. It was just below waist height, shockingly cold, and pulled strongly at me. I edged my way across the river, shuffling my feet to avoid tripping on an unseen stone and, in the meantime, striving to maintain my balance.

Halfway across, feeling dangerously top heavy and unsteady, I opted to throw my backpack to the far bank – a decision that almost cost me dearly, as the very throw itself unbalanced me. For an awful moment my arms windmilled as I strove to stay upright while the water tugged at my midriff. What felt like an eternity later, I had steadied myself and could proceed a little more easily than before across the remainder of the river's width. Pulling myself onto the riverbank, wet clothes clinging unpleasantly to me, I felt a relief that put seeing a rare orchid into sharp perspective.

The last stop in my foray through the complex and occasionally bewildering world of Britain and Ireland's marsh orchids was also off the west coast of Scotland. Where Rum had been unrelentingly cold and wet, North Uist was to be balmily kind to me. I stepped out of the airport at Benbecula into a day of hot sunshine and the promise of seeing one of Britain's most perplexing orchids.

If Pugsley's marsh orchid had charted a convoluted course to being formally recognised as a full species, Hebridean marsh orchid took the intricacies of *Dactylorhiza* genetics and identification to an entirely different level. Initially discovered by Maybud Campbell in 1936, it came to be considered part of what was, at the time, known as western marsh orchid – a marsh orchid found predominantly in western Ireland but also in a handful of outposts in north-west

Scotland. Latterly, genetic studies appeared to clarify matters – what had hitherto been simply western marsh orchid was, in fact, two species: Irish marsh orchid, representing the Irish populations while, at the northern extremity of the island of North Uist and the southern tip of nearby Berneray, a population of some two thousand orchids represented the world's entire population of Hebridean marsh orchid. Other formerly Scottish examples of western marsh orchid were now assigned to the *cambrensis* subspecies of northern marsh orchid.

Genetic analysis even went so far as to suggest an origin for Hebridean marsh orchid – it was the love child of a hybrid coupling of the *coccinea* subspecies of early marsh orchid and the *hebridensis* subspecies of common spotted orchid, both of which were to be found side by side in the area. Everything seemed about as clear as things can ever be where *Dactylorhiza* orchids are concerned.

That is to say, naturally, not very clear at all. No sooner had Britain's orchid flora been swollen by the addition of a new and extremely niche endemic species than the geneticists were at it again with a comprehensive paper published in the *New Journal of Botany* in 2013, and this time their conclusions were very different indeed. Hebridean marsh orchid had been demoted once more – and was now assigned to a wholly different species altogether.

Pugsley's marsh orchid, itself no stranger to a convoluted route to taxonomic acceptance, now had a new variation in its midst – the orchid formerly known as Hebridean marsh was now considered to be a variety of a subspecies of Pugsley's marsh orchid or, to give it the full Latin treatment, *Dactylorhiza traunsteinerioides ssp. francis-drucei var. ebudensis*. The former conclusions as to the species' origins were, it transpired, based on genetic analysis of just one plant. The authors of this latest analysis, Professor Richard Bateman and Dr Ian Denholm, used a larger sample but balanced their conclusions with the observation that their taxonomic decisions remained subject to future change in the light of further data and analysis – a caveat that, given these particular orchids' history, seems extremely prudent.

British orchidophiles welcome new additions to their lists, but are less enthusiastic about losing a species, no matter how well founded the intentions or science behind the loss. Simon Harrap's *A Pocket Guide to the Orchids of Britain and Ireland,* published in 2016, is typical in this regard – Harrap prefers to continue to treat the Hebridean marsh orchid as a full species in its own right, saying of Bateman and Denholm's paper, 'I suspect this might not be the end of the story and pending a definitive answer I prefer to maintain [Hebridean marsh orchid's] separate identity.'

I preferred to follow the scientists' lead and assume that, until the evidence suggested otherwise, the Hebridean marsh orchid was in fact an unusual variety of Pugsley's marsh orchid. As an amateur botanist, I knew I would not be adding anything to the debate as to what constituted a good, valid species – but nor could I afford to miss seeing a Hebridean marsh orchid this year, for it might yet prove to be a species after all. Most of all, I simply wanted to see a particularly beautiful and unusual marsh orchid at home in some of the finest remaining machair habitat in the British Isles.

Much of the confusion about this orchid stemmed from its distinctive appearance – the leaves in particular are heavily marked with purple blotches and can, in some plants, have the usual green colouration completely replaced with purple pigment. I wanted not only to see these orchids, but also to see the more extreme versions of them – those with the solid blackish-purple leaves.

A short drive across Benbecula and North Uist brought me to Port nan Long at the northern end of the latter island. The roads were narrow lanes just a car's width wide – these petered out on a sandy track that ran through the heart of the machair, a fertile, sandy-soiled, flower-rich grassland habitat. I parked beside a small cultivated plot, green potato haulms rising lushly above the bare soil. In their midst crouched a nesting lapwing keeping a watchful eye on me. Somewhere in the distance I could hear the rasping, monotonous call of a corncrake, like a fingernail run down the teeth of a comb. While it is for breeding birds such as these that the machair is justly famous, the botanical richness of the area is considerable too. I could already see a pinkish-purple flush of orchids amongst the grass only a little way from the track.

My first orchids proved to be the *hebridensis* subspecies of common spotted orchid – rose-pink pyramidal flowers heavily marked with dark cerise hoops and blotches. Nearby I found blood-red early marsh orchids – these were the *coccinea* subspecies, a startlingly different looking flower from the *incarnata* subspecies I had seen in Ireland and on Rum, both in colour and flower shape – the *coccinea* flower spikes were almost circular and grew low amidst the grass. I had never seen such a red orchid bloom before.

These two species had once been mooted as parents for the Hebridean marsh orchid – but what of that plant itself? It was moments later when I found myself in the midst of a loose colony of several dozen orchids that were, indisputably, Hebridean marsh orchid. Their flower spikes were haphazard, coloured and marked quite unlike the common spotted or early marsh orchids, and the individual flowers were large, loosely formed and richly magenta. Their leaves, meanwhile, left nothing to doubt – most were heavily blotched with dark purple spots, but three plants in particular were spectacular examples of their kind. Their leaves were almost solidly bruised with purplish-black pigmentation, above which a similarly dark stem arose, thickly clustered with deep purple bracts as sharply curved as tigers' claws. These were the extreme Hebridean marsh orchids I had so hoped to find.

It was easy to drown myself in these flowers – the short, springy turf around them was largely free of other flowers and it was possible to lie in their midst, surrounded by them, paying due homage with both naked eye and camera. I could hear droning bumblebees nearby, and meadow pipits calling unseen in the near distance. These Hebridean marsh orchids might only be a variety of a subspecies of Pugsley's marsh orchid, but I was more pleased to see them than I had imagined I would be.

Their beauty would have been enough in itself to make a day trip to North Uist more than worthwhile, but the island had a final trick up its sleeve for me that afternoon. I continued to walk the machair, heading north towards a sheltered, silver-sanded bay. I stopped time after time to examine more orchids – they were everywhere, studding the turf in discrete scatters of their own kind. Here were common spotted orchids, and there more blood-red *coccinea* early marsh orchids. Now still more Hebridean marsh orchids and, finally, my first frog orchids of the year.

These stubby, subtle orchids could have easily been overlooked. I had set myself down on a mound overlooking Clachan Sands to eat a picnic lunch before heading back to the airport on Benbecula when I noticed first one, and then more and more frog orchids rising unobtrusively from the short grass around me. Each was barely taller than the grass that surrounded it, just a few centimetres high, rising from a pair of glaucous leaves set flush with the turf. Their flower spikes were tight green cylinders suffused with burgundy, each individual flower tightly hooded by the petals and sepals, with a relatively long, unmarked red-fringed green labellum beneath. For years they were not known to be part of the *Dactylorhiza* complex, although they occasionally hybridised with other species in that family. It was only in the late twentieth century that molecular studies revealed them as a primitive *Dactylorhiza*.

I knew I would see more of them in the course of the summer, not only back home in Shetland, but also as far south as Sussex – they are widely distributed across the country. Nevertheless, they were a pleasant discovery here on North Uist, albeit not an entirely unexpected one, as I had heard they were present here in the same area as the Hebridean marsh orchids. What followed, however, was much more unanticipated. The sides of the mound were swathed in longer grass and, in the midst of this, hundreds of northern marsh orchids. They made for a handy comparison with the Hebridean marsh orchids, for both have deep purple flowers and the former was realistically the only potential source of confusion when identifying the latter here. It was while looking at the northern marsh orchids that one flower in particular seemed to leap out of the grass at me – there was something subtly, indefinably wrong about this orchid. The flower was not the usual deep, rich purple of a northern marsh – it was paler, but with a slightly yellowish cast in the sunlight. My heart beginning to race, I knelt to examine it more closely.

I had seen a photo of such a plant once before – this one also found in the Hebrides some years previously. I could hardly believe that I had found one too, but the closer I looked at the individual flowers, the more certain I became. The labellum of each flower was shaped and formed differently from those of the nearby northern marsh orchids, being longer and less overtly splayed. While the petals and sepals were purple, the labellum in particular had a sickly, isabelline hue that, combined with its unusual shape, betrayed the mixed origins of the plant. This, in the heart of a mixed colony of both parent species, was the hybrid between frog orchid and northern marsh orchid, known dryly to botanists as *X Dactyloglossum viridellum*.

Readying my camera, I found my hands were shaking – this was a rare hybrid, one infrequently found, and I had stumbled across it here on North Uist with not another person, let alone a botanist, anywhere in sight. I had this plant all to myself and I knew that this, selfishly, made the moment all the more special. Of course, I wanted to share the plant with anyone who would appreciate it, but that eureka moment of discovery and realisation? That was sweeter for being mine alone.

I took a series of photos before noticing that time had passed quickly while I was lost in the now familiar reverie that these plants seemed to induce. I had just enough time to hurry back to my hire car and head for the airport. This would have been a close-run thing even without finding a second identical hybrid some three metres away from the first plant – I could not resist spending a moment with this plant too. My departure from North Uist was to be a hot, sweaty and tense one – my return to the car was at a dead run, my camera and tripod bouncing on my back under the hot and unforgiving Hebridean sun, and my drive to the airport was interminable, hindered by guileless holidaymakers enjoying slow walks, cycles and drives through North Uist's patchwork crofting landscape.

The journey home passed in a pleasant haze. I had looked for, and found, our scarcest *Dactylorhiza* orchids in the western fringes of Britain and Ireland. The jewel in the crown had been a pair of rare hybrids, not even a full or disputed species in their own right – an unexpected but thrilling conclusion to my dive into the murky genetic depths of this complicated family of orchids.

7

The lady's slipper

If any orchid epitomises all of our preconceptions of what it is to be an orchid, it is surely the lady's slipper, *Cypripedium calceolus*. Its flowers combine beauty, intrigue, rarity and sexiness in one irresistible and, at times, tragic package. There is no other native British orchid quite like it. It is the sole British representative of a genus of temperate slipper orchids with a range that extends from North America to the Far East where, as early as five hundred years before Christ, they were coveted and grown in China during the time of Confucius. They are a feast for the eyes, their flowers a lush confection of deep claret petals as twisted as a Mobius band and an indecently bulbous, golden-yellow lip thrusting to the fore.

The name of their genus was the creation of Swedish taxonomist Karl Linnaeus, father of the system of binomial scientific names by which all species are identified to this day. *Cypripedium* featured in his *Flora Lapponica* of 1737, the name an allusion to *Cypris*, a Latin synonym of the goddess Aphrodite, and *pedilon* or slipper, referring to the popular common name, lady's slipper. Technically the genus ought to have been named *Cypripedilum* but Linnaeus, tremendous taxonomist though he undoubtedly was, was not such an adept with his Greek and Latin vocabulary – he instead employed the Latin genitive plural for feet, *pedium*. *Cypripedium* translates as Aphrodite's feet – whereas Linnaeus surely meant that it should be Venus's slipper, alluding to the folkoric tales attached to this beautiful flower.

Aphrodite's Roman counterpart, Venus, is intimately associated with the orchids – she was said to have been walking in woodland when she lost her slipper. A shepherdess found the slipper, but when she tried to pick it up, the slipper vanished, leaving the orchid we know today in its place. In time this classical myth evolved and adopted a more Christian persona – Aphrodite and Venus became supplanted by the Virgin Mary so, until Linnaeus renamed it, the lady's slipper orchid was referred to for centuries as *calaceolus mariae*.

Such distinctive flowers have evidently been well known for many years. Greco-Roman mythology aside, they were first formally described and illustrated in the mid-sixteenth century in Conrad Gessner's *Horti Germaniae* and Rembert Dodoens' *Florum* respectively. John Gerard heavily borrowed from Dodoens for his *Herball* of 1597, though Gerard did not appear to realise that lady's slipper was a native British species. He described it as 'our Ladies shooe or slipper', and referred to it growing in the mountains of central Europe. Gerard himself grew a flowering plant of lady's slipper given to him by his friend, the apothecary James Garret.

In 1629 John Parkinson, apothecary to James I, botanist to Charles I and close friend of the great gardener John Tradescant the Elder, wrote that it was to be found in Lancashire:

neare the border of Yorkshire, in a wood or place called
the Helkes, which is three miles from Ingleborough … as
I am informed by a courteous Gentlewoman, called Mistris
Thomasin Turnstall, who dwelleth at Bull-banke, near Hornby
Castle … [she] hathe often sent mee up the rootes to London
which have faire flowers in my Garden.

(This was, in a neat botanical coincidence, also the wood in which
the first British record of sword-leaved helleborine was noted in
1666.) By the eighteenth century the presence of lady's slipper
in England was well known, though the context in which the
plant was noted had changed somewhat from that of the pervious
herbals – Philip Miller, writing in his *Gardeners Dictionary* in 1731
noted it was to be, 'found in the woods of Yorkshire, Lancashire
and other Northern Counties of England … so the only Expense
is in the first procuring them, which is easily effected in many
Parts of England.'

Clearly by this stage our native lady's slipper was prized as an
ornamental garden plant and, following the example set the previous century by John Parkinson, Miller himself was growing it in
the Chelsea Physic Garden. In the first volume of James Smith and
James Sowerby's monumental *English Botany*, published in 1790,
the very first plate features the orchid in pride of place, an emi-
nence echoed in the accompanying text:

If the beauty or scarcity of a plant, or the singularity of its
structure entitle it to our notice, the Ladies Slipper certainly
merits the first place in a work on British Plants. It may
indeed be reckoned the queen of all the European *Orchideae*.
Accordingly, it has not only been cherished by the scientific
botanist, but it has been among gardeners always sold at the
highest price of any British Vegetable.

Whether lady's slipper orchids were ever a commonplace sight
in the north of England is moot, but their removal from their
wild stations and the slow reproduction of those that remained
will have accelerated their decline and, in the meantime, driven up

their price, as supply failed to match demand. A perfect Catch-22 situation developed – as the supply dwindled, the demand for, at first garden plants and, latterly, herbarium specimens grew exponentially. For those living in the vicinity of flowering plants the attraction of gathering plants for sale would have been irresistible. A letter written in 1781 to the botanist William Curtis records, 'Mr Birkbeck bought ten Lady's Slippers on market day from a man who had brought about forty to sell.'

This untenable situation was lamented by the Victorian gardener and plant collector Reginald Farrer, who said of the woman who had supplied John Parkinson with his plants in the seventeenth century, 'A worthy gentlewoman indeed! O Mistress Thomasin, if only you had loved these delights a little less ruinously for future generations!'

By the late nineteenth century the calamitous decline in the lady's slipper's fortunes appeared to be terminal, with only two extant locations recorded in *The Flora of West Yorkshire* in 1888. Reginald Farrer, who lived near the orchid's former stronghold of Ingleborough until his untimely death aged just forty, when plant collecting in Burma's Minshan mountains, related:

One old vicar kept careful watch over it, and went every year to pluck the flowers and so keep the plant safe, for without the flower you might, if uninstructed, take the plant for Lily of the Valley. Then one year he fell ill. The plant was allowed to blossom; was discovered and uprooted without mercy, and that was an end to him.

And worse is to follow: for a professor from the north – I will not unfold whether it were Edinburgh, or Glasgow, or Aberdeen, or none of these that produced this monster of men – put a price on the head of the *Cypripedium*, and offered the inhabitants so much for every rooted plant they sent to him. The valley accordingly was swept bare…

Farrer finishes his account of the lady's slipper with the following invective: 'Accursed for evermore, into the lowest of the Eight

Hot Hells, be all reckless uprooters of rarities, from professors downwards.'

It seemed as if this curse was too little too late as, in 1917, the lady's slipper was finally declared extinct in Britain. There, it seemed, the story had ended – an orchid gone the same tragic way as the flightless great auk, collected at first for its own sake and latterly, as it became ever rarer, simply because of that very rarity. All was, however, not quite as it seemed. Thomas Hey recounted an episode in *The Dalesman* in 1949 when a local man from Airedale met with him:

> [he] called in to describe some episodes concerning foxes,
> Cononley way. But I soon discovered that he had brought far
> more interesting news than that – he had chapter and verse
> for the existence of *Cypripedium calceolus* in the Grassington
> neighbourhood. I will not disclose the spot, but he left me with
> notes of the history of those few plants over three years – how
> many had flowered, how cattle nibbled back two of them, and
> how he was certain they still survived.
>
> If his story was true, and if those particular plants have
> escaped the collector's grasp in the intervening years, then
> assuredly the Lady's Slipper is still there. But I must say that
> I couldn't find it when I searched.[1]

That anonymous Airedale man, with his tales of miscreant foxes and extinct orchids, was probably Willie Jarman, a cotton weaver from Silsden. In early June 1930, Jarman and his brother were out walking near Grassington when they stumbled across a lady's slipper orchid sporting fourteen shoots, one of which was gloriously in flower. Lady's slipper orchids can live for decades, with some plants comfortably approaching or even exceeding a century in age – an individual plant in Estonia is said to be almost two hundred years old. This hitherto unknown plant in Yorkshire may have been there, unnoticed, for decades before the Jarmans happened across it. What is certain is that Jarman and, in later years, his son returned annually to monitor this precious plant while, in the meantime, they kept the plant's existence a closely guarded secret, sharing the information with only a handful of trusted confidants.

One cabal dedicated to protecting the safety of a lost orchid would be remarkable enough, but it seems as if there were other plants known to an entirely different local secret society – lady's slippers which, it appears, may have been discovered before the Jarman brothers' chance encounter with the Grassington plant. A secret society of local Dales naturalists formed in the 1920s, dedicated to conserving the lady's slipper – the extent of the membership and activities of the society remain unclear to this day, though it is certain that they met annually and were sworn to absolute secrecy about both the continuing presence of the orchid in the area and, naturally, specific site details for where those plants were to be found.

Precisely which plants they were aware of is equally unclear. Local flora accounts published in the latter part of the century provide clues that there may have been at least two additional plants in addition to the Grassington orchid – one was rumoured to have been found near Kettlewell in 1927, and a further site in Wensleydale was said to have harboured a plant until 1956 when, with a certain inevitability, it was dug up. Eventually both secretive groups became aware of one another, and their interests converged on the Grassington plant. By the late 1960s it seemed as if this was the only location that contained an indisputably English lady's slipper. (An isolated plant on the edge of the golf course at Silverdale in Lancashire had been known about for decades, though dogged by rumours that it had been planted there by persons unknown in the late nineteenth or early twentieth century. In recent years DNA tests have confirmed this plant is not of English origin, originating from Austrian or perhaps Pyrenean stock instead.)

In the meantime, a handful of botanists were trusted sufficiently to be brought into the circle of trust that surrounded this precious orchid. One of their number, John Raven, took his oath of silence extraordinarily seriously – on at least two occasions in the 1950s he passed within metres of the plant when botanising with friends in the area, but made no mention whatsoever of it at the time. He did, however, mischievously tell one of his companions, after the event, that they had been unwittingly been on the very cusp of seeing the lady's slipper in situ. The oath of *omertà*, however, worked for the most part and until the 1960s even prominent British botanists remained blissfully unaware that the lady's slipper clung on, precariously, in its former northern haunts.

The identity of one of the secret society is both known and infamous, as he eventually broke ranks and revealed to the world at large that the orchid was still growing in England. Eric Hardy was a naturalist with a keen interest in the fertilisation of lady's slipper orchids by *Andrena* bees, and also a journalist with a regular column in the *Liverpool Daily Post*. These two interests were to fatally coincide in 1966. Hardy's pollination studies had been repeatedly thwarted by the actions of at least one other member of the secret society who, in order to render the plant less conspicuous, habitually removed the forming flower buds from the plant before they could bloom. This was the cause of some ongoing disagreement amongst the society's members as, while it helped preserve the plant's anonymity, it also removed any possibility of the plant setting seed and reproducing itself. Hardy, meanwhile, was frustrated that his plans to study the pollination mechanisms of the lady's slipper were annually thwarted, and was growing increasingly resentful.

The first chinks in the lady's slipper's armour showed on 6 August 1965, in an article featured in *The Times* entitled 'Hunting the Lady's Slipper Orchid'. An unnamed correspondent related their search for this elusive lady of the Dales, a thrilling account culminating in the successful discovery of the plant. Then in 1966 it appears that Eric Hardy's mounting resentment finally got the better of him and the oath of secrecy he had sworn. He provided an approximate location for the orchid in his column in the *Liverpool Daily Post* and, if that were not enough, in a programme for Yorkshire Television. The lady's slipper's secret was well and truly out in the open.

The dismay of the other members of the secret society can only be imagined. Their disappointment manifested itself shortly afterwards when one of their number visited the orchid and discovered a hole in the ground where it had grown. The lady's slipper story appeared to have reached an inevitable conclusion. Dr Arthur Raistrick, one of the founding members of the society, was quoted in an article in the *Yorkshire Post*: 'This was an act of vandalism. Over the years we have done everything possible to preserve the remaining plants.'

Bob Jarman, son of the orchid's original finder Willie Jarman, visited the site on 11 June 1967. There he found, to his great delight, that at least some of the orchid's rhizome had been spared – four plants were present alongside the hole, with one of them coming into flower. The motives of the thief were, therefore, ambiguous – it is possible that the miscreant may even have been one of the secret society itself, reacting to the revelation of the orchid's location by removing part of its rhizome to plant at another secret, and presumably safer, spot in the Dales.

This attack, and the mounting public awareness and interest in the lady's slipper, proved the catalyst for the formation of a more organised body dedicated to the conservation of the species. A meeting was held at Grassington in 1969, chaired by Edgar Milne-Redhead, the deputy keeper of the Kew Herbarium. Attendees included representatives of the Botanical Society of the British Isles, the Nature Conservancy, the Yorkshire Naturalist Union, and Yorkshire Wildlife Trust. Amongst their number would have been members of the original secret society. These meetings became an annual event and, in 1971, a formal body known as the Cypripedium Committee was formed, dedicated to the conservation of the lady's slipper.

Their first decision was easily made: the orchids at Grassington needed to be allowed to set seed, if at all possible. It was not clear whether the plants, originating from one rhizome, would be self-incompatible – or unable to fertilise themselves – but the Nature Conservancy staff had brought fresh information to the table: there was at least one plant of known Yorkshire origin still surviving and flowering in a garden in the north of England. Those to be found at Hornby Castle in Lancashire, on the very doorstep of the notorious seventeenth-century orchid-digger Mistress Thomasin Tunstall, were understood to have been taken, originally, from the wild in the Ingleton area.

Should the Grassington plant prove self-incompatible, there would be a source of unrelated pollen that could be pressed into service. As pollination in the wild relies to some extent upon chance, and given the urgency of the task at hand, it was decided that the Grassington plant would be hand-pollinated whenever it flowered.

In 1970 Dr John Lovis attended the site to make the first attempt to hand-pollinate the orchid. There were two shoots flowering that year but, when he returned several days later to repeat the exercise, he found both shoots had been cut off at ground level and removed entirely. This could have been the action of the same person who had been infuriating Eric Hardy by removing the flowers, or it might even have been simple misfortune that someone had simply picked the pretty flowers they stumbled across during a walk in the countryside. Whatever the motive of the person who had removed them, a lesson was learned by the Cypripedium Committee – henceforth the lady's slipper would need round-the-clock protection during the flowering period.

In the years that followed, seed capsules formed and were allowed to naturally ripen, split and disperse their seeds into the local environment. This, while a step forwards for the orchid insofar as it now at least stood some chance of reproducing itself, was nevertheless not yielding immediate and tangible results in the form of new plants. The urgency of the situation was only reinforced in 1975 when, despite the surveillance guarding the orchid, yet another section of the plant was dug up and removed by an unknown perpetrator.

The vulnerability of the last wild lady's slipper was increasing as word spread of its whereabouts. In 1973 the tent-dwelling warden of the site recorded no fewer than thirty-five occasions upon which visitors came to see the orchid, in numbers ranging from lone individuals to a group of seven people. The site was becoming an open secret – there was even a form for visitors to complete, which featured the stark question: *Who told you?*. The orchid's custodians were attempting to unravel the grapevine along which news of the orchid filtered, but in their hearts they must have known that their efforts were best placed in terms of practical conservation rather than amateur detective work. John Lovis prefaced an article in *The Naturalist*, the periodical of the Yorkshire Naturalist Union, in 1976 with the following pragmatic summary:

> There can be by now very few readers of *The Naturalist* who are not well aware that the Lady's Slipper Orchid is still alive on a site 'somewhere in Yorkshire'. The existence of this site has now been so thoroughly publicised by articles in newspapers and a feature on television that it seems very unlikely that further harm can now come from admitting its existence in the pages of *The Naturalist*.[2]

What followed was an at times emotional plea for members of the Yorkshire Naturalist Union to confidentially provide details of any additional sites at which the lady's slipper was still growing in Yorkshire. Reading this *cri de coeur*, one is struck by the note of desperation in John Lovis's voice, and by his candour regarding the suspicion with which he knew members of the general public held the Nature Conservancy Council ('Council' was added to the agency's name in 1973). His closing remarks, highlighted in bold in the article for added emphasis, are a particularly heartfelt appeal to anyone withholding information that might help to conserve the lady's slipper:

> Anyone who is in possession of knowledge of a second colony and does not now inform the Nature Conservancy Council, should realise that they have contributed towards, and must bear some of the responsibility for, the ultimate disappearance of this species from Britain just as effectively as if they had cut the flower and put it in a vase or a plant press.

In the meantime, the Cypripedium Committee had begun to investigate the potential for germinating lady's slipper seeds in a controlled laboratory environment. Their initial experiments were unsuccessful, as they failed to germinate any seeds whatsoever. A ripe seed capsule from the Grassington plant was placed in the safekeeping of the Royal Botanic Gardens Kew seed bank in readiness for the day when techniques had advanced to a point at which the seeds might be successfully germinated even if, by then, the native parent plant had finally succumbed.

The Sainsbury Orchid Project initiative was launched at Kew in 1983 to investigate the mechanisms by which European orchid seed could be successfully germinated in a controlled environment. The hurdles involved were considerable as, in the wild, the seeds needed to be infected with a specific fungus species if they were to germinate. Circumventing nature had, hitherto, proved intractable. The first success came a few years later when the project team successfully germinated seeds of a different European orchid species in their laboratory. The loose-flowered orchid is essentially a widespread Mediterranean species but, as the alternative English name Jersey orchid suggests, it is found as near to mainland Britain as the Channel Islands. Kew's scientists successfully germinated loose-flowered orchid seeds collected from Crete in agar inculcated with a fungus found associating with a different orchid species and, once the resulting plants had grown and been hardened off, planted them out in their grounds at Wakehurst in West Sussex in 1987. Two years later these plants proved they had been successfully naturalised when thirty-five of their number flowered – they persist there to this day.

As befits an orchid as imperilled and glamorous as the lady's slipper, and one that hails from a county that famously places particular emphasis upon stubborn bloody-mindedness, success germinating Yorkshire seeds was not immediately forthcoming, as identifying the fungus that the lady's slipper seeds required to germinate proved a thankless task. Kew's scientists sought expertise from further afield and, in the form of a Swedish orchid enthusiast, Svante Malmgren, they had found their man.

Malmgren had cracked the *Cypripedium* code – he had developed an asymbiotic propagation technique that could germinate immature lady's slipper seeds without the critical fungal partner, in a culture of agar, amino acids and, most importantly of all, pineapple juice. The latter ingredient is critical – it appears a complex organic ingredient like pineapple contains plant growth hormones that the seeds need if they are to prosper. Malmgren's propagation process sounds disarmingly straightforward: 'Asymbiotic propagation can be done using just your own kitchen as a laboratory. A pressure cooker is the most expensive item in which you need to invest.'[3]

Armed with Malmgren's innovative techniques, immature seeds from the last known remaining lady's slipper in the wild in Britain were successfully germinated and grown in glass flasks, looking like a tangle of bean sprouts ready to be stir-fried, until they were big enough to be transferred into a soil-based compost. Malmgren recommends soil dug from the sort of habitat that looks right for the orchids in question, his pragmatism dispelling the myths that surround the cultivation of orchids.

> Guide books and scientific reports provide complex compost recipes and methods for adding fungi to the soil mixes, but mycorrhizal fungi are abundant in natural soils, and such procedures are unnecessary. The young plants might recruit a natural fungus from the soil when first potted up but perhaps they just don't need one.
>
> Myths and much-repeated dogma surround the suitability of different soil and compost types. With increasing experience, common garden sense will replace the incantations of complex soil recipes. In reality, no more than standard gardening problems are involved. If the soil is too hard, add a little sand; if it is too dry add a little peat. Some species prefer limestone soils, others prefer slightly acid soils. Some need a dry resting period in summer, others prefer a well-drained but never dry soil.[4]

In 1989, the first young lady's slipper orchids grown using Malmgren's techniques were planted out in Yorkshire near to their parent plant. Initially three quarters of these prospered, but none of the first planting survived in the long term. In the early 1990s, over a thousand more seedlings were planted out but with dismal results, as they all fell victim to voracious slugs and snails, hungry voles, and the rooting of thoughtless badgers. An article published by the BSBI in 1992 bemoaned the presence – and predilection for orchids – of the voles in the vicinity of the original plant. Something was still badly awry in the formula for successfully reintroducing lady's slippers into the wild.

Further research suggested that planting out more mature specimens would lead to a greater success rate – larger, sturdier plants would resist the attentions of malign mammals and molluscs better than delicate, barely weaned yearlings. Additional plants germinated from seed derived from both the original self-pollinated Grassington plant and Hornby Castle plants, or from cross-pollination of the two populations, were grown on in pots at Ingleborough for between five and seven years. These began to be introduced to sites in the orchid's former recorded range – the Cypripedium Committee had set itself a target of at least a dozen newly established colonies.

By 2003 nine such colonies had been successfully established, with mature plants enduring where immature ones had formerly failed and, by 2010, this had risen to sixteen established sites. In 2004 the first of these new colonies flowered for itself in the wild. Four years later one of the introduced plants bore a naturally pollinated seedpod and, by 2010, this encouraging behaviour had been seen at a further three of the introduction sites. Perhaps now, with a helping hand from the Cypripedium Committee, the technology and expertise of the staff at Kew, and the care and watchful eyes of a host of field workers in the north of England, the future of English lady's slipper orchids was once more assured.

I had decided to follow in the footsteps of the lady's slipper conservation story, beginning where the Sainsbury Orchid Project's first minor triumph had blossomed – at Wakehurst Place in West Sussex, where the remains of the pioneer loose-flowered orchids germinated by Kew's scientists had been naturalised.

My day began a little way away in East Sussex, on the top of the chalk downs at Mount Caburn National Nature Reserve (NNR). Here, on the flanks of the earthworks of the Iron Age hill fort, I had found my first burnt orchids, *Neotinea ustulata*, of the year. Short, delicate white orchids dotted lightly with fine spots the colour of black cherries, their unopened buds at the peak of the flower spike give the impression of a scorched, burnt tip. Their Latin name, *ustulata*, derives from the verb *ustulare*, to burn. I lay in heavy dew beside them, admiring these tiny wild things, many of which were the support for small spiderwebs festooned with prismatic sparkling droplets of water. This was an auspicious beginning to the day's orchid hunting.

My arrival at Wakehurst, however, felt quite unlike any other orchid hunt of the year thus far – paying to enter a formal garden in order to see orchids seemed uncomfortably like cheating. Previously I had seen loose-flowered orchids in the Channel Islands, though that too had a tenuous taint about it where botanising was concerned. Surely the Channel Islands, so close to the French coast as to be practically on the Continent itself, were about as biologically British as the Falklands?

The loose-flowered orchids had been planted in a wild area of the Wakehurst grounds known as the Slips, on the flanks of a series of cascading pools and streams that run down a shallow valley from the formal gardens above. I sought precise directions for the orchids from the Kew staff in the visitor centre where one enters the gardens, but was met with blank looks.

'Orchids? No. I'm sure we don't have any orchids growing here.'

I persisted – I had even seen a photo of a loose-flowered orchid taken in the Slips posted recently online. I knew they were there, just not exactly where in the Slips I should look. A hasty conversation between the Wakehurst staff yielded nothing more concrete than confirmation that yes, there was after all a loose-flowered orchid flowering this year, but I was too late – there had been only one flowering plant, and it would be over by now. And no, none of the staff present this morning knew where it actually was. I was on my own.

This was strangely heartening, as now my visit felt far more like a proper orchid hunt; with only the vaguest idea of where to look, and a real chance that I might not see the plant in question, I was on more familiar territory. I hurried through the beautiful formal planting of the main gardens, heading for the Slips.

The shallow valley echoed with the chatter and laughter of small children as a large school party was escorted by smiling Kew staff. While I searched for a loose-flowered orchid in the long grass on one side of the Slips, they were learning about plants and gardens. Somewhere behind me a frog was found, to a swelling chorus of shrill cries of wonder and alarm.

Perhaps my mental search image for this particular orchid was impaired by the news I had learned at the visitor centre, for it took me a moment to realise what I was looking at when I picked out a tall, graceful purple form in the long grass. I was expecting to find the loose-flowered orchid, if at all, in a post-flowering state. Instead what I had before me was in almost pristine condition. As their name suggests, they have a loose, scattered flower spike, with each individual flower distinctly apart from its fellows, and held well away from the stem by a slender, twisted, blushing green ovary. The flowers themselves had a loose appearance, as if thrown together half-heartedly from an orchid spare-parts bin – each flower was a rich magenta with only the large, sharply folded lip a startling and contrasting white. A long, upturned spur protruded from the back of the flower, while above, the purple lateral sepals stood piquantly upright.

The glory days of the loose-flowered orchids' naturalisation in the grounds of Wakehurst seemed to be behind them – this one flowering plant was a sorry remnant of the thirty-five that had bloomed there two years after their introduction in 1987 but, nearly thirty years after that, I could perhaps count myself fortunate to see it at all. Nearby I noticed something else nestling in the grass, something definitely orchidaceous, but very different indeed. This was the deliciously sculpted form of a greater tongue orchid and, nearby, there were more hiding in the grass. Was ever an orchid better named than this? Their short stems were surmounted by angular, ribbed and veined greyish-pink flowers with lascivious long, pointed, flesh-coloured tongues.

I had heard these were here, though I had not expected to find them so readily. Their presence is enigmatic; they are not a British native – if a single short-lived plant on Guernsey in 1992 and an unconfirmed record from Devon in the late 1990s are discounted – and they were not deliberately introduced to Wakehurst during the loose-flowered orchid naturalisation. Writing about them in the world's longest-running botanical publication, *Curtis's Botanical Magazine*, established in 1787 and published latterly by the Royal Botanical Gardens, Kew, Arthur Hoare described their discovery at Wakehurst as a surprise, and concluded that their seed was probably brought in with that of the loose-flowered orchids. Surely the plantsmen would have noticed the very different form of the young greater tongue orchids amongst the loose-flowered orchids? And would the former even have germinated amongst the latter? Yet here they were, happily flowering and looking healthy and at home in the rough grassy fringes of Wakehurst.

Despite a provenance that was, at best, no clearer than that of the sawfly orchid I had seen in Dorset, I felt I could not count them, really, in my quest, but I could still appreciate their gorgeous forms in their own right. I carefully set up my camera and tripod to take a series of photographs, attracting much curiosity from the passing children. It transpired that these orchids were a poor substitute for frog hunting, and I found myself left alone in peace with the flowers.

Having seen the orchids that blazed the trail for Kew's scientists to germinate the notoriously tricky, dust-like European orchid seeds, I now needed to see the ultimate goal of all of this research and applied horticulture – lady's slippers growing in the English countryside. Here I had a choice – I could go to see the original, parent plant near Grassington, or I could see that plant's successfully naturalised offspring, reared and introduced with loving care into the wild under the auspices of the Cypripedium Committee.

The location of the original plant, while closely guarded, is not too difficult to uncover. I knew of informed friends who I might ask directly, but did not wish to place anyone in an awkward position should I be asked by the plant's guardians the source of my information. Besides, ample clues to the plant's precise location are available online, if one only follows the orchid's trail carefully enough. Knowing where to go was not the issue – what concerned me was the morality of seeing this particular plant. The Cypripedium Committee discourages anyone from visiting it, and even its members have been known to minimise their visits for fear of compromising the security of the site. History alone suggests this caution is well founded, and I decided that it would be irresponsible to risk drawing needless attention to the plant's exact whereabouts. I concluded it would be very wrong of me to see this orchid, not least because it would involve leaving a nearby public footpath and actively, knowingly, trespassing thereafter.

What I wanted to see were the fruits of the successful lady's slipper conservation story – those plants that were flourishing at their northern introduction sites. While I knew of several such locations, one of them in particular is reasonably well publicised and accessible for visitors, so I headed north to Cumbria, where I would see my lady's slippers on the slopes of Gait Barrows NNR.

Managed by Cumbria Wildlife Trust, this nationally important nature reserve is a mosaic of limestone habitats, varying from damp fens to pristine limestone pavements via deep yew forest and open water. For the visiting naturalist it is a jewel of a reserve – and for the carefully nurtured lady's slippers that call this home, it offers pockets of ideal habitat in which to flourish.

I walked uphill from the small car park that serves the reserve, following a dry path that skirted through thinning trees as I climbed. Emerging into an open clearing abutting an area of limestone pavement, I found myself suddenly surrounded by patches of deep burgundy and gold – the flowers of small clumps of lady's slipper orchids, their heads nodding in a hilltop zephyr wafting above their lush emerald-green leaves. They were shockingly obvious, and I realised now why they had been so easily found and removed from the wild in centuries gone by. These were no shrinking violets – their beauty verged on the brash, almost improbably extravagant for the restrained British countryside.

Illustrations did their flowers scant justice: the reality was far more dramatic, the colours more intense and the spectacle more arresting than I had anticipated. I understood not only why they were so easily found by those early plant collectors, but also the lust that drove the demand for them in the first place, the acquisitive orchid mania that gripped the gardeners of the eighteenth and nineteenth centuries. These were undeniably sexy plants that besotted botanists and greedy gardeners simply had to have.

Reginald Farrer, writing in *My Rock-Garden*, his 1907 paean to the appreciation and cultivation of delicate alpine wildflowers, describes the consuming *Cypripedium* hunger vividly:

> Then, one ominous day, I caught sight of [*Cypripedium*] ...
> beautiful beyond the tongue of man to express. In that instant
> I understood *Romeo and Juliet* better than I ever had before.
> But my doom was sealed; as cruel engines draw in, first one's
> coat-tail, and then by degrees the whole body, so the Orchids
> have now enveloped me densely in their web.
> I am engulfed in Orchids and their dreadful bills; nor do
> I see the slightest chance of ever tasting solvency or peace again.

Farrer was a man who knew all too well the heights of euphoria and the depths of despair that rare, exquisite and unusual plants could induce. His passion for alpine plants was barely tolerated by his parents, and certainly not encouraged. It was partly sheer expediency that drove him to plant hunt commercially in remote reaches of China, as he was dogged by financial insecurity and could not settle on another more conventional career. His father, perhaps seeking to encourage his son to conform, provided him with £1,000 in 1911 to cover the expenses involved in standing for election as the Liberal MP for Ashford, in Kent – Farrer failed to win the seat, and was rumoured to have spent his father's money on rare flower bulbs. I knew how Farrer felt – when I was at university I poured whatever money I had into travelling to see rare birds and orchids, much to my parents' combined frustration and incomprehension.

A homemade sign stopped me in my tracks, and shockingly reminded me that the darker side of orchidelirium was, sadly, not consigned to the past. Around a colour photograph of a magnificent flowering lady's slipper orchid was the stark message:

This Lady's-slipper Orchid has been stolen!

It should have had 4–5 double flowers but was dug up by persons unknown sometime this past winter. Such a greedy and criminal act has lessened your enjoyment today.

Feel angry!

If the sign shocked me, it did not surprise me. After the Grassington plant was partly dug up following Eric Hardy's ill-advised decision in 1966 to publicise the location, it had been pro-tected by the wardens appointed by the Cypripedium Committee. That had not, however, marked the end of *Cypripedium* theft in England.

In 1980, a peat garden was created in the grounds of Kew Gardens, in an area of shade cast by the Jodrell Laboratory. This proved to be an excellent site for growing a variety of hardy *Cypripedium* species, albeit not for long, as they were all stolen in an overnight raid by an unknown orchid thief. Kew already enjoyed a track record where orchids and nocturnal criminality was concerned. On the night of 8 February 1913, a member of staff discovered that panes of glass in the Orchid House had been smashed and, inside, a number of orchids had been attacked, their remains strewn on the glasshouse floor. While the perpetrators were not caught, 'Votes for Women' leaflets were found scattered nearby, including a note that read, 'Orchids can be destroyed, but not a woman's honour.'

The suffragette link seemed confirmed two days later when Emmeline Pankhurst addressed the weekly meeting of the Women's Social and Political Union. Knowingly drawing her audi-ence's attention to a bouquet of orchids set on the table before her, she said:

We are not destroying orchid houses, breaking windows, cutting telegraph wires, injuring golf greens, in order to win the approval of the people attacked. If the general public were pleased with what we are doing, that would be a proof that our warfare is ineffective.

We don't intend that you should be pleased.

A fortnight after this orchid attack, the suffragettes struck again in the grounds of Kew, on this occasion burning down the Tea Pavilion. Olive Wharry and Lilian Lenton were caught fleeing the scene and were subsequently sentenced and imprisoned for their part in the arson. They might also have been behind the attack on the orchid house, though this was never proven. The motives behind the Orchid House vandalism are as elusive as the perpetrators themselves. It is tempting to speculate, given the traditional association between orchids and testicles – the very name orchid being derived from the Greek *orchis*, or testicle – that the choice of the Orchid House was an act of symbolic emasculation by the suffragettes against their male oppressors.

It is also possible that botanical artist Marianne North's treatment by Kew may have had something to do with its choice as a target for the suffragettes. This astonishing woman devoted her life to botanical illustration, travelling widely around the world and suffering considerable privations in pursuit of her art. Her paintings pop with passion and vibrancy, and are housed in a purpose-built gallery at Kew – North wrote to Kew's director, Sir Joseph Hooker, offering to fund the gallery's construction provided he agreed to display her life's work in it. She also asked that the gallery might serve tea and coffee, a request that Hooker refused to countenance. North was nothing if not determined, so she took her case to the House of Commons, where it foundered once more. Undeterred, North painted coffee and tea plants, quietly ensuring these particular pictures went over the gallery's doors.

I wondered whether this strong, inspiring woman, having foundered against the patriarchal bastions of Kew and Parliament over something as seemingly trivial as the serving of hot drinks, might have inspired the suffragettes a few years later – was the choice of Orchid House and Tea Pavilion for their attention more than a mere coincidence?

The suffragettes' initial target may, however, have been more broadly inspired by the largely male preoccupation with orchids in the preceding decades. While Queen Victoria was famously besotted with orchids, it is said that other Victorian women were discouraged from taking an interest in them – the sexually suggestive shapes of their flowers being considered too explicit for their feminine eyes. Certainly, the vast majority of Victorian and Edwardian orchid breeders, collectors and enthusiasts were male. Perhaps striking at Kew's Orchid House was considered on a par with attacking the apparatus of that other popular male pastime, the golf greens that Emmeline Pankhurst mentioned in the same breath as the orchid houses.

Those two traditionally male preoccupations, golf and orchids, were to collide in Lancashire in the early years of the twenty-first century. A lady's slipper orchid had been growing quietly there for decades behind the sixteenth green of the golf course at Silverdale when, in 2004, it was partly dug up and removed. This was the plant that had long been rumoured to originate from Continental stock before genetic analysis confirmed once and for all its immigrant status, no more a native British wildflower than the sky-blue *Meconopsis* poppies beloved of Alpine gardeners. Whatever its origin, it had proved irresistible to somebody – as unfortunately, in the winter of 2015, had one of the plants at Gait Barrows NNR.

Not far from these fatally beautiful, beleaguered flowers was an orchid that was as unassuming and subtle as the lady's slippers were floridly extravagant. Coralroot barely sounds like the name of an orchid, only looks like one with the very closest of scrutiny, and is remarkably easily overlooked. It is small, not at all colourful, and grows hidden away from all but the most determined orchid hunter's gaze. Even the most impressive specimens typically fail to top ten centimetres tall, with individual green and white flowers barely five millimetres in length. I had never knowingly seen one before, though I had spent time in the habitat they prefer. Growing deep in the midst of patches of creeping willow, they take a practised eye to find them readily. Fortunately, I had enlisted the help of Jamie Armstrong, one of the guardians at their English stronghold, Sandscale Haws NNR, a national nature reserve on the edge of the Duddon Estuary in Cumbria, managed by the National Trust.

In the weeks beforehand, I had spoken with one of Jamie's National Trust colleagues, Neil Forbes. Neil had been helpful, but not particularly encouraging.

'It's almost certainly not going to be a good year for coralroot orchid this year. In a typical year, if such a thing still exists, we would be expecting to see the first orchids around now, but numbers vary dramatically from year to year and we do have occasional years where we don't find any at all.

'This year the winter rainfall has led to increased flooding of the dunes slacks and some of the main coralroot sites are still under water. The last time we had similar conditions, in 2013, we didn't find any, although this doesn't of course mean that there weren't any flowering spikes that year. The site is pretty vast, so the chances of finding them in poor years obviously decreases.'

I did not like the sound of this at all. Coralroot appears to be in decline in Britain, with the orchid now absent from almost half its former historical range – perhaps a reflection of climate change and the recent preponderance of wet winters, something coralroots evidently do not like. Sandscale Haws provides a typical snapshot of the species' fluctuating fortunes – from a heyday in the late 1980s and early 1990s, their numbers have slumped with the passage of time. Over three thousand plants were recorded there in 1990 – but with none found in 2013, and only 177 flowering orchids noted in 2014, it seemed that not only were there fewer flowering plants in the maturing dune slack habitat they favoured, but there was also a distinct possibility that following a wet winter I might struggle to see any whatsoever.

I arrived at Sandscale Haws to find Jamie and Emma, his colleague, gathering litter and worse from the small car park and the paths that led from it to the beach beyond. Judging by the cars that jammed the parking area and crowded the sides of the lane approaching it, and the ample evidence left unclaimed in their pets' wake, Sandscale Haws was first and foremost a popular recreational destination for families and dog walkers. Jamie and Emma ruefully agreed that gathering abandoned litter and dog faeces was not what they had in mind when they considered a career in conservation.

We walked parallel with the beach for a short while until the sounds of the visitors spilling onto the sand faded behind us and, once we passed through the ramparts formed by the rippling sand dunes that fringed the Sandscale Haws headland, vanished completely. Signs of the wet winter Neil had alluded to were all too evident. Jamie paused beside a large pond.

'That's normally not there at all. We've got so much standing water still on the reserve this summer. I was worried we wouldn't find any coralroots this year, but I found the first ones last week. You need to look out for coloured pencils – I've marked the plants I've found so far with them.'

Looking for coloured pencils pushed into the ground along-side the invisible orchids seemed an easier prospect than spontaneously and independently finding a coralroot, though I desperately wanted to do just that. While I was deeply appreciative of Jamie's assistance, I wanted to believe that, had I not had it, I might have managed to find a flowering coralroot for myself. In the event, I did not manage to find either a flowering orchid or a coloured pencil marker before Jamie announced we were coming up to one of his marked plants – though, making me feel a little less inept as an orchid and a pencil hunter, we had collectively failed to find the first marked plants in the dune slacks, only noticing them later when we retraced our steps.

The dune slack in question was a slim, shallow valley formed between two large dunes. A narrow path meandered around the edges of large patches of creeping willow – a low-growing silvery-leafed shrub with which coralroot orchids have formed an intimate and inextricable bond. Many of our native orchids rely, to a greater or lesser extent, on mycorrhizal fungi in the soil around them – either to assist seed germination, or for obtaining nutrients – but very few orchids take this relationship to quite the extreme of the coralroot. Their name perfectly describes their underground rhizome – though I would, of course, not see this for myself. The rhizome is a branched, creamy mass of knobs and protrusions, appearing exactly like the orchid's underwater namesake.

The only time the orchid appears above ground is when it throws up a flower spike and, all being well, sets seed. The stem is sheathed with barely discernible scale-like leaves and these, the stem itself, and the individual ovaries of each flower contain some chlorophyll – but while coralroots presumably can photo-synthesize to a limited extent, their main source of nourishment comes from a very different source indeed. Their rhizome is heavily infected with mycorrhizal fungi of a very particular family, the *Thelephora-Tomentella* complex. Coralroots are fussy, and for good reason – these fungi form symbiotic relationships with the roots of trees – birches, pines and willows, and the orchids obliquely, badly, need those trees. In the case of the dune slacks I was exploring, the fungi in the soil would be partnered with the abundant creeping willow. The relationship between fungus and tree is mutually beneficial – the fungi coat the roots of the tree, with many hyphae extending centimetres away from the roots into the soil. In effect, the fungi multiply the root network of the tree, increasing the tree's ability to absorb water and nutrients from the soil. In return, the fungi can extract carbohydrates from the host plant – theirs is an ectomycorrhizal relationship.

Coralroots, while belonging to a small genus of orchids with a widespread global range, are found in Britain only in the north and only where the right mycorrhizal fungi and their tree partners are to be found. Their relationship with their fungal partner is less benevolent, however – the orchids' rhizomes are infected with the same fungi as the trees, but the flow of nutrients is exclusively one way – they draw carbohydrates from the surrounding creeping willows via the fungal interface, but give nothing in return to fungus or tree alike. Coralroots are the ultimate orchid parasite, rivalled only by the bird's-nest orchids I had seen in the aqueous half-light of Surrey's beech woods.

Above ground, the flower spikes are the picture of innocence, revealing nothing of the cheating nature of the orchid. Carefully parting the tiny branches of the surrounding creeping willow, I was face to face with my first flowering coralroots. Each stem was a rusty red that extended onto the flowers' twisted ovaries. The flowers themselves were surprisingly attractive, even with their diminutive stature and muted colours – the chartreuse sepals and petals were relatively long, surrounding the heart of the flower-like bared cat claws. The tongue-shaped lip was snow white, blotched at the base with crimson spots like blood on a sheet. Each flower spike bore only a few flowers, exploding like a firework at the very top of the slender stem.

While I busied myself examining my first coralroot, Jamie and Emma continued to walk slowly around the edges of the creeping willow, looking for further orchids. In the time we were there, they added no more to the handful Jamie had previously located; as had been gloomily predicted, this did not look like being a good year for flowering coralroot at Sandscale Haws. I could count myself lucky to have seen them there at all, and realised that without the help of Jamie, Emma and Neil I would almost certainly not have managed to find a flowering plant. It was a chastening thought to carry away with me as my attention switched once again back to the south of England.

We made our way back through the dunes towards the car park. I had seen less than a dozen coralroots, but was glad of every single one. We began meeting visitors once more, labouring their way to the beach with children, dogs and bags in tow. I reflected that almost all of them would be completely unaware of the biological riches Sandscale Haws conceals in its vastness. While I could understand that an orchid as unassuming and well hidden as a coralroot might struggle to catch their attention, I felt sad as I realised that most of the visitors were even oblivious to the small ponds beside the car park that swarmed and writhed with the tadpoles of natterjack toads. When had children stopped being fascinated by tadpoles?

I tried to tell myself this did not matter – the presence of the orchids and the toads was, perhaps, enough in itself. At least they were valued enough to warrant specific conservation measures to protect, maintain and grow their populations. Maybe that was the most important thing – after all, I could hardly criticise visitors to Sandscale Haws for being unaware of the natural history to be found there, for I had come myself unaware of the social and military history of the area. Sandscale Haws had, I discovered, played a critical part in Britain's war effort. It was here that a vast decoy harbour was constructed in the Second World War to lure German bombers away from the nearby, strategically vital Barrow docks. I left Sandscale Haws concluding that we are all partially blind to what is around us until we take an active interest, seek to learn more and, crucially, are shown what was there all along by those who already know better and are happy to share that precious knowledge.

This had been a day of contrasts in Cumbria. I had explored vastly different habitats, from the damp sea-level dune slacks at Sandscale Haws to the bare rocky limestone pavements of Gait Barrows. I had seen orchids that represented polar extremes of their kind, from the subtle, tiny and easily overlooked coralroot to the blousy, sublime beauty of the lady's slipper. Starkest of all, though, was the contrast between the kindness and generosity of the National Trust staff who had shown me my coralroots at Sandscale Haws, and the selfishness of the unknown orchid thief who had dug up one of the precious lady's slippers at Gait Barrows.

The words of Reginald Farrer, plant hunter, gardener and chronicler of the iniquities perpetrated on the most beautiful of the north of England's orchids echoed down the years: 'Wickednesses untold have been perpetrated upon this plant. He has suffered most terribly at the hands of the despoiler.'

A sentiment that was, apparently, as true today as when Farrer wrote it in 1907.

8

Military manoeuvres

The year 1597 was a good one for British publishing. A number of Shakespeare's plays were released in print for the very first time, including the superbly brutal, warring and duplicitous *Richard III*. The first edition of a very different work was released that year too – John Gerard's *Herball, or Generall Historie of Plantes*. This book was to cement Gerard's reputation down the intervening centuries as a botanist, but his background in science was, in reality, somewhat less specialised – he had been apprenticed at the age of seventeen to a barber-surgeon, a confluence of professions that, while incongruous, hints strongly at the limits of what passed for medical knowledge in the late sixteenth century.

In 1597 Gerard was appointed junior warden to the Barber-Surgeon's Company, and it was in this year that his *Herball* was published. A lavishly illustrated description of several hundred species of plant, running to almost 1,500 pages in length, this was destined to become a popular reference book in the seventeenth century. Indeed, there is even evidence of it still being used sparingly as late as the early nineteenth century.

It is unsurprising, then, that today Gerard is remembered as a botanist but, although he produced his *Herball* during the early years of Renaissance natural history, his contemporaries in London viewed him with some disdain. While the renowned Lime Street community of natural historians seems to have looked down upon him as something of an outsider, he was on good terms with a Flemish botanist, Matthias de l'Obel, and the two are known to have undertaken field trips with one another.

The reality of Gerard's popular *Herball* is that it contained comparatively little original material – Gerard was asked by the Queen's printer, John Norton, to complete a translation of a popular Continental herbal of the day written by Rembert Dodoen. An initial attempt by Norton to publish an English-language translation of this work had foundered when his translator inconveniently died.

Gerard did as he was bid, and incorporated some new material – unknowingly provided by his Flemish friend, l'Obel. When an apothecary neighbour of l'Obel, James Garret, in a twist worthy of a Shakespearean plot, happened to see the proofs of Gerard's *Herball* in John Norton's workshop, he felt compelled to bring to Norton's attention numerous errors he found in the text – and also material he considered appropriated from his neighbour, l'Obel. John Norton promptly hired l'Obel, as a renowned botanist of international acclaim, to proofread and correct Gerard's translated text. When he learned of this development, John Gerard displayed a ruthlessness that would have done Richard III credit, promptly conspiring to have l'Obel dismissed.

What emerged in 1597 was a book that was to have popular appeal for well over a century and, while the unfortunate and slighted Matthias de l'Obel later claimed that Gerard was little better than a plagiarist, Gerard's reputation as a botanist was henceforth secured.

Carl Linnaeus, the great Swedish taxonomist, even named a plant genus *Gerardia* in his honour.

For me, Gerard's *Herball* represents the first serious attempt to produce an illustrated field guide to the plants that one might have encountered in sixteenth⁻ and seventeenth-century England. While it was intended primarily as a pharmacopeia for the barber-surgeons of the day, it serves now as a window through which we can glimpse some of the plants our forebears were aware of, and the regard in which those plants were held. Among the many beautifully detailed species accounts is one that is recognisably of an orchid – what Gerard referred to as the Souldier's Satyrion, or Soldier's Cullions. This latter name was a reference to the large and hairy-rooted underground tubers from which this orchid grows – *cullions* were testicles. This was a name that would neither stand the test of time nor sensibility – the Soldier's Testicle Orchid became, in the intervening centuries, what we now know as the military orchid.

This contemporary name is said to be a reference to the anthropomorphic flowers – the purple-suffused white sepals and petals form a coal-scuttle helmet, striped delicately purple on the inside, while the purple spots that stud the length of the centre of the flower's white lip are said to resemble the buttons on a soldier's tunic. Gerard's original text noted these points, but his preferred name for the plant was the earthier choice, a decision that reflected the centuries-old reputation of orchid roots as a source of male potency. Certainly, his description of the species is graphic: 'Souldiers Satyrion bringeth forth many broad large and ribbed leaves ... among the which riseth up a fat stalke full of sap or juice ... The rootes be greater stones than any of the kinds of Satyrions.'

I doubt whether the homoerotic undertones of this phallic description would have been wasted on the military orchid's greatest admirer, the writer and naturalist Jocelyn Brooke. Brooke's first book was named after the subject of a lifelong obsession – published in 1948, his semi-autobiographical *The Military Orchid* recounted his attempts to see the species, largely in the south-east of England, touching time and again upon his attempts to reconcile his homosexuality with the constraints of the day. *The Military Orchid* reads like an impassioned, unrequited love letter – a search for a vision that remained tantalisingly beyond Brooke's reach.

His story began in Kent, where earlier in the spring I had walked in Brooke's footsteps – his shade had accompanied my orchid hunting through the depths of the Elham Valley. There I had seen, amongst others, Britain's finest colonies of lady orchids – but in order to see military orchids I would need to travel further afield.

Brooke recounted how he strove to find a military orchid in Kent and further afield; he came close, seeing cut specimens of his prize on several occasions, but in the course of his school years in England and military service abroad, he failed to find a flowering plant. Small wonder though in England, as the military orchid was by all accounts never widespread in its occurrence. Largely restricted to the Chilterns, it declined rapidly in the 1850s. George Druce recounted wistfully in his *Flora of Oxfordshire*, 'I have only found it during the last four years very sparingly. It only appeared in a barren state in 1886.'

This cataclysmic decline seemed to have culminated in extinction by 1929, when the last specimen was collected in Hertfordshire. Collecting certainly contributed to the species' decline, as did fluctuations in rabbit populations, changes in land use and the ploughing of downland for agriculture. What is certain is that, by the time Jocelyn Brooke wrote *The Military Orchid*, the subject of his quest had become a near-mythical entity for British botanists. Many, like Brooke, sought it in its former strongholds and in other likely habitat. But until 1947 there was no further sign.

It was in May of that year that the botanist Job Edward 'Ted' Lousley rediscovered the military orchid at Homefield Wood, near the small village of Hambleden in Buckinghamshire. This was a site at which the species had not previously been recorded, and Lousley evidently was not expecting to find them there. He recalled, 'The excursion was intended as a picnic, so I had left my usual apparatus at home and took only my note-book. But I selected our stopping points on the chalk with some care, and naturally wandered off to see what I could find. To my delight I stumbled on the orchid just coming into flower.'

Lousley found eighteen flowering plants in Homefield Wood, with a number of non-flowering plants in the vicinity. He speculated that their appearance had probably been caused by an increase in light levels following the felling of trees during the Second World War. It is sad and ironic to think that Jocelyn Brooke, a man consumed with seeing a military orchid in Britain, was writing his *cri du coeur* at the same time that Lousley was rediscovering the very orchid Brooke craved so badly. Lousley, however, was deeply principled and concerned that, were he to reveal his great find's whereabouts, the colony would suffer the common fate of so many rare British orchids, and would be collected to the point of extermination. He kept the site at Homefield Wood a closely guarded secret, shared only with a handful of trusted confidants.

For years, those British orchidophiles outside Lousley's circle of trust who had learned of the colony's existence tried to track the location down for themselves, but with no success. Rex Graham, the finder in Buckinghamshire in 1953 of England's largest ever colony of ghost orchids, *Epipogium aphyllum*, sent Lousley a postcard with a playful yet plaintive plea for information regarding the whereabouts of the military orchid, *Orchis militaris*:

I've searched the Chilterns high and low,
I know where each dark lair is,
I know where Epipogiums grow,
I've frightened all the fairies.
I've searched each valley, hill and dell,
My life just one despair is.
Dear Lousley, if you'd only tell
Where Orchis militaris!

Finally, in 1956, Lousley received another postcard – this one sent by the botanists Richard Fitter and Francis Rose. It bore the cryptic but telling message: 'The soldiers are at home in their fields.'

The secret was out, after a fashion. Fitter and Rose had systematically searched for the mythical military orchid and, eventually, their diligence had been rewarded. News that the military orchid was flowering once more in England was only released to the public in 1975, but it was not until the end of the 1980s that their presence in Homefield Wood finally became widely known. Growing up in the 1970s and 1980s, I had no idea that military orchids were still to be seen on British soil – like Brooke, they were the stuff of fantasy for me. Now, finally, I would see them in Buckinghamshire for myself.

Befittingly for an orchid that remained shrouded in secrecy as long as this one did, there is little fanfare or announcement made when one approaches the wood. A small layby off a narrow country lane provides parking for a few cars. On the sunny morning I arrived, the layby was empty. A track leads into the woods down a wide avenue of trees and there is little to suggest what might lie beyond. A red kite called stridently somewhere out of sight, nearby but invisible above the tall canopy above me. Unlike the military orchids, these glorious raptors had not prevailed without human intervention – common during Gerard and Shakespeare's time, they suffered centuries of persecution at the hands of man until their eventual extinction as an English breeding bird. It is only in recent years, following a successful reintroduction programme, that one can now see their dynamic, rufous tail-twisting forms hanging in southern English summer skies once again. I took this calling bird for a good omen.

At the end of the track I found myself entering a small, enclosed meadow in the form of a shallow valley fringed with ash, sycamore and whitebeam. Male brimstone butterflies dashed and jousted sulphurously with one another around the lists formed by stands of buckthorn. Narrow pathways of shorter grass meandered off the main thoroughfare and it was off these twisting diversions that I could immediately see what I had hoped for – tall, stately, purplish-white forms soaring above the surrounding grass. I ran uphill to them, unable to contain my excitement. I felt like a boy again – here was an orchid I had never seen before in Britain, something genuinely new for me. Something rare, something special, and something compellingly beautiful. I dropped to my hands and knees in the style of Lousley himself – he was famously short-sighted and often botanised on all fours, a posture known to his contemporaries as 'Ted at his prayers' – and revelled for a good, long while in the first flowering plant I had come to.

This flower was everything I had hoped it would be, and so much more besides. This was more elegant than the superficially similar, but more brashly hued and contorted monkey orchid, and as large as a lady orchid, yet more delicate and graceful. These military orchids had everything – and in the warm early-morning sunlight they were luminous. Each flower was just as Gerard had described over four hundred years previously: 'little flowers resembling a little man, having a helmet upon his head, his hands, and legs cut off; white upon the inside, spotted with many purple spots, and the backe part of the flower of a deeper colour tending to redness.'

Each flower was a masterpiece in its own right. With my nose almost touching the blooms, I could see in exquisite detail the 'soldier' formed by the flower's elements, right down to the tiny buttons on each tunic, rich purple papillae as carunculated as the spikes on the back of a fritillary caterpillar. The lobes that formed the soldier's arms and legs were richly suffused with rosy purple. While these soldiers would pass muster on any parade ground one cared to mention, in the interests of conservation I would just have to assume that 'the rootes be greater stones than any of the kinds of Satyrions'. I gladly chose not to see what lay beneath the soldiers' uniforms, and left the plants undisturbed in the ground.

Lousley's original eighteen flowering plants were still flourishing in Homefield Wood – a rough count revealed an army of over a hundred plants either in flower or in bud, and I knew there would be more unseen in the depths of the wood's clearings. My careful scrutiny of the meadow revealed a few shy fly orchids too – Homefield Wood's secrets still remained well hidden, but would give themselves up to the dedicated searcher nowadays.

I lay down in the grass, surrounded by military orchids, imagining what it must have felt like for Lousley when he discovered them here in this sheltered corner of Buckinghamshire. Not so very long before the urgent sound of British fighter planes, Hurricanes and Spitfires, would have been heard drumming overhead while, down here at ground level, men would have been felling trees for the war effort. Freed from the shackles of their shading canopy, those long-suppressed orchids would have finally found licence to bloom. Surely Lousley must have felt those newly liberated orchids represented hope and revival in the tough years immediately after the Second Word War. Perhaps the irony of their name and the well-rehearsed parallels between the shape of their 'helmets' and those worn by the German army did not escape him either.

While the *Wehrmacht* never invaded Britain, the flowers that bore bonnets with such an uncanny resemblance to their *Stahlhelme* were no respecters of our borders. In 1955 another colony of military orchids was discovered in Suffolk at Mildenhall, a location already synonymous with hidden treasure following the finding there in 1942 of a sizeable hoard of magnificently ornate solid silver Roman tableware – an event commemorated in Roald Dahl's short story 'The Mildenhall Treasure'. (Dahl was yet another author bitten by the orchid bug – in 1963, while his actress wife, Patricia Neal, was in Hawaii filming *In Harm's Way* with John Wayne, Dahl scoured the island for *Phalaenopsis* orchids to bring home to England, while orchids also figured prominently in one of his finest short stories, 'Bitch'.)

These latest military orchids were, in their way, no less precious or significant. Found in an old chalk pit in an area with no prior historical records of the species, there were over five hundred plants present with at least a hundred flowering at the time. Not only were they numerous, their flower spikes proved very different in appearance to those in the Chilterns, being taller, paler and more loosely flowered, and were more typical of the appearance of the widespread military orchids of mainland Europe.

Recently, genetic profiling of both the Buckinghamshire and Suffolk colonies has been undertaken. This research concluded that they are unrelated to one another, representing independent colonisations of British soil from the Continent. The armies of the Third Reich may never have landed in southern England, but right under our noses there have been waves of more welcome invaders – a benign fifth column of rare and graceful orchids.

The fortunes of Lousley's military orchids have waxed and waned since their discovery in 1947. By the time Richard Fitter and Francis

Rose stumbled upon them in 1956, their numbers had dwindled to just a fraction of the colony nine years previously. Rabbit numbers crashed in the 1950s with the devastating onset of myxamatosis, and the subsequent lack of grazing pressure almost certainly led to an increase in scrubby vegetation that swamped the fussier and less competitive orchids. By 1984 only twenty-eight plants remained, with a mere five flowering.

The 1980s saw a change in the management of the woods, with removal of encroaching scrub and new areas clear-felled, deer and rabbits excluded during the growing season, and managed grazing introduced during the autumn and winter. Under this more thoughtful regime, the soldiers have found their feet – in the summer of 2016 a record total of over seven hundred flowering plants were recorded throughout Homefield Wood. As I wandered through Homefield's meadows, I knew I was in the presence of an orchid that had stared into the abyss of local extinction and, with some careful and thoughtful conservation measures implemented, stepped away from the edge and recovered. It felt like a privilege to be in their presence. Jocelyn Brooke's words played on my mind: 'The Military Orchid had taken on a kind of legendary quality, its image seemed fringed with the mysterious and exciting appurtenances of soldiering, its name was like a distant bugle call, thrilling and rather sad, a *cor au fond du bois*.'

While John Gerard was aware of the military orchid when his *Herball* was published in 1597, it was not until 1666 that any reference to Britain's other pugnaciously named orchid was made. Sword-leaved helleborine was first noted by Christopher Merret in *Pinax Rerum Naturalium Britannicarum* ('A Picture of British Natural History'). The very title alone tells us that the focus on Britain's natural history was tightening to identification for identity's sake rather than simply as a means for highlighting a plant or an animal's perceived medicinal qualities.

What remained immutable was the process of decline in many instances, as the decades and centuries unfolded. Revolutions, agricultural and industrial alike, placed increasing pressure on our native flora and fauna, and none perhaps more so than upon our specialised orchids with their very specific habitat requirements. In that number must be counted sword-leaved helleborine, as since Merret acknowledged its existence, this most statuesque and sculptural of all the woodland orchids has suffered a predictably dramatic decline.

This would be another new orchid for me; there were none to be found when I was a boy searching for orchids in the south-west of England, nor in Kent during my days as a student. My island home of Shetland had no helleborines whatsoever. Like the military orchid, sword-leaved helleborines favoured chalky soils, but unlike the military orchids, these were plants that positively embraced shade and cool, moist conditions.

Not far from Selborne in Hampshire, former home of the eighteenth-century pastor-naturalist Gilbert White, running parallel to the sort of narrow country lane whose hedges reach with hungry branches for the sides of passing cars, is a small wood that White would surely have loved. Leaving the lane, an earthen track led a little way into the wood, the ground bulging and rolling as if some hidden subterranean beast were flexing its coils beneath my feet. The real secrets of Chappett's Copse are on the surface though, and only concealed from prying eyes by a short walk from the road. Here, in small clearings surrounded by beech trees, I would find my sword-leaved helleborines.

A day that had started bathed in sunshine was concluding drenched with rain. My arrival in Chappett's Copse coincided with a torrential, warm downpour that seemed to gather itself on the beech leaves above me before falling in streams rather than mere droplets. The ground steamed around me as I walked into the aqueous green light of a wood clothed in newly minted leaves.

Within just a few hundred yards I found myself surrounded: an armoury of sword-leaved helleborines bristled on the woodland floor, their many sharp, spiky, upheld leaves a vibrant and vigorous green bursting out of the rich fruitcake brown of last year's shed leaf litter. They looked a little like pineapple tops from a distance, but no pineapple was ever supplanted by a bloom as graceful as that of these helleborines – a starburst of purest white flowers that glowed in the watery gloom as if lit from within. Each flower was as sharply attenuated as the leaves of the plant beneath, and all were hung with glistening droplets of rainwater.

I sheltered at the base of the trunk of a large beech, my camera stuffed inside my shirt for some measure of protection from the gradually easing downpour. Sitting back on my haunches, I could see a constellation of helleborines stretching away from me beneath the trees. Two plants, like supernovas, soared above them. Their leaves seemed different too, somehow larger than those of their peers. I was puzzling what this could mean when, while shifting myself to a more comfortable pose, I found the answer within touching distance of me – a small, barely flowering white helleborine.

I had seen these already back in Surrey, but it was only seen alongside many sword-leaved helleborines that I could really appreciate how very different their respective structures were – the white helleborines had much broader and less spiky leaves than their rarer counterparts, and were feeble shrinking violets compared with the parade-ground magnificence of the sword-leaved. My two giant helleborines, I now realised, could only be hybrids between the two species, growing with hybrid vigour taller than either parent. While superficially similar to sword-leaved helleborine, their broader leaves betrayed their white helleborine influences.

While I had heard that this hybrid, known catchily to botanists as *Cephalanthera x shulzei*, had occurred in Chappett's Copse in the past, I'd not expected to find them here. I had been told that these unusual hybrids were not flowering this year – yet here they were. I felt flushed with a sense of some small discovery, the thrill of stumbling across the unexpected. Nothing, of course, like how Job Lousley must have felt back in 1947 when his family picnic was torn asunder by the startling rediscovery of Britain's lost military orchids, but a modest triumph nonetheless.

A bumblebee appeared as if from nowhere and began to vigorously probe a nearby sword-leaved helleborine. Snapping out of my reverie, I hastened to take some photographs of this infrequently witnessed activity. It was as well that the camera was mounted on a tripod as I found my hands were shaking – a rare orchid hybrid had once more set my heart racing.

9

Butterfly collecting and the fight for the Fens

My days invested in exploring Kent's ancient woodlands had yielded a cornucopia of orchids of many kinds, including my first tremulously emerging greater butterfly orchids of the year. These graceful, arching flowers have a related, smaller cousin in the British Isles – the unimaginatively named lesser butterfly orchid. I could not help but feel that both species had been badly let down by those who bestowed their names upon them. Our native orchids would never approach the richness of nomenclature that graces our moths – nothing comes close to species names like setaceous Hebrew character or merveille du jour – but they nevertheless generally have names that at least complement their colour and form. Not so our two native *Platanthera* species. Granted, both have a passing resemblance to a large insect, with clearly defined cruciform wings and abdomen, but the greater and lesser prefix seemed like a wasted opportunity for such striking and elegant flowers.

It is a different story in North America. There, orchid enthusiasts have many more species to describe, yet have done their native orchid flora justice. Their many *Platanthera* orchids revel in names worthy of the plants they describe: north wind bog orchid, slender spire orchid, wood rein orchid ... names that flow beautifully.

It was hard, then, not to feel that our butterfly orchids had been slightly short-changed by their modern English names. Older local names for them were much more evocative. Greater butterfly orchids were known in Wiltshire as night violets, almost certainly a reference to the plants' habit of emitting a strong, heavy scent at night to attract their pollinators, large night-flying moths such as hawkmoths. Meanwhile in Somerset they were known as white angels – arguably a better description of the appearance of each individual flower than the butterfly epithet that Gerard noted in his *Herball* of 1597, when he described the plant as, 'That kinde which resembleth the white Butter-flie.'

Kent is as good a county as any in which to see greater butterfly orchids but, unusually for a county as generously endowed with orchids as Kent, the lesser butterfly orchid remains an elusive wraith within the county bounds. Fortunately, I would be spending a day with an old friend in Hampshire who would help me to find them, and another orchid besides – the vanishingly subtle and easily overlooked musk orchid.

Naturalists tend, in my experience, to fall into one of two categories – the vast majority being relatively quiet, unassuming souls with just a small minority being the obsessive, tightly focused individuals one would think twice about taking home to meet one's parents. Jeff Picksley falls into neither category – we had been firm friends for over twenty years now, and I had never met his like elsewhere. A handsome, chain-smoking, fast-driving polo player with a laconic way about him that belies his ready wit, it would be easy to dismiss him as a latter-day James Hunt

of the New Forest. That would be to do him a terrible injust-
ice, for Jeff is a naturalist possessed of prodigious breadth and
depth of knowledge. A former Forestry Commission ranger, he
has spent over a decade working around the UK as an environmental consultant. That pedigree aside, Jeff knows Hampshire's
wildlife intimately, and I could think of no better companion for
a day's orchid hunting in the county.

We began at an unprepossessing roadside car park in the heart
of the New Forest. Lesser butterfly orchids are much less fastidious
than their greater butterfly cousins. While the latter is often found
in deep, moist woodland, lesser butterfly orchids can be found
in a wide variety of habitats – in woodland, but also in ancient
meadows, woodland fringes, acid moorland and on open heaths. It
was in this last habitat in which we would look for my first lesser
butterfly orchids of the summer.

We began to walk through the low, gnarly heather that carpeted
the open areas opposite the car park. A small party of New Forest
ponies moved slowly ahead of us, faintly inquisitive but with a
finely tuned sense of which humans might offer an apple core. The
warm air was thick with the scent of heathland, a heady cocktail of
heather, the faint honeyed-coconut traces of gorse, and pony dung.
A tiny butterfly darted along the narrow winding path we followed,
flashing fragments of electric blue before us. It settled briefly on
a patch of damp soil, proboscis probing the ground for minerals,
allowing us to see the distinctively spotted dove-grey underwings –
the first silver-studded blue I had seen for years. My last had been
in Dorset over a decade previously, on a hot afternoon that faded
into a dusk punctuated by the dim light of glow-worms and the
churring calls of nightjars. I would not have time to look for either
insect or bird later that day, for I had an appointment the following
day in East Anglia, but this small butterfly was a welcome sight.

'I think these are what you're looking for.'

Jeff, with characteristic understatement, was pointing into the
heather a short way ahead of us. There, growing through a knotted
twist of heather wood, was a small, densely flowered white orchid.
Beyond it, peeping through the heather, I could see more flowers
still. They were, in the flesh, not the virginal white of photographs

and field guides – these flowers had a creamy yellow cast, the colour of antique ivory chess pieces.

Each individual orchid was a masterpiece of sculpture and form. Rising from two fat, oval, shiny green leaves, a flower spike held around sixteen individual blooms, spaced about the upper half of the stem, each one a miniature white angelic figure when viewed head-on. The long, green-tipped labellum formed the body between two spread white lateral sepal wings, while the upper sepal and the petals formed a cowl about the angel's face. Behind each heavenly body extended a long, slightly down-curved spur – just like those of the tropical orchids that Charles Darwin had predicted would be pollinated by a moth with a suitably long proboscis, albeit these spurs were considerably shorter. The lesser butterfly orchid spurs were long enough to exclude all but a select band of long-tongued pollinators from getting anywhere near the sweet nectar the spur contained.

While they are not exclusively the preserve of hawkmoths, it is members of this dramatic moth family that are particularly attracted to lesser butterfly orchids' prolific nectar and alluring night-time perfume. Hovering in front of the flowers like miniature hummingbirds, they uncoil their proboscises and insert them with a surgeon's precision into the flower's spur, resting their forelegs on the lateral sepals in order to steady themselves. Each flower has two pollinia waiting stickily at the mouth of the spur, ready to adhere to the moth and be carried in due course to another flower where, having rotated forwards while glued to the moth, the pollinia are positioned such that they should make contact with the new flower's stigma, ensuring pollination occurs.

In North America, our butterfly orchids' *Platanthera* cousins deploy similar perfumed lures to attract their pollinators, though the scent in question varies from pollinator to pollinator. Hawkmoths are partial to sweet, enticing odours, but tiger mosquitoes prefer something meatier. Researchers have found that blunt-leaved orchids emit a scent that contains chemicals usually found in human body odour, all the better for attracting a pollinator that usually seeks out warm-blooded prey.

Having eventually had our fill of the sweeter delights the lesser butterfly orchids afforded, we continued our walk across the heath. In the heart of one boggy area, further white orchids glowed alluringly against the black peaty water in which they flourished on partially submerged tussocks. I recognised them from Ireland – I had last seen two *leucantha* variations of the early marsh orchid in the midst of Ballyheigue's immense colony of Irish marsh orchids. Those Irish *leucantha* had been approachable but slightly past their best – these Hampshire individuals were in pristine condition, but like Aesop's fox pacing beneath grapes just beyond his reach, I strove fruitlessly to find a way of getting close enough to them to allow for a good photograph. The water in which they sat was inky black and gave nothing away about what lurked beneath. I had a shrewd idea that it would be both deep and suckingly muddy were I to go in. Had it been towards the end of the day I might have been tempted, but I had no wish to inflict the drama and odour of bog immersion on either myself or Jeff. We had plenty more orchids to look for before the day was out. With woodlarks rising from the heath around us, we headed back to Jeff's car for the inevitably rapid journey to Selborne.

If I were asked to name any town or village that was inextricably linked with the study of natural history and my own particular journey to becoming a lifelong committed naturalist, it would be Selborne in Hampshire. I was a deeply reluctant and rather unhappy boy when sent to a boarding school in Dorset – I struggled to see the point of much of what we were taught in lessons, and took every opportunity I could to vanish into the Dorset countryside to see what birds, butterflies and plants I could find. Those opportunities were, unfortunately, relatively few and far between, as almost every hour of my waking day was tightly prescribed by the school. I particularly loathed games, especially sports that involved enforced teamwork. In very little time I became a serial skiver, a team-sport conscientious objector. I took the consequential punishments with what, in hindsight, must have been an infuriatingly blithe insouciance and, in due course, my housemaster had a quiet word with me.

'I can't force you to play rugby, much as I might like to. If you're not bothered about letting the House down, you could at least try to stay out of sight when you're meant to be participating.'

This, he went on to clarify, did not mean wandering around the countryside near Sherborne. While in the burgeoning days of spring and summer this was an impossible stipulation for me to honour, in the cold, wet days of the winter the stricture was more easily complied with – I found a small second-hand bookshop in the town, and spent every afternoon holed up in there, working my way systematically through the extensive natural history section. The bookshop owner was a kind, older gentleman and, I think, recognised that I had found a sanctuary amongst his bookshelves. In time, he let me sit in an armchair tucked in a small storeroom, and provided mugs of hot, sweet tea while I read there.

'You might enjoy this,' he said one day. 'If you've not read it already, I think it might be your sort of thing.'

He handed me a copy of a large hardback bound in faded green fabric. This was *The Natural History of Selborne* by the Reverend Gilbert White. Written two hundred years previously, it described White's natural-history observations around his home in the vicarage of the village of Selborne.

I was immediately transported – White was an astute and gifted observer of the natural world around him, making up for the relative contemporary lack of knowledge with a careful and systematic eye for detail and a questioning disposition. It seemed as if he was speaking to me across the centuries – this was exactly how I felt as I explored the Dorset countryside. White combined his keen naturalist's eye with an adept turn of phrase and a gift for description of place, people and wildlife that I was far from the first to find impressive and compelling – Virginia Woolf summarised, 'No novelist could have opened better. Selborne is set solidly in the foreground.'

The Natural History of Selborne takes the form of a series of letters, ostensibly written by White to two close friends, although this is, in fact, a literary device. I did not realise this at the time, but after a spell of feeling sorry for myself that I did not have any correspondents to write to about the wildlife I was seeing, I settled upon keeping a nature journal in which I wrote about what I had seen on any given day. It was the beginning of a habit that has lasted a lifetime.

Much of the wildlife White described was what I was seeing and learning about for myself in and around Dorset's Blackmore Vale. White was the first person to realise that a small bird known at the time as a willow wren was, in fact, three wholly different species of warbler altogether – chiffchaff, willow warbler and wood warbler. Even today, despite having binoculars the likes of which White could not have imagined, some birdwatchers struggle to differentiate these warblers. They were the first identification challenge I mastered for myself as a novice birdwatcher, and could only imagine how pleased White must have felt at the time he realised what he was seeing.

With my then nascent passion for orchids, one particular passing comment made by White on 3 July 1778 struck a chord with me, a chime that never entirely faded away with the passage of subsequent years. On that day White recorded three orchid species in the vicinity of Selborne, '*Ophrys spirales*, ladies' traces; *Ophrys nidus avis*, birds' nest ophrys; and *Serapias latifolia*, helleborine.'

White concluded that these flowers were 'neither unacceptable nor unentertaining'.

This masterful understatement fired my imagination. I, too, wanted to see orchids that were neither unacceptable nor unentertaining, and the more of them, the better. As Jeff and I passed through Selborne on our way to nearby Noar Hill, I remembered my schooldays and Gilbert White's inspiring words. They were not written for me, but it had always felt as if White had the likes of me in mind. Would he have regularly walked out of Selborne and up onto Noar Hill? He described the hill as 'a noble chalk promontory' – it is an imposing feature in the local landscape and it seems inconceivable that the good reverend would not have spent some happy hours ministering to his botanical studies on the hilltop.

Viewed from the small lane that runs to its base Noar Hill gives nothing of itself away; the hill's flanks are clad thickly with trees and the hilltop itself is lost from sight behind the smothering green canopy. A rough stony track leads towards the woods and, from it, a narrow, muddy pathway wends uphill. I followed Jeff as he led the way into the woods. The path was not calculated to inspire, being churned, sticky mud interspersed with much evidence of the passage of dogs and, in a final touch of pathos, a freshly dead mole.

A wooden gate brought us through the trees and into the hilltop itself. Once above the treeline, Noar Hill reveals itself in fits and starts. The hilltop is a succession of deep grassy hollows and small scrubby thickets linked by a spider's web of meandering grassy paths that thread their way around the site. In medieval times the hilltop was extensively quarried for chalk to spread on local fields as a fertiliser – ironically, it was this agricultural purpose that spared the hilltop itself from being ploughed and used for agriculture in later years, as the landscape that remained was too deeply pock-marked to lend itself to easy cultivation. What remains is one of the finest chalk grassland habitats in southern England.

The myriad craters and declivities make the hilltop a series of enclosed microclimates – the temperature at ground level in the sheltered hollows was noticeably warmer than elsewhere. Noar Hill is famous amongst British orchid enthusiasts for support-ing a large population of approximately twelve thousand musk orchids but, as we set about searching for them, they were not immediately apparent to me. I knew they were in flower, but my mental search image was not yet tuned in to them. Naturalists the world over would sympathise with this, as when searching for something subtle, hidden or well disguised, it can take a while before one starts to see them, even when the species in question is numerous. Jeff was quietly amused by my evident frustration, and took delight in pointing out other orchids – common spot-ted, pyramidal and chalk fragrant orchids in particular abounded amidst the grass.

Eventually I found my first musk orchid of the summer. It had been over twenty years since I last saw one in Kent in a meadow where they were, even then, extremely rare and now appeared to have vanished altogether. On Noar Hill, however, they continued to thrive. I no sooner had knelt to examine this first individual closely than I began to see first one, then several more in the grass nearby. It was as if I was looking at a stereogram where, from a mass of random visual noise, a sharp and recognisable image suddenly emerges. Now I could not look at any area of grass without seeing yet more musk orchids. There were hundreds in my immediate vicinity.

Most were barely as large as a modest stem of grass, with only a small number of particularly vigorous specimens exceeding ten centimetres in height. The flowers themselves were equally self-effacing, each flower spike comprising a neat column of tiny, compact chartreuse flowers each no more than a few millimetres wide. No wonder they were hard to see when walking through their midst – finding them took some care and attention to detail. Here in southern England they were at the very extremity of their global range: musk orchids can be found across northern Europe and into Asia as far east as China, and even in the lower reaches of the Himalayas. Noar Hill was no Kangchenjunga, but they had an orchid in common.

I cupped my hands around a clump of three flower spikes. The orchid's name is slightly misleading – while they are scented, they do not smell of musk. I could not recall ever having smelt the musk orchids I found while living in Kent, so was not going to let this opportunity to inhale their scent pass me by. I breathed in deeply. Sure enough, there was a rich, sweet odour, like buttered toast and honey.

Jeff, meanwhile, continued to wander nearby, searching for further plants of interest. His efforts were rewarded with several pure-white chalk fragrant orchids. In common with their close relatives, heath and marsh fragrant orchids, these flowers were usually bright, vivid pink. Var. *alba*, the scarce snow-white variation, was a more refined and less brash flower altogether. We paused while I took some photos, distracted only by marbled white butterflies that flirted shamelessly with my camera – in the hot sunshine they were active and alert, rarely settling for long to nectar on a flower. Try as I might, I could not get a sharp portrait of one. They dashed in flight around us, black and white wings flashing like cursors. Each was newly emerged, lustrous and unblemished, and busily courting in the open spaces between the numerous dark green juniper bushes that studded the hilltop.

As we made our reluctant way down, we found a large plant that, from a distance and to the unwary, looked very much like the bird's-nest orchids I had seen in Surrey's beechwoods. This, though, was no orchid and, in some regards, was all the more interesting for it. Broomrapes are parasites, their seeds stimulated to germinate when in proximity to their specific host plants' roots. Once connected to the root system of the host, the broomrape robs it of all the nutrients the broomrape requires. Broomrapes, the pale vampires of the plant world, lack chlorophyll of their own. This particular knapweed broomrape was a magnificent specimen of its kind – a thick, straw-coloured, hairy stem rising some thirty centimetres high, surmounted by a flower spike of veined, frilly purplish-brown flowers. There was something faintly creepy yet, at the same time, compelling about this plant's vigour.

We moved on to our final orchid site of the day, Jeff navigating increasingly narrow and overgrown lanes with an ease borne of long familiarity.

'Our timing's about right, but I don't think they've been seen here for years…'

The last orchid we were to look for was the longest of long shots. Red helleborines were first discovered at this site in north Hampshire as recently as 1986. Clinging to the steep sides of a beech hanger, the helleborines were last seen in flower in 2008. Botanists had suggested that they might still be present, the orchids' rhizomes surviving unseen in the soil, so our visit was a speculative one; there was a slim chance that we might be fortunate enough to find a flowering plant after an absence of almost a decade.

The wood in question was heavily shaded by the beech canopy overhead, the late afternoon sun watered to a soupy, algal green light that barely illuminated the floor beneath. The steep ground itself was slippery and muddy underfoot, our progress rendered unsteady as we traversed the valley side, clutching at beech trunks to arrest our descent. The first signs of any orchids were the dried dark brown stems and seed heads of year-old bird's-nest orchids and, nearby, a handful of fresh flower spikes, each the translucent pale brown of freshly carved horn. Heading uphill, we came to a path that led across the hillside towards a small sunlit clearing in the midst of the trees. At the sides of the path, still in deep shade, were three weedy, slender orchids, their oval green leaves immediately betraying their kind, if not their precise species. I had heard that narrow-lipped helleborines were present in this wood, but for now it was too early in the season for them to be in flower. They were certainly *Epipactis* helleborines, but which species would have to remain a mystery.

The clearing that had once been graced by red helleborines was small and almost choked by long grass that had flourished in the absence of a suppressing tree canopy overhead. We searched the area carefully and methodically, but with no joy. If the helleborines were here, they were still keeping a low profile. There was consolation to be had – the day was to finish as it had begun, with a butterfly orchid. In one corner of the clearing we found a greater butterfly orchid blooming. With the lesser butterfly orchids we had seen earlier still fresh in our minds this was a good opportunity to compare the two very similar and closely related species. The best way to tell them apart is to examine the size and shape of the pollinia – in the lesser butterfly orchid they should be close together and parallel with one another. These greater butterfly orchids, meanwhile, had revealingly large pollinia positioned widely apart and leaned towards one another at the top. The two species are believed to occasionally hybridise, so in due course I planned to visit a site that boasted orchids with pollinia positioned somewhere between those of either parent species – a level of orchid esoterica that, had I considered it at the start of this quest, I would surely not have countenanced. My orchid tastes were evolving.

Although I had dared to hope we might rediscover red helleborines blooming in this quiet wood, I had not really held out much hope that we would be so blessed. They have always been a sporadic and capricious orchid in Britain, notoriously shy and fussy, and never abundant or flourishing wherever they were found. In the absence of these Hampshire plants they were known to flower at just two locations in England, in Buckinghamshire and

Gloucestershire respectively – I had arranged a visit to the latter site, so could leave Hampshire without feeling too despondent at our failure to see the species here.

It was, besides, quite impossible to feel downbeat after a day orchid hunting in Hampshire with such success and in such good company. We had seen both species of butterfly orchid in a single day, some beautiful white variations of relatively common early marsh and chalk fragrant orchids, and many hundreds of a nationally important colony of subtle green musk orchids. Above all, I had much to look forward to the following day, for then I would be seeing another green orchid, and a rarer one still – my first ever fen orchids.

Seeing musk orchids in England is a relatively straightforward proposition. Fen orchids are a different matter altogether – as their name suggests, they are predominantly found in wet, boggy places. Britain boasts two subspecies, one of which, subspecies *ovata*, is found in south Wales and is at home in damp dune slacks. Our second subspecies is *loeselii* and is found in East Anglia at just a handful of saturated Norfolk fens – two adjacent sites, Catfield Fen and Sutton Fen, hold 90 per cent of the British population of the species.

For a while, keen orchid enthusiasts had suggested that the two distinct British populations were, in fact, similar but separate species – their leaves had slightly different shapes, while those in the dunes grew a little shorter and had fewer flowers than those in the fens. Research eventually proved that they were, genetically, almost indistinguishable from one another. I planned to see *ovata* in due course at Kenfig NNR in Glamorgan, but wanted to see my first fen orchids of the year where they flourished in habitat worthy of their name. Access to the Norfolk sites is strictly by invitation only, in order to protect their delicate ecosystems from inadvertent damage by visitors. The site manager of Sutton Fen RSPB, Richard Mason, had kindly agreed to take me onto the reserve to see the fen orchids – an honour that I deeply appreciated and one that, in the weeks leading up to this day, I had looked forward to with all the excitement of a child in the weeks before Christmas. It had been many years since I had waited for a natural history event with quite this degree of anticipation – and all this emotion was generated by an unassuming green-flowered orchid found in a waterlogged fen.

Many of the orchids I had seen so far this summer had developed sophisticated pollination strategies that intimately depended upon insects of one species or another. I had seen fly orchids that lured male wasps to them by imitating the smell of a virgin female wasp, and greater butterfly orchids that, in the dead of night, played court to long-tongued hawkmoths with their copious nectar. Fen orchids, meanwhile, have a refreshingly simple, elegant pollination mechanism that appealed deeply to me – they wait for rain.

Each flower on the flower stem points up to the sky, the long strap-shaped sepals and threadlike petals held horizontally in supplication to the gathering clouds above, while the tongue-shaped flower lip is upturned as if yearning for release. When rain comes, self-pollination can occur – raindrops hit the anther cap, knocking each flower's pollinia towards the receptive stigma. It is believed that the raised lip may even serve to deflect raindrops towards the anther.

In common with so many of the naturalists I had met in the course of the summer, Richard's passion for his charges was infectious.

'It's an exciting time in the world of fen orchids!' he said, fairly bubbling with enthusiasm as we chatted over a mug of tea in the open barn that served as his office. Much of his time in the preceding months had been spent preparing evidence ahead of a public inquiry that would consider the renewal of two water-abstraction licences that threatened the very future of the fen orchids. Habitat loss of one form or another has accelerated their decline as a British species, and since 1890 fen orchids have been lost from over forty sites. They now remain at just four localities in England and Wales, three of which are found in Norfolk.

Changing land management has not helped, as traditional activities such as reed and sedge harvesting, turf-cutting and extensive grazing had all, in the past, contributed to a mosaic of damp and wet habitats that suited the orchids. The drying-out of suitable habitat has compounded matters. This is either deliberately done, to reclaim land for use by agriculture, or inadvertently done, as collateral damage of water abstraction, often for watering nearby crops. The effects of this are a change in the height or acidity of the immediate water table, disastrous for those species that depend upon keeping their feet wet, fen orchids amongst them.

In the case of Sutton Fen, and the nearby Catfield Fen that the RSPB managed on behalf of Butterfly Conservation, a local farmer had abstracted water from two boreholes nearby since 1986. The farmer in question had applied to renew his licences to extract up to 90,000 cubic metres of water a year for his salad and potato crops, but the Environment Agency had refused his application. The farmer had appealed, and it was the subsequent public inquiry that Richard had been preparing for.

As we walked out onto the watery expanse, it immediately struck me just how special this place was. Primrose-yellow and jet-black swallowtail butterflies sailed past our heads as we waded slowly through water that reached to our calves. Marsh harriers languidly quartered the reeds in the near distance, while occasional grass snakes sinuously threaded the water's surface ahead of us. The rich smell of disturbed sediment combined with aromatic bog myrtle to make a heady, intoxicating perfume. While I marvelled at the abundance of life around us, Richard warned me to follow in his footsteps, for the fen was deeper than rubber-boot height in places.

'I can't imagine working anywhere else,' he said. 'It's an incredible place.'

When the RSPB bought the 365-acre mosaic of fen and grassland that comprises the reserve in 2006, they acquired one of Britain's hidden fragments of wilderness. Sutton Fen had fallen off the map, unknown to all but a handful of fen tigers, the countrymen who had for centuries cut sedge for thatch in its watery fastness, netted plovers in flooded pastures and, when the winter brought vast flocks of ducks from the near Continent, gone wildfowling there. Set to one side of the River Ant, water flowed as slow as the passage of time across the fen, passing through a tapestry of reeds, alder copses and sedge. The landscape had stood still here while the world moved heedlessly on.

'Pretty special, isn't it?' asked Richard rhetorically as we paused and I took in the immensity of the fen before me. I understood immediately what he meant – I had felt the same sense of rightness of place the moment I set foot in Shetland. For me it had only been a matter of time before I moved to the islands, and I could not envisage living anywhere but there. Sometimes a landscape connects deep within a person and establishes a hold that is all but impossible to sever.

We were standing in an open area that looked like a patchwork quilt, with rectangular plots of differing appearance all around us. Some areas were thickly vegetated, while others were almost bare. In association with Plantlife, Kew Gardens and the Cambridge University Botanic Gardens, the RSPB have been monitoring the growth and abundance of fen orchids in response to differing management techniques at Sutton Fen, hoping to identify the very best habitat management regime under which the orchids would flourish and, ultimately, how fen orchids might be successfully reintroduced to some of their former haunts.

In common with many of our rarer orchid species, fen orchids are fastidious to the point of fussiness in their requirements. If they are to do well they require very specific ecological conditions – a water pH in excess of 6, a water table near the surface year-round, an abundance of tussock-forming brown mosses and, to improve their reproductive success, a level of physical disturbance sufficient to assist the dispersal of seeds and bulbs. They are unusual amongst orchids in that they do not rely entirely on seeds for their reproduction – fen orchids hedge their bets by growing tiny, detachable propagules on the stems of their pseudobulbs. These propagules can, when dislodged, form an entirely new plant in time if they lodge on a suitable mossy tussock – a clone of the original parent plant formed by vegetative reproduction and a generous dose of good luck. Many of these propagules will, inevitably, not find themselves in a suitable habitat and will perish, their potential unfulfilled, but it seems as if propagation by seed in the fens is even less successful. Disturbance, perhaps unintentionally by browsing deer, or deliberately by the benevolent hand of man, seems vital if they are to prosper.

Richard began showing me my first fen orchids, each growing in the heart of tussocks formed of brown moss rising barely above the surface of the water that surrounded us. It had rained recently, so the water level was a little higher than would be usual in midsummer, an inconvenience only for the would-be orchid photographer rather than the water-loving orchids themselves – I had to be careful not to submerge the body of my camera as I began to take a series of images. Richard explained that the orchids only thrived on these tussocks, and did better on plots that had had most of their vegetation removed in previous years.

'The cutting reduces the vigour of the dominant plants like reed and sedge. That lets the smaller plants, including fen orchids, have better access to light, water and the nutrients they need.'

We discussed how precarious the continued presence of fen orchids was at Sutton and Catfield Fens. Their existence, with their particular ecological requirements, rested on a knife edge. The extraction of water for agriculture nearby was already influencing the ecology at Catfield Fen, allowing a proliferation of sphagnum moss – conditions in which fen orchids cannot persist for more than a few years. The outcome of the public inquiry regarding the local farmer's attempt to renew his water abstraction licences would be pivotal. If the decision was overturned, this could lead, in time, to a catastrophic change in the fortunes of the vast majority of Britain's current fen orchid population.

This remote corner of east Norfolk is home to a variety of rare breeding birds, many of which have responded well to efforts on the part of conservationists to improve the habitats upon which they depend. Not least amongst their number are Britain's pioneering common cranes – a small breeding population established itself in the area in the late 1970s and has, incrementally, increased in number with the passage of time. They had been lost as a British breeding species over four hundred years previously due to a combination of hunting and the draining of their wetland homes.

In recent years, with considerable effort and at no small cost in terms of time and money, a collaboration of conservation bodies under the umbrella of the Great Crane Project have reared and released almost a hundred common cranes into suitable habitat on the Somerset Levels. As a birdwatcher, such an initiative filled me with joy – it is impossible not to be uplifted by such majestic birds as common cranes. From their elegant tall forms with shaggy bustles of powder-grey feathers, to their courtship dances and bugling calls, these are iconic birds.

Yet a small part of me, hearing first-hand the precarious situation in which the Norfolk fen orchids found themselves, and the largely unsung efforts of those dedicated to their conservation, wondered at the place in which we had collectively found ourselves. Was it right that such efforts should be focused on crowd-pleasers like common cranes? Or perhaps, more damningly, was it right that we, the public, appeared to care more about those cranes than the diminutive green orchid that shared the fens with the birds? It was heartening to learn of the considerable efforts being expended in the defence and conservation of the fen orchids, and the plans to reintroduce them to other sites in East Anglia. It simply felt a little sad that this story would never attract the same sort of public attention and support as the cranes' reintroduction. The Fen Orchid Steering Group was a name that would never fire the public's imagination in the manner of the Great Crane Project, but I felt perhaps it should.

It was easy to shake off this pang of melancholy in surroundings such as Sutton Fen. With water threatening to overflow the tops of my boots, I followed Richard as we walked through this saturated world, pausing time and again to examine clumps of fen orchids flowering from soft, bronzy, moss tussocks. Each rose as a slender stem between two long, prominently keeled and sharply pointed green leaves, held like a fresh green V above the moss. The pale jade-green flowers were relatively large in comparison to the stem, and were few in number, with ten being typical for each flower spike, allowing me to appreciate their delicate cruciform shapes held yearningly skyward in anticipation of rain.

Nearer to the alders that fringed the fen we found my first southern marsh orchids of the year – I had not thought beyond the fen orchids, though of course I should have known that a site as biologically rich as this would have other orchids besides. Southern marsh orchids are widespread across much of England and Wales, and I would see many more of them in the coming weeks, even on the embankments of motorways, for they are tough and more catholic in their choice of habitats than their name suggests. They were the very antithesis of the delicate green fen orchids – each flower spike was tall and robust with a thick column of blowsy purple flowers that erred towards pink in the bright sunshine. While I paused to take a last photo of the fen, a Norfolk hawker dragonfly clattered past us like a chitinous biplane, all dry rustle and hunting intent. Life was abounding here in all possible forms.

Three months after I visited Sutton and Catfield Fens I was pleasantly reminded of my day with the fen orchids in Richard's company when, in September, the outcome was announced of the public inquiry into the Environment Agency's decision to refuse the local farmer's application to renew his water abstraction licences. In the end, the Planning Inspectorate upheld the decision to refuse the licence renewals. The inquiry was held in April and May, just weeks before I had gone to Norfolk. During the inquiry the Environment Agency had robustly defended its initial decision, presenting evidence from Natural England with the RSPB acting as an expert ecological witness. All three bodies provided a significant and compelling body of evidence demonstrating that refusal of the abstraction licences was the only option to safeguard the vulnerable Sutton and Catfield Fens and the species, not least fen orchids, that depended upon them.

Phil Pearson, the RSPB senior conservation officer for the Eastern region, said: 'We are very happy with the positive outcome of the appeal. The planning inspector's decision ensures protection for this crucial wildlife habitat and marks a significant milestone in our work with Butterfly Conservation, Plantlife and other partners to restore Catfield Fen to the best condition. Failure to address the adverse impact of water abstraction on this site now would have been disastrous for its longer-term protection and management.

'Catfield Fen, along with nearby Sutton Fen, is the "best of the best" within one of Europe's most important areas of wetland. Strong legal protection for the site has been an important factor in achieving a positive outcome, and highlights the need to maintain such protection for our finest wildlife sites in the future.'

It seemed as if the planets had aligned favourably that week where publicity for the fens was concerned, for they also featured prominently in the *State of Nature 2016*, an audit of the health of the UK's wildlife undertaken by a coalition of over fifty wildlife and research organisations – including those champions of Sutton and Catfield Fens, the RSPB, Plantlife and Butterfly Conservation. East Anglia was highlighted for the importance of the habitats it held – 80 per cent of the nation's fenland, 50 per cent of our reed-beds, 31 per cent of our saltmarsh and 22 per cent of our estuaries – and the wildlife that depended upon those habitats, not least 90 per cent of the British population of fen orchids.

However, launching the report at the Royal Society headquarters in London, Sir David Attenborough issued a stark warning: 'The natural world is in serious trouble and it needs our help as never before. Landscapes are being restored, special places defended, struggling species being saved and brought back. But we need to build significantly on this progress if we are to provide a bright future for nature and for people.

'The future of nature is under threat and we must work together – Governments, conservationists, businesses and individuals – to help it.'

The refusal to renew the water abstraction licences adjacent to Sutton and Catfield Fens was, predictably, not universally popular – the farming press decried it at the time, while the farmer himself described the decision as catastrophic. Meanwhile, I felt this decision represented a small yet significant triumph for conservation in the face of an increasing clamour from the agricultural industry as a whole for fewer restraints on their activities.

During my summer of orchid hunting I had seen hundreds of signs erected in farmers' fields supporting Brexit, but not one advocating that Britain should remain in the EU. The writing for the subsequent referendum result had been on the wall for months – many farmers, regardless of the many millions they received annually in subsidy payments from Europe, felt shackled by the environmental and husbandry regulations that came with those payments. They decided to bite the hand that fed them, hoping subsidies direct from the British government would not be dependent upon similar levels of legislation and environmental compliance.

What would the future hold for fragile, vulnerable habitats like Sutton Fen in a post-Brexit world? For now I could celebrate a more assured future for the fen orchids I had seen this summer, but I feared for the longer-term future they and their like now faced. It only takes a tiny shift in water pH to effect a catastrophic decline in a fen orchid population – what would the outcome of such a monumental political decision be for Britain's natural world as a whole?

Time alone would tell.

10

Orchid hunting in the simmer dim

The preceding few weeks of my quest had been hectic. What had started as a trickle in the mild south-west of England, with the first tentative emergence of early purple and early spider orchids, had rapidly turned into a flood as the flowering season got into full swing with the lengthening of days and the warming of the soil. A plethora of orchids had nosed their stems skywards, buds swelling with the promise of colour, perfume and deceit.

I had lost myself in the kaleidoscope – gladly submerged in a rainbow of wildly divergent shapes and forms. My journey began in my childhood haunts on the lush Somerset Levels and had returned to another former home on the rolling Kentish chalk downs – and meanwhile I had abandoned myself to the current, swept weekly to the far reaches of the British Isles in pursuit of my dreams and the rarest and most achingly beautiful of our wildflowers.

It felt strange to wake up on a Saturday morning in my own bed, with nascent golden sunlight and the moaning call of love-lorn red-throated divers filtering through the blinds. I was over halfway through my journey, and the law of diminishing returns was shortly to start to bite with a vengeance – seeing most of the remaining orchid species would involve travelling to specific sites for just one species at a time. Sites that would be, in many cases, on opposite sides of the country to one another. Today, however, would be a pause for breath of sorts, an opportunity to see new orchids closer to home.

My move to Shetland had always felt like a homecoming. It was a chance to live in the midst of one of Europe's remaining unspoilt wildernesses, surrounding myself with wildlife of all kinds in this remote outpost of the British Isles, closer to the Arctic Circle than London. Twenty years before it had been Shetland's reputation as one of the best places in Europe in which to see rare migrant birds that had lured me up here, but with every visit I found more reasons besides to compel me to return.

When eventually I moved to Shetland for good, I sank roots deep into the island of Whalsay and the old, white-painted stone croft house I rescued from dereliction. I immersed myself in the islands' wildlife in all shapes and forms – the harbour porpoises that rolled blackly and glossily through the waves outside my window, the otter cubs that whistled and squabbled on the bladderwrack at low tide, or the pellucid jade-green bog orchids to be found in the spongy vastness of sphagnum bogs.

Shetland spoke to something deep inside me. Mine was a love affair with the islands themselves, a passion that drew me inexorably to this wildest and remotest of places. Eighty years before me it was the same compelling urge that washed the Scottish poet Christopher Grieve up in Whalsay. The landscape, the geology, and the prismatic air invigorated this pillar of the Scottish Renaissance, and he created some of his most lyrical work under the pen name

Hugh MacDiarmid while eking out a frugal existence on the island I now call home.

While the islanders struggled to understand why a man as well educated as Grieve could be so poor, eschewing conventional employment for a life of letters, it was his Cornish wife Valda who scandalised the locals with her lasciviously scarlet-painted toenails – they initially mistook her nail polish for blood. One woman recalled: 'We tocht she'd caa'd her toes apön a stane! Aye, aye ... When Valda arrived dat wis da start o' da emancipation o' da wives o' Whalsa!'

My time in the islands has been much less scandalous. Over the years, I had invested my time exploring the many islands that make up the Shetland archipelago, and this was to pay dividends at this point in my quest. I was heading to Britain's most northerly outpost of all, the island of Unst – home to a small community of six hundred people and a tiny but choice selection of orchids I had yet to see, all within an area measuring a mere twelve miles long by five miles wide. Nowhere else on Shetland could I easily find lesser twayblades or early marsh, frog and heath fragrant orchids – on Unst I could hope to find them all in one compact but botanically rich island.

Nevertheless, I had a lot of ground to cover on the island if I was to find all of my target species. A good job, then, that the hours of daylight stretch out interminably this far north in midsummer. Known in Shetland as the 'simmer dim', it never gets truly dark during the height of summer – the sun barely dips below the horizon at midnight before rising again for another nineteen hours of full daylight. Some hardy souls play golf in the opalescent light of midnight at this time of year, while I, meanwhile, intended to be hunting for orchids late into the day.

In crystal-clear conditions I could just make out the elegant Georgian fascia of Belmont House on Unst from my kitchen window on Whalsay. Most of the time, however, Unst was just below the horizon, separated from Whalsay by an expanse of over twenty miles of restless sea and shielded from view by the haze between the islands of Fetlar and Yell. For me, visiting Unst involved three individual ferry crossings – it might be relatively local, but that didn't mean it was easy to reach. I hoped that it would be worth the effort.

Shetland's geology is magnificently varied – the fragmented archipelago is over a hundred miles long, and is spectacularly diverse. Red granite cliffs tower within sight of glittering crystalline limestone crags nosing their way through lush, green, sheep-dotted pastures. Small wonder Christopher Grieve found such inspiration in the landscape that surrounded him. The opening lines of 'On a Raised Beach' remain as timeless as the rocks that they describe:

All is lithogenesis – or lochia,
Carpolite fruit of the forbidden tree,
Stones blacker than any in Caaba,
Cream-coloured caen-stone, chatoyant pieces,
Celadon and corbeau, bistre and beige,
Glaucous, hoar, enfouldered, cyathiform,
Making mere faculae of the sun and moon.

Each island has a distinct character all of its own, but Unst is, even by Shetland's standards, the eccentric cousin that lurks on the periphery of the family gathering. The geology of the island is like a mosaic, patches of wildly divergent rocks millions of years apart crammed together like tesserae. From a botanist's perspective, this is a heavenly accident of nature, providing fragments of different habitat – and thus different plants – in one tightly confined area. Yet Unst looks like a hard place upon which to exist. Swathes of the island are bleak stony areas of what, to all intents and purposes, are the nearest thing to lichen-clad Arctic tundra the British Isles have to offer. Nowadays promoted by its inhabitants as 'The Island Above All Others', less kindly folk have been known to liken it to J.R.R. Tolkein's infamous fictional wasteland Mordor.

I find it hard to imagine that Unst has changed all that much since the days when a presumably rather disgruntled Robert Louis Stevenson set foot on Britain's most northerly island. Sent there by his father to put his fanciful dreams of writing firmly behind him, and to pursue instead the family trade of building lighthouses in wild and remote outposts of the British Isles, I am fairly certain young Robert Louis was taken aback when he first saw what was to be his home while he studied the building of the so-called 'impossible lighthouse'. The Admiralty had challenged the engineers of the day to build a light to ward ships off the sea-swept Muckle Flugga rock at Unst's most northerly extremity. Conventional wisdom had it that this could not be built, so challenging were the sea conditions around Muckle Flugga, but the Lighthouse Stevensons were determined to prove otherwise.

Today, the graffiti at the island's ferry terminal greets visitors and speaks volumes – scratched deeply into the wood of the toilet doors is the heartfelt sentiment 'Unst is a shithole'. It is rumoured locally that Robert Louis Stevenson might have felt that way too. Legend has it that he based a number of the less salubrious characters in *Treasure Island* upon locals he met during his stay on the island. Looking at the map of Treasure Island, one is immediately struck by the similarities between it and the shape of Unst. What is certain is that after an all-too-brief sojourn, he left the island to pursue his career as a writer, the family trade of building lighthouses dashed on the rocks of a Shetland winter. The Muckle Flugga lighthouse was completed without him and continues to ward ships off Unst's brutal coastline to this day.

By mid-morning I found myself standing at the back of a small, rust-streaked ferry as it groaned away from the pier on Yell in a shimmering swirl of diesel fumes for the last short leg of my journey. Unst lay just ten minutes ahead of us, most of the landmass hidden behind the brow of the first of many rocky hills. Off to one side in the choppy, tidal waters lay the considerably smaller island of Linga, once home to Shetland's only resident bear. I had heard the story years ago during a party in Unst, when the fiddle player, too drunk to play on, fell into an armchair and told the tale of Jan and the bear.

He recounted how, in the twelfth century, while Shetland was under Norse rule, a local man, Jan Tait, enraged by the unreasonable demands of the Norwegian king's tax collector, who was assessing how much butter he should yield by way of levy, struck the unfortunate man with his own *bismar,* or weighing beam, killing him with a single blow.

Arrested and taken to Norway to stand trial for murder, Jan was standing in front of the king, who remarked upon the prodigious size of the suppurating corns on Jan's bare feet. Jan seized an axe from one of the king's bodyguards and promptly set about cutting them off himself, impressing the king with his tenacity, his tolerance of pain, and his lack of regard for his own flesh. Jan was clearly a man to be reckoned with. The king offered Jan a deal: if he could capture, alive, a particularly troublesome bear that had been bothering a nearby district, the king would pardon Jan and stay the inevitable capital punishment he faced.

Being from Shetland, where there were no mammals more fearsome than an otter, Jan had no idea what kind of an animal a bear was, merely that it was said to be fierce and unapproachable. Undaunted, he set off into the woods and, upon meeting a local woman, explained his predicament and asked how such a beast could be overcome. Such a tale is never complete without a wise woman and, having explained to Jan the scale of the creature he had been tasked to tackle, she was said to have prophesied, 'Butter got you into this mess, and butter shall get you out of it.'

Jan purchased a large barrel of butter, tracked down the bear, and set the barrel before it. Much taken with this delicious easy meal, the bear consumed the lot, licking the barrel spotlessly clean before curling up beside it to sleep, gorged quite senseless with butter. Jan seized the opportunity to tie up the beast's feet and jaws and, thus secured, he brought the bear before the king.

The king kept his word, and Jan was allowed to return to Shetland. The only condition set upon his pardon was that he take the bear back with him. His neighbours, while delighted to see Jan return safely to the community, were said to be rather less thrilled at the prospect of sharing their home with a bear so bothersome the king of Norway had seen fit to exile it across the sea to Shetland. Jan, feeling he owed his life to the bear, took it to the offshore island of Linga, where it lived out the rest of its short life chained to a stout post, sustained only by what fish Jan could catch for it.

It is said that to this day one can see the circle worn deep into the ground where the bear had circled the post that kept it from swimming back to Unst. The only signs of life I could see on Linga as the ferry passed it were a pair of greylag geese shepherding their downy grey young through the profusely flowering red campion above the shore. Of Jan's bear there was no discernible trace. Shetland, an isolated scatter of low-lying islands whipped by intense storms born deep in the salty cauldrons of the Atlantic and Arctic Oceans, would not have been a particularly comfortable habitat for a bear more accustomed to roaming the dark and sheltered recesses of Norwegian forests, but today it would provide plenty of scope for the keen orchid hunter.

Our arrival on Unst involved no small theatre. The elderly ferry's groaning reached a shuddering crescendo as the heavily bearded and taciturn crew brought it effortlessly into the dock. Ahead of us onshore lay a small marshalling area, a large colourful billboard welcoming visitors to the island and, incongruously, a large homemade xylophone formed from an old wooden rowing boat strung inside with lengths of copper water pipes culled from redundant central heating systems, making an effective, if somewhat out of tune, musical instrument. A sign nearby exhorted visitors to 'hae a tön on da plinky boat'.

I eased the car gingerly off the ferry and, three hours after leaving home on Whalsay, I rolled onto Unst. Today's orchid hunt would begin now in earnest. Just a few minutes' drive from the ferry terminal lay one of Unst's more lush corners. While much of the island appears barren and infertile, here and there are to be found some greener, less uncompromising areas. It was in one such sheltered, hidden nook that two years previously I had discovered a small colony of early marsh orchid of my favourite subspecies, *incarnata*, sporting creamy white flowers with a blushing suffusion and tracery of the most delicate rosy pink. I had already seen some this year, but who can possibly resist second helpings of an orchid that looks like raspberry ripple ice cream? I knew I certainly couldn't.

I abandoned the car and set off along the coast. The tide was falling and, for now, the sun was winning the battle against a threatening mass of cloud. Wet pebbles shone at the water's edge and a small flock of nervous turnstones moved ahead of me, searching for invertebrates hiding amidst the stones and seaweed. These birds should have been up in the Arctic by now, settling down to the serious business of rearing a brood of chicks in the short northern summer. This handful hadn't made it that far, and my heart lifted to see their calico-cat plumage so bright against the dark, wet stones. The springy turf above the shore upon which I made my way was littered with spiky pink and purple fragments of shattered sea urchins left there by feeding gulls at the last low tide. It took a moment for me to realise that amongst them were flowers of similar hue – small, stunted heath spotted orchids were blooming right up to the edge of the banks that overhung the coast. These are the commonest of all the orchids to be found in Shetland, and I would be seeing plenty more of them as the day wore on – for now, I had much scarcer orchids on my mind.

Presently I headed inland along a rough track that took me past a sheep crö, or pen, where a crofter in the traditional crofting garb of a blue boiler suit and bright gorse-yellow rubber boots was steadily shearing a stoical Shetland sheep. The ewe was set back on her haunches and supported by one powerful arm while the hand shears whispered through her tawny brown fleece. Her flock members huddled as far away from their half-nude companion as the pen would allow them, their discomfort made little easier to bear by the close attention of a fixated border collie. The dog ignored me, but the crofter looked up from his work at my approach and greeted me.

'Hi aye. Fine day.'

'It's better here than on Whalsay. We had fog when I left home.'

I was keen to establish my credentials as a local. While my English accent sounded nothing like the broad, elastic Whalsay tones, I didn't wish to be taken for a tourist. I was, after all, wandering across his croft unannounced. Maintaining a firm hold on the recalcitrant sheep, his interest was evidently piqued.

'Du bides in Whalsay? Whar does du stay?'

The Shetland accent was pronounced, yet I knew he was knappin' – the Shetland dialect expression for 'speaking clearly so an incomer can understand you'. So far we were on safe ground, as we were exchanging the expected formalities to allow him to establish my place in the community. It was only if we went conversationally off-piste that I might find myself in trouble following accent, dialect, or both. I explained where I lived, and that I had been there for over ten years now. He looked pleased.

'Du must like it yondrew. I doot yon's an ower windy spot, no?'

I agreed that it was indeed a very exposed location, even by Shetland's admittedly high standards where extreme weather was concerned. It is a rare day here in the isles when the wind is not blowing keenly, even in the height of summer.

'Is du one o da birdy men? Here tae spy twartree phalaropes?'

He had noticed my binoculars and was alluding to the presence of breeding red-necked phalaropes in the islands. These delicate wading birds breed around the edge of the Arctic Circle, with just a handful of pairs nesting each year in Shetland at locations kept a closely guarded secret amongst their local custodians. It was a good job I was not an egg collector.

'Well, yes, I'm a birder, but it's orchids I'm here to look for today. You've got some really good ones on your croft.'

'Orchids? Boy, boy. Du's come aa dis way fur peerie flooers?'

He looked incredulous. While Shetland has a long history of birdwatching in the isles and many islanders, while not birdwatchers, could certainly recognise an *unken* or unfamiliar bird, should they happen across one, a grown man expressing an interest in wildflowers was apparently an unexpected turn of events.

'Ah well. Good luck ta dee.'

And with that he bent over and resumed clipping the half-shorn sheep between his legs. I had been dismissed. Feeling rather chastened, I made my way further along the coast. Was it so very odd to be looking for flowers? It was probably just as well I'd not explained that a day trip to Unst from Whalsay was the very least of my orchid-hunting adventures this summer.

The early marsh orchids were where I'd hoped they would be, a loose scatter of some thirty flowering plants growing in a damp, humid area flanking a small stream that threaded a meandering course in a sheltered valley. Unusually for Shetland, one could not see the sea from here. Small hillocks clad in rough grass and heather enclosed the valley and a tiny diamond-sparkling lochan into which the stream seeped; these rocky hillocks would once have been considered trowie mounds, the homes of the trows that featured prominently in Shetland's folklore. Some Shetland people still believe in these little people – Maurice, a local friend younger than me, hearing where I was going orchid-hunting this weekend, had seriously warned me, 'Mind du taks care. Yon's a muckle trowie place.' His face was stern, and he was being deathly serious. Shetland's folklore was riddled with stories of wanderers in the hills meeting the trows, being invited to share hospitality with them in their trowie mounds, and returning to the hill the following day to discover time had passed more quickly outside the trowie mound, with decades having elapsed in their absence. I could not afford any such chance encounters – in these few precious months of summer I needed to see all of our native orchids. I couldn't afford to miss a decade or two carousing with da trows.

The early marsh orchids shared their saturated home with numerous carnivorous plants, round-leaved sundews with ruby-red leaves sparkling with fatally sticky 'dew', and lilac-flowered butterworts with pale yellow leaves looking like so many anaemic starfishes washed up in the dark mire. Most of the orchids were already past their best, their petals beginning to brown and curl up as the ovaries beneath each flower head began to swell to form a seed capsule. One or two plants still had flowers in their prime, though, each floret crisp and bright as a gem. On either side of the stream were myriad heath spotted orchids – compared to the refined early marshes, their purple-flecked blousy white flowers seemed brash and vulgar.

Where the early marsh orchids had come from, or how long they had been growing here remained an unfathomable mystery. I had heard rumours of sightings of other early marsh orchids elsewhere in Shetland, and had seen some faded photographs of what purported to be the species, but most of these relics were as unreliable as childhood memories, blurry and inconclusive photos taken on slide film with old-fashioned cameras and lenses, and labelled with only the most general reference to the locality in which the plants had been found. I had never found any until I stumbled across these ones in Unst by pure chance one day while photographing golden plovers.

At the time I had spent hours fruitlessly searching the surrounding area for more early marsh orchids, and had concluded that this small colony was a one-off and not part of a larger, scattered population. How had they come to be here, of all places, and nowhere else? How long had they persisted here? I could only surmise that they might have arrived as airborne seed from an otherwise undiscovered parent colony elsewhere on the island.

Shetland's capricious wind has a habit of dispersing colonists to new lands. Back in 1745 two young Unst women were believed lost at sea when their small boat went missing in a sudden violent storm. In due course it transpired that they had been blown across the sea to Norway, washing up on the island of Karmøy, where they settled and eventually married local men. Their descendants live there to this day. Perhaps these early marsh orchids had been blown into Unst from much further afield.

I took some photos of the few remaining pristine flowers, and then made my way back to the car by a circuitous route that avoided the sheep crö. A field at the side of the narrow road harboured thick, tall purple flower spikes. These appeared at first glance like reasonable candidates for northern marsh orchid. I had already cut my teeth with the *Dactylorhiza* genus in Ireland and the Hebrides, and knew never to readily accept them at face value. Their genus spans Europe, North Africa and the Middle East, and follows the historic Silk Road deep into the heart of China and the former Soviet Union. There are myriad species of *Dactylorhiza*, and for every species there appear to be numerous distinctive subspecies and innumerable hybrid combinations between species and subspecies alike. This makes them the stuff of taxonomists' dreams, but for the casual observer hoping to identify definitively a target species, potentially a fiendish challenge in which certainty is an elusive chimaera. While in the grand scheme of orchids Britain and Ireland has relatively few species of *Dactylorhiza*, the ones we do have behave entirely typically for their genus – they hybridise freely and promiscuously with one another. The sheer size and thrusting phallic vigour of these flower spikes by the Unst roadside was ringing familiar alarm bells. Hybrid offspring between northern marsh and heath spotted orchids are often much larger and more striking than either of their parents, and these flowers were easily the largest *Dactylorhiza* I had seen all summer. A closer examination was needed.

Kneeling on the wet ground, I parted the lush grass and stiff mare's tails that surrounded one of the orchids. Sure enough, the flowers were not the necessary deep royal purple of a northern marsh orchid, revelling instead in a lighter pastel shade like that of blueberry yoghurt. Most damning of all, the green leaves were heavily blotched with dark purple markings, a sure indication of some heath spotted orchid in this orchid's ancestry. I examined the surrounding plants one by one, and while each was different from its fellows, they were none of them a satisfactory candidate for a northern marsh. I found myself in the middle of a hybrid swarm of *Dactylorhiza x formosa*. This indicated to me that there should be plants of both parent species nearby, if only I cast my net a little wider.

Heath spotted orchids were ubiquitous – I couldn't miss them if I tried, myriad constellations of flowers studding the roadside verge and the moorland beyond it. Try as I might, though, I could not find any northern marsh orchids. Perhaps they had been here once and, like the indigenous Picts at the unforgiving hands of the Vikings who took Unst from them, subsequently died out, leaving behind just faint traces of their passing. Alternatively, a wandering insect may have brought northern marsh orchid pollen from further afield to cross-pollinate one of the many local heath spotted orchids.

Where I was quick to dismiss the numerous heath spotted orchids, centuries ago the people of Shetland were said to have valued them as part of a cure for a child that had been burned, a recipe for recovery that leavened Christian symbolism with a salty pagan touch. A cross would be made of barley straw, and covered with dried flowers. The healer would touch this three times beneath the child's bed, and three times at the head of the bed. Approaching the fire, the healer would say,

'From the fire he leap't,
Inta da cradle he crept,
Ta heal da bairn brunt
O Guid's name.'

The child's burns would then be touched by the cross, and would apparently then heal without any complications. While it's easy to scoff at such leaps of faith with the benefit of hindsight, the world's myriad orchids provide a rich vein of material to mine for medical researchers hoping to unlock beneficial compounds from their enigmatic genetic depths.

A further short drive brought me over the centre of the island to my next destination, a stony hillside on the eastern seaboard known as the Keen of Hamar. Shetland's Viking heritage is carved deeply into the landscape and there are many archaeological sites that bear witness to the centuries during which the islands were an outpost of the kingdom of Denmark; the outlines of longhouses, boat burials and field systems are slowly being absorbed by the landscape through the passage of time and the vegetable growth of centuries of grass. There are traces, too, of a more ancient human presence, Pictish defensive brochs, Bronze Age hut circles, simple burial cists … but the place names in use today give the lie to this having been a harmonious displacement of the Picts by the Norsemen. Of 1,200 place names in Shetland, less than fifty have a non-Viking root. The Keen of Hamar is 'the rocky hill belonging to Hamar'. History does not record quite what Hamar would have made of his rocky hill – it certainly would have had little agricultural value for the Viking settler of the day, as the soil is desperately thin and lacking in nutrients.

From a distance the Keen of Hamar is striking – surrounded by green fields that slope gently down to the sea, the domed hillside looks like a satellite image of the surface of some arid, ochraceous alien world. It's as if part of the island's surface had been scoured off by the weather of millennia and the material beneath had begun to rust. What from afar could be Mars is, on close inspection, Europe's finest example of a particularly unusual habitat, serpentine debris, a name that's every bit as dry and arid as the landscape it describes. The hillside encompasses some twenty hectares of ferrous fragments of serpentine rock bound together by a thin, clayey soil, and seems utterly devoid of any meaningful life. When I was leading a wildlife-watching tour here in the past, one of my guests stood aghast at the gateway to the reserve.

'There's literally nothing here,' she complained.

Fortunately for all concerned, she was very wrong. For thousands of years the effects of rain, frost and the salt-laden air have combined with the thin layer of heavy-metal-infused soil on the hillside to create a habitat that is unique. Plants that otherwise scale the giddy heights of a few centimetres high elsewhere in Shetland are stunted dwarves here. Alpine species more at home in the high peaks of Scandinavia and Iceland are found just a few metres above sea level on the Keen. Most importantly of all, a handful of orchids eke out a precarious living here, in particular frog orchid and heath fragrant orchid, the one as plain as the other was ostentatiously beautiful.

I walked happily out onto the hillside. While the wind was blowing briskly from the sea and there was the merest promise of some drizzle, down at ground level the stony soil provided a warmer microclimate. What at first glance looked desolate was, on closer inspection, studded with flowering plants. I had to be careful where I trod for fear of crushing something delicate. Tiny tufts of sea pinks and kidney vetch flowers of the palest lemony yellow nodded in the breeze. Here and there clumps of moss campion looked as if someone had scattered myriad vivid emerald-green pincushions in their wake.

It took a little while to get my bearings on the featureless face of the hill, but before long I had relocated my faithful colony of frog orchids – while there are individual plants scattered all across the site, one particular otherwise unremarkable small area some twenty feet in diameter holds a dense colony of these unassuming flowers.

I had discovered them there five years previously and their numbers held firm year after year – there were usually as many as fifty plants to be found in close proximity to one another.

Like all the flowering plants in this challenging habitat, the Keen of Hamar frog orchids are much smaller than their counterparts elsewhere. Had I tracked some down on the British mainland, I might have expected them to be as tall as thirty centimetres; these plants, however, were five centimetres tall at best, with no visible stalk to speak of – their deep burgundy and dark green flower spikes sat upon their leaves like modest pyramids in the desert. From a standing perspective one could so easily miss them – but once one lay down and looked at them from ground level, their numbers became more apparent and the understated beauty of the flowers was appreciable.

Quite where this particular orchid got its name is a matter of conjecture. Unlike the monkey orchids I'd enjoyed near my former home in Kent some weeks previously, the individual flower heads look nothing like the animal after which the plant takes its name. With a great deal of imagination one could just about convince one-self that the hood on each flower, formed by the sepals, resembled the slit-eye of a frog, but this seemed pretty tenuous as explanations go. That the flowers are partly green seems more far-fetched still as an origin – both bog and fen orchids have much greener flowers, and both favour damper, more frog-friendly habitats. The name remained as mysterious and inexplicable as ever.

The plant, meanwhile, appealed deeply to me. For a long time I'd carried a torch for the underdogs of the natural world: the plain, the small, the downright ugly – the species that other enthusiasts were quick to dismiss in favour of more glamorous alternatives. You could keep your dramatic plunging ospreys, your myopic badgers, your iridescent purple emperors – I would champion the shy and declining willow tit, the beleaguered mountain hare, or the marsh fritillaries with wings the clashing palette of an *Abigail's Party* dinner set.

It was precisely this sort of inverse snobbery that drew me inex-orably to love the frog orchids on the Keen of Hamar. Obscure of name and without the bright candy colours or spectacular structures of many of their orchid counterparts, to make matters worse (or more appealing, in my eyes), these individuals were stunted and smaller than their southern cousins, and they grew in what looked like the most exposed and forbidding area of Britain's most northerly outpost. Like so many of the orchids I was to see this summer, their numbers nationally had plummeted over the years in Britain and Europe – casualties of intensive agriculture and habitat loss. I couldn't fail to love them and, naturally, I spent a good while with them.

Eventually I dragged myself away from these perversely pleasing flowers, and set off across the scree to the opposite side of the reserve, overlooking the abandoned chromite mines that once fed Britain's explosive-making industry. Above me I could make out the tracks left in the hillside by the Royal Air Force engineers who installed a short-lived radar station on the hilltop during the early years of the Second World War.

While the extant traces of Jan Tait's pacing bear on nearby Linga were, of course, just a fanciful tall tale, these impressions of heavy machinery moving across the land had endured for three-quarters of a century. In such a fragile and infertile place as the Keen, plants grow but slowly, and the traces of man's passage fade slowly. Traversing the slopes, I came across the remains of one of the concrete anchor points for a radar mast. There is something irresistible about wet, unset mortar, and beside the inscribed initials of the men who served in the RAF unit at the time was the name of the unit itself and the date – *3 TRU 1940* – picked out in fragments of soapy-green serpentine set into the concrete. Above that legend a skull and crossbones was inscribed. More chillingly still, beside that was a swastika frozen in time and set in concrete. It is said that Flight Lieutenant Len Pittendrigh, the commanding officer of the radar station, feared that some of the men in his command were at best German sympathisers or, at worst, saboteurs. The swastika and accompanying death's head suggests his fears may not have been entirely groundless. Three months after it was commissioned, the Keen of Hamar radar station was suddenly closed down without explanation.

At the height of the conflict some twenty thousand troops were stationed throughout Shetland, and the crumbling remains of their radar stations, pillboxes, gun emplacements and barracks provide archaeology of a different kind from that of their Viking forebears. If most of the legacies of the war are relatively benign, some are rather less so. A few years ago, two schoolboys out playing on the hills found some lumpy brown objects amidst the heather. After playing football with them for a little while, one of the boys noticed that they looked a little like the hand grenades he had seen in the movies. The boys caused mild consternation in the local police station when they produced one of the grenades (for that was indeed what they were) at the reception desk. The bomb-disposal squad were duly called up from the Scottish mainland, and a controlled explosion was carried out. Had the Germans invaded, small caches of arms like these in the hills would have allowed a guerrilla action to be fought – orchids are not the only hidden treasures in the countryside, it seems.

Below me, on the lower slopes of the Keen, a gradual accretion of soil had allowed a slightly more verdant community of plants to flourish. There were small patches of wiry, bluish grass, silvery areas of sea plantain and, somewhere in the midst of this jungle – by the Keen of Hamar's standards – a handful of heath fragrant orchids. Logic suggested that their lurid pink flowers ought to be easy to spot. The reality was that there were less than a dozen flowering plants somewhere in an area encompassing a couple of hectares, and I had only the vaguest recollection of where I had seen them in the past.

Meanwhile, I was easily distracted. Here and there amidst the shattered stones of the hillside were the delicate white flowers and hairy purple leaves of Edmonston's chickweed. Found nowhere else in the world but on this exposed, lonely hill in Unst, the discovery of this lovely plant in 1837 remains one of my favourite botanical tales.

Thomas Edmonston was the son of the island doctor on Unst, and the nephew of the laird of the island. Buness House, the family home, is an imposing grey edifice a mile down the coast from the Keen of Hamar, as strikingly different from all the surrounding properties today as it was back then. Where the island's crofters and fishermen lived in simple single-storey dwellings, the laird's house was a grand affair – a statement of wealth and power in this otherwise humble place. In those unhappier days the lairds' control in Shetland was absolute, and many of the islanders would have been little more than serfs, their daily activity tightly prescribed by the need to generate income for their less than benevolent landlords. Failure to do so would leave them without a roof over their heads and no means by which to feed their family – the laird owned the crofter's land, his house, and his fishing boat.

Young Thomas Edmonston, hailing from this privileged family, would have had time on his hands, a luxury that would not have necessarily been afforded to other local boys, who would be expected to contribute substantially to their households' productivity. It is easy to imagine that the nephew of the laird may have cut a rather lonely figure, one who had to find his own amusements in the austere surroundings of Unst. The Keen of Hamar would inevitably have drawn him away from the farmland that surrounded his home at Buness, the orange stone hillside that looms over the coastal community proving a magnet for a bored young boy.

What remains remarkable is that at the tender age of twelve, Thomas not only recognised that the small white flowering plant he found amidst the orchids on the hill was something different – especially bearing in mind that he would not have had the benefit of the many well-illustrated field guides we have nowadays – but also that he took matters into his own hands to bring his discovery to the attention of the eminent botanists of the day. He would have been supported in this by his father, the laird's brother Laurence Edmonston – also a naturalist and a pioneering conservationist who championed the preservation of the nascent great skua colony on the nearby Hermaness headland, the site that I was to visit shortly in search of lesser twayblades.

Nevertheless, in the face of scepticism from the botanical establishment at the temerity of his claims to have found a hitherto undescribed species, it was not until 1843 that Thomas formally announced the chickweed that was to bear his name in

The Phytologist. The paper he published, 'Notice of a new British Cerastium', began:

> Having for some years entertained the opinion that the plant, although generally referred to as *Cerastium latifolium*, was distinct from the plant called by that name in Britain, I have paid considerable attention to our *Cerastia*, and am disposed to conclude that my plant is truly distinct from the *C. latifolium* of Smith and Hooker.

Thomas was eighteen when the chickweed he had discovered six years previously was formally accepted as a new species to science. Within a year he had been elected, with the support of the pre-eminent botanist of the day, Sir William Hooker, to the position of professor of botany at the Andersonian University of Glasgow. The testimonial written by Hooker, then the director of the Royal Botanic Gardens at Kew, in support of his application shows the regard with which this precociously talented young botanist was now held, and commended Thomas's 'most uncommon zeal in the cause of Natural History'.

Buoyed by his appointment, Thomas gladly grasped the thrilling opportunity to follow closely in Charles Darwin's footsteps, accepting an offer to sail on HMS *Herald* as a naturalist on a government expedition to California, following in the wake of Darwin on HMS *Beagle* only ten years earlier. The two men corresponded prior to his departure and, upon arriving a year later in the Galápagos Islands, Thomas made a collection of as many plants and animals as he could, in part augmenting Darwin's existing research that would inform the pivotal *On the Origin of Species*. Hailing from Shetland, the young naturalist would have found the Galápagos archipelago made a powerful impression, and the parallels between the two island groups would have been striking, insofar as both had limited flora and fauna. But the strangeness and exotic nature of the Galápagos wildlife must have been intoxicating for one used to the austere surroundings of Unst.

Leaving Galápagos, the *Herald* returned to the South American coast and anchored during the evening of 23 January 1846 in Sua

Bay, off the coast of Peru. From the ship the officers were taken to the shore by boat. While Thomas was being carried from the boat to the beach, someone accidentally caught the hammer of a loaded gun in their trousers and discharged it. The ball passed through the arm of a nearby sailor, and struck Thomas on the temple. He died instantly.

Thomas Edmonston burned brightly and briefly, and it was the flower that bears his name that I found myself walking past. I felt a kinship with him – as a boy growing up in the rural south-west of England I had not shared my peers' dreams of being either a professional football player or a banker in the City. All I had wanted to be was a naturalist, one who travelled to distant lands and saw strange new things. I wondered what, had he not been tragically killed at just twenty years of age on a distant South American shore, Thomas Edmonston would have achieved in the world of science. As it was, the chickweed that bore his name was readily found on the Keen of Hamar, although the heath fragrant orchids were proving a rather trickier proposition.

I criss-crossed the dour north-easterly face of the hill in the general area in which I knew the orchids should be flowering. Here and there were the dried, desiccated stalks of spent early purple orchids, their flowers long gone to seed, their stems and seed capsules now blackened husks. From a distance, the pale pinkish-white flowers of heath spotted orchids looked superficially promising, but they flattered to deceive. I began to despair of finding heath fragrant orchids in Unst after all. The species had always been extraordinarily rare in Shetland, and had but a tenuous grasp as a member of the islands' flora. I had only been able to find a handful of flowering plants the last time I had looked for them. Perhaps they were all gone now?

Finally though, on the brink of giving up, I found myself almost treading on one that nestled by my feet in the short dense grass like a bright-pink jelly baby. From just a few feet away it would have been invisible, so well hidden was it in the surrounding vegetation. A careful search in the immediate vicinity yielded just two more individuals. My patience had been rewarded, but I could so easily have missed these heath fragrant orchids altogether.

The smell of bruised wild thyme hung heavily in the air while I examined them closely. Each flower glittered with a crystalline, sugary hue of acid, unblemished pink. Elongated curved spurs protruded from the back of each flower head with the bittersweet promise of a dentist's tools. There was nectar deep inside here, but what insect on the Keen could possibly extract it?

Heath fragrant orchids were first recorded in Britain in 1634 when Thomas Johnson published his *Mercurius Botanicus* (*Botanical Mercury*), in which he noted the '*Orchis palmata minor calcaribus oblongis*' or 'lesser palmate Orchis with oblong spurs'. When I had first started to explore the herb-rich chalk downlands of Kent as a student in the 1990s, I had seen what were then merely known as fragrant orchids aplenty – and had noted for myself the flowers' long spurs and sweet clove-like scent. In nearly four centuries nothing had changed.

But if there's one thing botanists appear to abhor, it is an unchanging status quo. Just as Thomas Edmonston had noticed his local chickweed seemed rather different from the more widespread *Cerastium latifolium*, now contemporary botanists turned their attention to fragrant orchids. What had seemed like three extremely similar-looking subspecies of one species was proven in the late 1990s to be three genetically distinctive species – chalk fragrant orchid, marsh fragrant orchid and heath fragrant orchid. Just to make matters that little bit more complicated, all three species were not only physically very similar, but were known to hybridise freely with one another. Evidently it was not just the marsh orchids that liked a bit of interspecies action.

I knew from my research that these Shetland fragrant orchids were said to be heath fragrants, but I really needed to satisfy myself that this was indeed the case. I felt I owed it to Thomas Edmonston's memory to make a bit of an effort on his home turf to get to grips with their subtleties. It was time to embrace my inner taxonomist – and to self-consciously unleash both my newly acquired hand lens and slide rule. The featureless landscape felt like my friend in this regard – after thirty years of being a birdwatcher and shouldering the mild scorn that went with wearing binoculars in public, I had developed a thick skin where putting myself up for ridicule was concerned. That said, I was acutely aware that measuring the individual florets of an orchid and examining the angles and shapes of an orchid's lip with a dinky little hand lens was, even by my standards, pretty nerdy stuff. It was reassuring to glance around and know with absolute certainty that there was not a soul within a radius of half a mile of me in any given direction. Lying flat on my belly, my face mere inches from that first orchid I'd almost squashed underfoot, I set about measuring and assessing with a vengeance.

What I discovered was – apart from the difficulties involved in taking the measurements of a wind-vibrating orchid with a shaky hand where millimetres were critical – reassuring. My orchid's florets were satisfyingly small, it had a barely lobed lip that was longer than it was broad, and that lip was sufficiently narrow. All in all, my plant could only be a heath fragrant orchid. Pleased with myself I straightened up … and then, just to be on the safe side, I repeated the exercise with both of the other flowers I'd found. All three measured up, I cross-checked my identification with the list of field characteristics in my field guide – and, pleasingly, everything tallied. In such a windswept location as the Keen of Hamar I was not particularly confident that I would be able to discern the perfume from which the plant took its name, so it was with little expectation that I cupped my hands around one of the candy-pink flower spikes and inhaled deeply. And there it was! I could smell a faint, cloyingly sweet, carnation-like scent. My heath fragrant orchids were indeed fragrant. Standing back upright and brushing serpentine grit from my knees, I was pleased with myself – but a little disconcerted to notice that the sky was now suffused with grey cloud and the temperature was noticeably cooler. It was time to hurry further north to the very tip of the British Isles, to the massif that was Hermaness.

My return to the car took me back across the face of the hill. A rusting wire fence separated me from a field in which a small herd of bullocks watched me with impassive, rheumy eyes. The grass in their field was cropped short – no lush pasture, this. A few decades ago their field had been identical to the botanically rich moonscape on which I had spent the past couple of hours hunting for and photographing orchids. But for a twist of fate, the entire hillside could have been covered with grass – and where there was pasture, there could be no chickweeds or orchids.

After the Second World War, successive British governments strove to make the country more self-sufficient in food production. In the post-war years grants became widely available to assist the intensification of agriculture, so land that was of marginal productivity was 'improved' by the subsidised application of heavy doses of fertiliser and lime. Large swathes of Shetland were transformed for ever, changed from agriculturally unproductive but biologically rich habitat into monocultures of pasture – pasture that, as it was growing on soil that had for millennia been relatively infertile, required regular top-ups of yet more lime and fertiliser to keep it growing with any sort of vigour.

Half of the hillside here at the Keen of Hamar was thus improved. Had the crofter who owned the other half of the hillside that is the nature reserve today been similarly inclined, the entire hillside would now be sterile pasture for disinterested bullocks; the serpentine debris would have been clad with a thin skin of grass, and with it would have been lost the entire world population of Edmonston's chickweed and a host of other scarce and rare species, orchids included. I drove away towards Hermaness reflecting upon how lucky we are that at least some of the Keen of Hamar remains, and just how fragile and easily damaged or entirely lost such habitats can be. My journey to Norfolk to see the beleaguered fen orchids at Sutton Fen had demonstrated all too clearly how, even in these more environmentally conscious days, the competing interests of agriculture and conservation remain uncomfortably at odds with one another.

My final target for the day was one of Britain's most inconspicuous orchids. Lesser twayblades are almost laughably feeble – they are unassuming orchids with two basic leaves at the base of their flowering stem, these being the 'twayblades'. Growing just a few centimetres tall, their stem is grass-thin, and their flowers are small and a dull, reddish green. Examined closely, those individual flowers resemble a tiny, elfin figure with arms and legs, an enticing blend, for me, of counter-intuitively pleasing drabness allied with charming anthropomorphism. What they are not is easily found. In addition to being highly inconspicuous, they favour wet moorlands or peat bogs – difficult places for the orchid hunter to access at the best of times – and even there they have the unhelpful habit of growing out of sight, tucked snugly underneath mature heather plants.

I had found lesser twayblades on Hermaness before, and the site had one significant advantage in its favour for me – there was a carefully maintained boardwalk that allowed one to walk easily out into the midst of the boggy mires that made up the body of the moor. This, insofar as any orchid hunting was easy, should have been relatively straightforward.

This presupposed that the great skuas would leave me alone to search unhindered for the lesser twayblades. As guardians go, great skuas leave a lot to be desired for the would-be orchid hunter. Known in Shetland as bonxies (a name derived from the old Norn language, a legacy of the Vikings that persisted in the islands until the late seventeenth century, meaning 'a stout and aggressive fellow'), they are ferocious and determined in the defence of their breeding territories. Woe betide anyone who strays too near to a bonxie nest; the adult birds will readily employ considerable force to drive away the interloper, and have been known to draw blood from human trespassers. Shetland is home to over half the world's breeding population of great skuas, and many of them consider Hermaness their exclusive domain.

I left the car parked beside the white-painted shore station that once housed the Muckle Flugga lighthouse keepers' families and supplies. The towering Hermaness headland juts out from the body of Unst itself, separated from the adjacent Saxa Vord headland by a narrow, deep voe – the Shetland equivalent of a sea fjord. The shore station nestles at the side of this sheltered voe in the flanks of Hermaness, overlooked by the remains of the Cold War radar station up on the heights of Saxa Vord, a jumble of concrete bunkers, blockhouses and gun emplacements. This was once NATO's eyes and ears in the North Atlantic: the radar swept the seas on the very edge of Europe while Russian-speaking listeners eavesdropped on the Soviet Union's radio communications. At the height of the Cold War, an article in the *Daily Express* began with the heart-felt sentiment: 'If God had not made the island of Unst, then the MOD would have had to invent it' – recognition that not only were the military men and women stationed on Unst doing sterling work, protecting us all from the Communist threat, but that God was on our side, too.

As I walked up the steep footpath that carried me over the brow of this looming headland and into the heart of the moors beyond, I found myself surrounded by great skuas. These pugnacious broad-chested birds, as large as a modest goose, stood on the heather with mottled brown wings stretched up above them to their full extent, barking an aggressive warning at me with all the swagger and well-founded confidence of a pitbull terrier.

Agg-agg-agg-agg-agg!

While I eyed them warily, a sheep careered across the path ahead of me, a bonxie swooping after it, striking the ewe on her back with both stout hooked beak and heavily taloned feet. The ewe made heavy work of running through the deep heather, her eyes rolling madly. The airborne skua swung around for another pass at her, white flashes on its broad wings like a parody of RAF roundels.

Agg-agg-agg-agg-agg!

More bonxies took up the refrain across the moor as the deranged sheep laboured her way out of the breeding colony and I hastened my way uphill. Below me the Muckle Flugga lighthouse clung tenaciously to the top of the rock that gave it its name, a leaden sea roiling around the base of it, scythed by the passage of innu-merable snowy-white gannets making their way to and from their nests on the vertiginous Hermaness cliffs. The wind was picking up and, with it, seabird activity – puffins were making heavy weather of riding the rollercoaster updrafts at the clifftops, while fulmars hung mid-air with all the balance and poise of a carnival's waltzer operator.

What had already been a cold excuse for a summer day was now deteriorating rapidly as time wore on, and intermittent drizzle gave way to steady face-stinging rain. A dark, bruised sky stretching to the far horizon held little promise of the weather improving.

With an agitated chorus of watchful skuas and these uncomfortable conditions, I did not want to stay out here on the moor for too long – the weather can break down rapidly in Shetland, and it is a foolish man who takes bad weather lightly in this remotest of British outposts. The highest wind speed ever recorded in Britain was logged here in 1992, a frankly terrifying gust of 173 mph; while on an oil rig a few miles north-east of the island a gust of 194 mph was reported that same night. It was a sobering thought to recall that two birdwatchers lost their lives that night on Hermaness when the hut they were staying in blew over the cliffs.

That was in midwinter; such extreme weather was highly unlikely in midsummer, but barely a year goes by in the islands without the coastguard helicopter having to rescue a lost or injured walker in inclement summer conditions. At the very least, Hermaness was becoming an uncomfortable place upon which to linger. Home, a hot bath and a chance to look at the day's orchid photos were calling. This all hinged on getting lucky with a twayblade … I turned back from the cliffs and concentrated my search on the fractionally more sheltered lea of the headland. I impatiently lifted heather at the side of the path in order to peer underneath it – and eventually found a dainty pair of lime-green leaves that looked familiar. But no flower. Could this be a 'blind', non-flowering lesser twayblade? It certainly looked good. I really needed a flower to be sure and, if this was a twayblade, there should be others nearby – they usually occur in small colonies and are rarely found alone.

More heather lifted and, finally, success. There, amidst the wet, gritty black peat and beneath a gnarled heather branch was another pair of those distinctive sharply oval green leaves and above them an impossibly delicate short, slender flower stalk. Each individual flower was a minute pale burgundy homunculus, the petals textured on close examination like the pores of skin under a microscope. Did an orchid ever pick such an uncompromising, unpromising environment in which to flower than this sea-spray-lashed dome of rock and bog?

As water ran down the back of my neck and bonxies scudded watchfully low overhead, I huddled over this precious plant, all discomfort temporarily forgotten. Somewhere nearby, beyond the swirling grey curtains of rain, was the Muckle Flugga lighthouse that had brought Robert Louis Stevenson to Unst all those years ago. Dubbed the impossible lighthouse at the time, it was regarded as unbuildable by other engineers, so inhospitable was the terrain and so treacherous the sea around it. Yet the Stevensons had built it. I, meanwhile, had managed to find an orchid no taller than my little finger, as slender as the stem of a garden daisy, in the middle of a 965-hectare blanket-bog nature reserve. I was cold and wet – and couldn't have felt happier about my own modest achievement if I'd tried. I had a feeling Unst's unsung botanist hero Thomas Edmonston would have been pleased for me as I began the long walk back to the shore base and the journey home.

11

Reptiles and old goats on the Royal
St George's

A return to the Garden of England marked the next stage in my travels and with it a sense that my quest was entering a new phase. My botanising on home turf in Shetland had felt like a chance to catch my breath after the dizzying maelstrom that had been the spring – it had seemed, for a while, as if new orchids were bursting into flower faster than I could possibly hope to see them. Heading back to Kent, the scene of so much of that frantic, wonderful activity, meant my orchid hunt was now in more peaceful territory. For the next few weeks, until the enigmatic *Epipactis* helleborines began to flower, some of the pressure had, at last, abated for a while.

I headed east through the Kent countryside towards Sandwich with a pleasing lack of urgency. My target today was an easy one – a large and showy orchid that grew in tremendous profusion in this area. Known only to grow in Kent in the nineteenth century, during the following century the fortunes of lizard orchid, *Himantoglossum hircinum*, waxed and waned in England. From a point in 1900 when it was feared in danger of imminent extinction as a British orchid, it spread, rapidly, from Kent in the early decades of the twentieth century as far west as Devon and north to Yorkshire, with approximately thirty individual populations known to botanists across England by 1930. Writing in June 1927, the botanist Eleanor Vachell recalled in her diaries, 'a visit was paid to the golf links [near Burnham, Somerset]. Amongst plants noted were … *Himantoglossum hircinum*.'[1]

Yet ten years later that had all changed, and the population had contracted once more to a third of the coverage it had enjoyed at its peak, with the stronghold once again being in the south-east of England and, in particular, in Kent. This population remained largely stable until the mid-1990s, at which point the lizards began scuttling outwards once more, with pioneer colonies found again as far west as Somerset.

Our first record of lizard orchids dates back to 1634, when Thomas Johnson noted *Orchis saurodes* in Kent 'nigh the highway between Crayford and Dartford' in his *Mercurius Botanicus*. Shortly afterwards, in 1641, this population was recorded as lost when the road in question was widened – surely one of the first recorded instances of road improvement to the detriment of rare wildlife. It is hard to imagine that orchids as distinctive in both appearance and stature as these would have been overlooked in the intervening years until the early twentieth century – it appears that the Dartford plants, perhaps colonists from France, where they are relatively commonplace, bided their time for a few centuries before finally finding their feet and advancing into pastures new.

Their spread would have undoubtedly been constrained by the attentions of gardeners or those who sought to profit from the passion, growing at the time, for planting wild orchids in private gardens. Peter Collinson, an eighteenth-century Quaker, and his son

Michael were the proud possessors of an 'Orchis bed' in the garden of the family house at Mill Hill – populated with plants taken from the wild, their botanic garden boasted at least fifteen British orchid species, including some that we now consider extremely rare. Their notes in their copy of John Blackstone's *Harefield Plants* of 1737 speak volumes both of the contemporary gentleman gardeners' approach to removing orchids from the wild and, surely, their role in accelerating the decline of some our native orchids. For military orchid, Michael Collinson notes, 'Found near the great Beech-trees, so remarkable a landmark in Kent, as you go to Sevenoaks: this in 1758, and it flowered finely in my garden at Mill Hill, in 1760.'

Other species are recorded as flowering 'annually in our Orchis bed' – but inevitably some, removed from their specific habitats and mycorrhizal fungal partners, flowered once or twice, or not at all. Collinson was nothing if not persistent in his removal of orchids from the wild for, when they failed, he would try time and again with further plants; he bemoans his lack of success with transplanting bee orchids.

Michael Collinson's recollections of lizard orchids show that the species was both extremely localised in its occurrence and highly sought after by gardeners – small wonder the species took such a long time to spread beyond the bounds of the Dartford area:

> The Tragorchis [lizard orchid] is a most noble plant, but it is a very rare one. I never saw it but once, and that was a little beyond Dartford, on the road to Greenstreet Green, very sparingly. I removed a large sod of them to Mill Hill in 1759, which consisted of three distinct bulbs, and which I carefully separated, but to my great mortification not one of them ever appeared.
>
> My father formerly removed into his garden at Peckham this curious plant, and it flowered there with him for several years.

Ironically, given father and son's predilection for digging up orchids of all kinds for their garden, Michael Collinson recalls one occasion when he found several 'Tragorchis' in an old chalk pit near Dartford Heath:

There had been a destroyer in the same pit a little before me, who had (by the holes in the turf) carried away with him in full flower near seventy roots, most of which would undoubtedly perish, and thus this species of Orchis rare to be met with here for the future.

Such rapacious removal of orchids from the countryside was not universally regarded as acceptable by the Collinsons' contemporaries. One of these, Lewis Weston Dillwyn, recalled:

July 4th, 1757. Went to the Duke of Portland's, at Bulstrode; stayed to the 11th. In returning we found the great Fly Orchis on the declivity of a chalk-pit in Esquire Cook's park, in the parish of Harefield, Middlesex; but there is one Miles, a parson, of Cowley, near Uxbridge, who is Orchis-mad, and takes all up, and leaves none to seed, so extirpates all wherever he comes, which is cruel, and deserves chastisement.

Chastisement would not have been forthcoming for many of those who stole orchids from the wild at the time. Perhaps it was fitting that Peter Collinson himself should have been the victim of an 'Orchis-mad' plant thief – an entry in the *Daily Advertiser* on 4 July 1768 records the theft of a large quantity of 'hardy Orchises' from Collinson's garden. Peter Collinson died shortly afterwards on 11 August 1768 – perhaps the trauma of losing his beloved orchids proved too much for him bear.

That Eleanor Vachell found lizard orchids on a golf course on the Somerset coast in the early twentieth century was, perhaps, not entirely surprising – the species appears to like the open, grassy habitat afforded not only by old chalk pits, but also managed coastal golf courses. Their English stronghold is in just such surroundings, on the golf courses that flank the small town of Sandwich. I planned to see my lizard orchids at one of their most illustrious stations on British soil, in the august surroundings of the Royal St George's golf course, home – in addition to a burgeoning population of lizard orchids – to the Open Championship on no fewer than fourteen occasions. The Royal St George's Golf Club boasts that visitors are greeted with a warm, friendly welcome, and I sincerely hoped that this would extend to casual orchid hunters as well as keen golfers.

My last visit to Sandwich Bay had been over twenty years previously, on an unforgiving November day in 1993 when an easterly wind scythed off the sea and scoured the flat fields that surround the golf courses and the nearby Sandwich Bay Bird Observatory. I was not looking for orchids: the purpose of my visit had been an attempt to see an isabelline shrike, a rare vagrant bird blown to Britain on those easterly winds. The young shrike, migrating for the first time, should have been in the Middle East or sub-Saharan Africa rather than haunting the wire fences that divided the fertile agricultural land around Sandwich. By the time I left that afternoon I, too, wished I was anywhere but Sandwich Bay.

The shrike proved an elusive quarry, vanishing for long periods of time while it hunted small rodents in the depths of interminable drainage ditches. I wandered for hours through this monotonous landscape, trudging aimlessly along field boundaries hoping to stumble across the wary bird. When night began to fall as hard and fast as the rain that persisted all afternoon, I was glad of a pair of headlights that bounced their slow and erratic way towards me across a grassy field, and a friendly Kentish voice from the open window of an elderly blue Transit van that asked, 'All right, mush? You want a lift?'

Having explained that my car was parked at the bird observatory I was told, 'Jump in the back, mush. Don't stick your fingers in the ferret boxes – they'll bite you for sure.'

I did as I was bid, and clambered in the back door of the old van. Dimly illuminated by a small light on the van's plywood bulkhead, the inside was filled with the paraphernalia of a day's furtive country sport – a strong, musty aroma and ceaseless scuffling announced the presence of the promised ferrets, travelling in cages stowed beneath a crude wooden bench that ran along one side of the van. Coils of wire and finished snares gleamed above them, hanging from wooden pegs jammed roughly into the vehicle's flanks. Dead ducks and rabbits pendulumed on short lengths of orange baler twine from the ceiling as the vehicle began to move. I hung grimly on to the bench as we lurched across the bumpy field, keeping my fingers well away from the ferrets. It was only when the van braked hard to stop at a gateway that its final secret was revealed – a heavy white mass shifted across the floor from beneath the bench opposite me, sliding awkwardly out into the open. My companions had crowned their day's poaching by shooting a swan.

I had high hopes that my return to Sandwich Bay would be altogether less marred. The walk from the bird observatory onto the Royal St George's golf course is a short one, crossing the private road that serves the Sandwich Bay community and almost immediately placing one within the boundaries of the links. A grassy pathway quickly leads onto the golf course itself – signs are stationed regularly warning non-golfers not to stray from the footpath. In the event, I had no need to wander, as I soon began finding lizard orchids standing proudly above the surrounding long grass along the path's edges. These were orchids like no other I would see this year – compared to their peers they were colossi, many approaching half a metre in height, their thick stems swathed with pointed leaves as patinated as bronze sword tips thrusting upwards from some ancient burial.

From a distance their flower spikes appeared hairy, a diffuse mass of straggling pale amethyst tendrils. At closer quarters the flowers resolved themselves into the faintly reptilian forms that lend the plant its English name. Each flower appears like the hindquarters of a lizard clambering in towards the stem, the long, twisting central lobe of the flower's labellum forming the lizard's mauve tail, and the shorter side lobes giving the impression of the animal's hind legs. Each sinuous lizard tail diffuses into snow white where the tail meets the legs – a brilliance offset by the inclusion of a number of brilliant cerise tufted papillae as spiky as miniature thistle leaves. The lizard's hindquarters vanished inside the large hood formed by each flower's pale jade-green sepals, lined inside with a fine tracery of dark aubergine.

I thought these flowers sinuously gorgeous, but Belgian poet Maurice Maeterlinck perceived something darker and altogether more sinister about them. His description in *The Intelligence of Flowers*, published in 1907, is a Gothic marvel:

It is symmetrically adorned with vicious three-cornered flowers
of a greenish-white stippled with pale violet. The lowest
petal, decorated at its source with bronzed caruncles, with
Merovingian moustaches, and with ominous lilac buboes,
extends endlessly, crazily, improbably, in the shape of a twirled
ribbon, of the colour of a drowned person whose corpse has
been in a river for a month.[2]

These flowers were exquisite, but simultaneously quite repul-
sive – in the warm morning air their scent hung, cloyingly, around
them. It was this ripe perfume rather than any passing resemblance
to a lizard that informed the French name for *Himantoglossum
hircinum*. *Orchis bouc*, or billy-goat orchid, is a name that accur-
ately describes the flowers' odour – a ripe, rich, tangy aroma that
was, after a while, impossible to shift from my nostrils. The smell
would linger in my memory all day long, reminding me of them
long after I had left the orchids.

An association with goats – and hence, presumably, the Greek
half-goat half-man fertility god Pan – doubtless influenced John
Gerard and, before him, Dioscorides. Of all the orchids detailed
in his *Herball*, Gerard considered the lizard orchid to be the most
effective aphrodisiac of all. He helpfully informed his readers that,
'the bulbs or stones are not to be taken indifferently, but the harder
and fuller, and that which containeth most quantitie of juice: for
that which is wrinkled is less profitable...'

Lying on the short grass of the path, I tried in vain to shift the
goaty scent by inhaling deeply of another flowering plant that vied
with the orchids' plenitude in this corner of the golf course – clove-
scented broomrape is one of those plants that does exactly what its
name suggests, producing pink and white hairy flowers on a straw-
yellow stem smelling sweetly of spicy cloves.

'Is that an orchid?' asked a passing woman, out for a walk with
her husband and boisterous young granddaughter. I looked up
from my prone position, slightly embarrassed to have been caught
sniffing so lustily at a flower. Realising she meant the broomrapes
rather than the surrounding lizard orchids, I explained that the
broomrape, while looking rather like an orchid flower spike, was

in fact a very different plant altogether – each broomrape species is a specialist parasite, drawing nutrients from the roots of particular host plants. I then showed them the nearby lizard orchids, much to the delight of the young girl, who promptly picked one to give to her grandfather. He had the grace to look rather sheepish as he took the gift, and began to explain to his granddaughter that one should not pick wildflowers, and especially not rare orchids like this one.

This reluctance to pick flowers, especially those of orchids in general and lizard orchids in particular, is one that surfaces time and again in botanical literature – though it is a sentiment sometimes only grudgingly allowed or, on some occasions, wilfully ignored. On 27 May 1926 Eleanor Vachell's diary recalls stopping with botanical companions at Goodwood in Sussex to see a lizard orchid, the only one of its kind at that particular location. She describes the event in the third person:

> There was one plant only, a special treasure, and no one was to touch it. E.V.'s excitement can hardly be described when it was found a rabbit had bitten off the flower-head and had laid it at her feet, a votive offering to be added to her collection![3]

Vachell's glee at this serendipitous rabbit intervention is unconcealed. Jocelyn Brooke meanwhile, lifelong orchidophile and Kent native, recounted in his semi-autobiographical *The Orchid Trilogy* an encounter with lizard orchids in wartime Italy that needed no helpful third-party interference. Once again we are reminded of just how rare this orchid was in Britain at the time, as Brooke describes fruitless years of searching the Kent downs for this 'most celebrated of English rarities'. One day, while orchid hunting in the Tuscan countryside, the narrator finds a patch of lizard orchids. He is unable to resist the temptation to pluck them, though he knows it to be wrong:

> To pick a Lizard Orchid – the action had about it something unholy, something rather blasphemous ... I picked several more; examining with a wondering delight the long slender

lips, two inches long, cleft at the tip like serpents' tongues, unfurling themselves in delicate spirals from the opening buds.[4]

Listening to the grandfather scolding his granddaughter, I was uncomfortably reminded of the one occasion I had picked an orchid, the early purple orchid I found as a young boy in Somerset in the early 1980s. I was not admonished for this minor transgression at the time, though I felt guilty about it some years later, but the seed that orchid sowed within me had lasted a lifetime and contributed, I was sure, to my broader interest in natural history.

'Your granddad's right – we really shouldn't pick them,' I said to the girl. 'But really, just this one flower – it doesn't really matter. And it's lovely, isn't it?'

Overcome suddenly with shyness, she hid behind his legs to peep mutely at me. We said our goodbyes and they walked away towards the coast, the grandfather self-consciously carrying the orchid stem before him. I wondered whether he would discreetly dispose of it before he earned the censure of someone less constrained than me by personal history. Judging by his granddaughter's close attention, I fancied he would be taking it home with him to suffuse the house with a reproachful reek of billy goat.

I wandered away from the main path, following the drifts of orchids through the long grass. Each flower promised to be better than the last so, camera and tripod in hand, I lost track of just how far I had strayed. I was orchid-blind once more.

'Oi! What do you think you're doing?'

The shout came from uncomfortably nearby. At once I was transported back to childhood and the innumerable occasions on which I had been caught by zealous landowners trespassing through their fields and spinneys looking for birds, butterflies and wildflowers. A wave of overwhelming guilt washed over me; I knew I was somewhere I ought not to be, and had absolutely no reasonable excuse to be there, although I was doing no harm. Two elderly male golfers were on a nearby green, one of whom was visibly agitated to have noticed me meandering through the rough.

'You can't walk here, you know! This is private property!'

I tried to apologise, telling him I had simply lost track of my whereabouts while looking for orchids on the edge of the golf course – and I was, if anything, less than fifty yards from the public footpath. If I had hoped that explaining this inoffensive activity and the very minor nature of my transgression might mollify him, I was to be sorely disappointed. His indignant, quivering face grew an angrier, bantam-wattle red.

'Well, you can't look for flowers here! This isn't a bloody nature reserve, you know. Bloody tree huggers…'

There was no reasoning with this blind fury – I turned my back on him and began to retrace my steps.

'Don't you walk away from me, you little sod!'

His strained voice quickly faded behind me. It sounded as if he was sorry to see me go – while we had both been enjoying our respective morning activities, I had a feeling that, far from disrupting his golf, I had obliquely enhanced the experience. This was a man who enjoyed having something to complain about and, unwittingly, my enjoyment of the lizard orchids on the Royal St George's had provided him with just that. Back on the side of the path, where the sweet, spicy scent of broomrape mingled cloyingly with the pervasive orchid tang, I paused once more to lose myself in an entanglement of lizard orchids. As many as thirty thousand are estimated to grow in the area – they even rise, unbidden, from the front lawns of the scatter of houses along nearby King's Avenue. Once relentlessly dug up by eighteenth-century gardeners keen to augment their botanic gardens, here at Sandwich Bay they have colonised gardens for themselves.

If lizard orchids were rare in Britain until comparatively recently, red helleborine appears to have always been, at best, very scarce and, in recent times, vanishingly rare. Found only in a handful of closely guarded woodlands in Britain, the name is a misnomer, as the flowers are a delicate rose pink. Confined to ancient beech forest, these orchids do not produce nectar and instead appear to rely on attracting bees to pollinate them by their structural resemblance to certain nectar-rich blue *Campanula* flowers – a deception that, as bees' eyes are not sensitive to the red end of the colour spectrum, works well where the right species of bees are present and do not realise they are visiting the wrong-coloured flower.

Unfortunately, it appears as if bees of the correct species, and hence size and shape, are largely absent from Britain, meaning our red helleborines tend not to be successfully fertilised, their flowers falling off complete with their ovaries as the flowering season concludes. For a family of plants so intimately associated with sexual potency, virility and love, it seems this particular orchid is pathetically poor at reproducing itself, at least in Britain.

First reported here in 1797 at Hampton Common in Gloucestershire, red helleborine is at the very cusp of its global range at its few stations in southern England. It is found widely throughout mainland Europe and further east still, as far away as Iran. They may, once, have been found in suitable habitat throughout the south of England, but since the time of their first noted discovery, they have only been seen sparingly, mostly in the Cotswolds and Chilterns, but also in the ancient beech hangers of north Hampshire. Genetic analysis of the three extant British populations in Buckinghamshire, Gloucestershire and Hampshire shows them to be unrelated to one another – as such, they probably represent the remaining fragments of three separate migrations from mainland Europe. If some of our orchids are bold pioneers, colonising pastures new in Britain, red helleborines hang on precariously, teetering ever closer to the brink of extinction as a British native species.

If their pollination mechanism were not fussy enough, they are also unhelpfully intolerant of anything but precisely the correct environment in which to grow. They appear to be happiest in dappled shade with only a few hours of direct sunlight, usually in clearings or other open areas. It seems likely that they have evolved to be opportunistic, flowering where conditions have recently become favourable for them – perhaps in the aftermath of a fallen tree opening a window in the woodland canopy, or in the wake of the grazing and rooting action of wild boars. These animals were formerly a British native species and only recently become extant in our countryside once more, though always commonplace on the Continent. The orchids' opportunism seems supported by their longevity and feeding habits, as they are known to persist underground for years on end before suddenly flowering once again. For example, a plant that flowered, magnificently, in Hampshire in 2003 did so after an absence at the site spanning seventeen years. Red helleborines derive much of their nutritional requirement from mycorrhizal fungi in the soil so, while they lie dormant underground, apparently waiting for conditions on the surface to suit the production of flowers, they continue to be sustained in large part by the fungi and, hence, the trees all around them.

While we have, for centuries, lacked wild boar in our woodlands, the opening up of woodlands by accidental tree-fall or the activity of man has continued regardless. But it seems that the unavailability of a suitable pollinator and perhaps a limited gene pool play a large part in impeding the red helleborines' success as a British orchid – in a ten-year period in the Chilterns just one mature seed capsule was recorded. Following hand-pollination efforts by conservationists, the situation improved dramatically, with almost half of those flowers going on to produce seedpods.

Unfortunately, analysis of seeds from the Chilterns revealed that approximately 20 per cent of their seed was actually viable – while the scientists at Kew, able now to create a production line of lady's slipper orchid seedlings, have not been able to replicate that success with red helleborines. Conservation for this graceful but fatally choosy orchid seems for now to be limited to cherishing and protecting those few that cling on in southern England – though even this is fraught with uncertainties. In years with moist and warm springs and early summers, slugs and snails flourish in woodlands, and are extremely partial to succulent red helleborines. Conservationists have agonised about how to keep them at bay. Slug pellets, while an obvious solution, are not without their detractors. Debate rages about how they might change the soil chemistry or adversely affect the subterranean mycorrhizal fungi upon which the orchids rely so heavily.

While I had already speculatively looked for red helleborines at their former Hampshire site, I had assumed that I would see my helleborines this year at their secluded Gloucestershire home. The news in the days preceding this visit was not at all encouraging, as the weather had been both damp and warm; this was a good year for slugs and snails, and that meant a bad year for red helleborines. The latest reports I was hearing on the orchid grapevine were not at all encouraging – the few plants that looked as though they might form flowers were already suffering heavily from slug damage. It was entirely possible that no red helleborines would flower at all in England this year. I had assumed, perhaps blithely, that ghost orchid would be the trickiest orchid to track down, but maybe it would be another shy woodland orchid altogether that undid my quest.

When I learned that, against all the odds, one helleborine was coming into bloom in Gloucestershire, I knew I could not afford to wait. I needed to see this flower at the earliest opportunity. One wandering, hungry slug could undo everything. I arranged to meet Tim Jenkins, a National Trust ranger who cared for the sole known Gloucestershire population, early one morning at the end of a long, dead-end lane deep in the countryside near Stroud. Such is the secrecy that surrounds this small, vulnerable population of orchids that I was forbidden to reveal the wood's name. I had, however, heard of this place – amongst British orchidophiles it has an almost mythical status for the level of security that has been set in place to protect the precious plants.

The small corner of woodland in which they cling on has been caged, surrounded on all sides by a high mesh security fence, with access possible only through a locked gateway. I had heard a story of one orchid fanatic who had scaled the fence for a closer look at the helleborines – a story I had not fully appreciated until, following Tim up the steep track that led to the enclosure, I actually saw the fence in question. It was well over six feet high, so would take a particularly determined botanist to consider tackling it. Tim explained that it was as much to keep deer at bay as it was humans, though he ruefully warned me that I would need to follow his footsteps precisely.

'There's only one plant coming into flower, but there are a few more, smaller plants in the area. Step exactly where I do and you won't crush any of them.'

I did as I was told, straining to catch my first glimpse of a British example of a red helleborine. I had seen them in France and Germany where, if not exactly common, it was certainly not the hallowed orchid on the brink of extinction that it was here in this dark English wood. While Tim bemoaned the activities of the local slugs and snails, it struck me that the fence, while keeping browsing deer and clumsy humans at arms' length from the orchids, could do nothing to keep molluscs at bay. Meanwhile, suddenly, there it was – a small, tremulous flash of pink in the surrounding riot of green undergrowth. The orchid was just coming into flower; the pink was visible, though the flowers themselves had not yet opened fully. I would need to return in the coming days to gaze, from outside the protective cage, up at the mature flowers.

Tim stood like a protective parent alongside me while I carefully took some photos of this rare and critically endangered British orchid – I did not dare use my tripod for fear of inadvertently damaging some small, unseen seedling in the surrounding undergrowth, so simply held the camera at arm's length beside the flower spike and hoped for the best. In that moment I realised that capturing pleasing, beautiful images of this – or, for that matter any – orchid was not what my quest was about; it was seeing and appreciating the plants themselves, and understanding the efforts that went into protecting them, that mattered. My approach to my orchid summer was evolving as surely as the plants themselves.

12

Highland fling

When I made the decision to move to Shetland it was not a decision driven by orchids. Scientists have a name for the compulsion to migrate, *Zugunruhe*, a compound of the German *Zug* or move, and *unruhe* or restlessness. Birds preparing for migration are visibly agitated, their behaviour modified by their overwhelming need to move on to someplace other, someplace better. My *Zugunruhe* was primarily borne of those transient birds themselves – Shetland is without equal in Britain as a place to witness bird migration. While other aspects of the islands' ecology were very much in my mind at the time – how could they be otherwise, with abundant opportunities to watch marine mammals, and some of the country's finest breeding seabird colonies present here – seeing orchids was not high on my agenda when I arrived.

Time is said to be a healer, but I found it is also a teacher, if one is prepared to learn. The first summer I spent in my new home revealed thousands of heath spotted orchids growing in the grass and maritime heath all around the house, and I could not fail to see the rich purple phallic spikes of northern marsh orchids on roadside verges and in boggy former hay meadows. It took a little longer to hunt down Shetland's remaining orchid flora, years in which I discovered more about the other flowering plants the islands had to offer. By the time I had lived in Shetland for a decade, I had seen all but one of the orchids recorded in the islands. That last species, the small white orchid, has subsequently come to be imbued for me with qualities and emotions quite out of proportion to the plant itself. It is after all, as the name suggests, rather underwhelming, being both small and white.

Small white orchid was first recorded in Shetland on the island of Bressay around 1845. The date and the precise location are vague, and the plant itself more enigmatic still, for it has not been seen subsequently in the archipelago. This seems surprising, as small white orchids are found throughout Scotland, remain in small numbers on neighbouring Orkney and, more tellingly, are found even further north in Faroe, Iceland and Norway. Logic alone told me that small white orchid ought to be found somewhere in Shetland, overlooked in a remote grassy meadow somewhere, spared the reseeding of the ground by subsidised crofters and the overgrazing by subsidised sheep during the worst excesses of the Common Agricultural Policy.

Yet, try as I might, I have never found one. It has not been through lack of effort, for every summer I spend time searching, hoping that one day I may stumble upon a flowering plant. My search has certainly not been without its pleasures, as I've found new colonies of small adder's-tongue hiding in the short turf, a benign and tiny snake in the grass of a fern. I have discovered autumn and field gentians thrusting mauve flowers skywards like the cones of missiles emerging from their silos, and I have marvelled at the pearly, veined flowers of grass-of-Parnassus. But I have never found a small white orchid in Shetland. As long as I remain in the islands my annual search will continue, but for the purposes of my orchid quest this year I needed to search for them in more certain circumstances on the British mainland. Peter Stronach, an ecologist friend living in the Scottish Highlands, had promised me a private field 'thick with small whites' – a truly mouthwatering prospect.

Shetland could, however, be relied upon to furnish me with one further species of new orchid. Conveniently, I would be able to stop for this latest addition to the summer's tally on my way to Sumburgh airport to catch the small plane that would take me to Inverness, my gateway to the Highlands. The site in question lay only a mile as the crow flies from the main road that forms the spine of mainland Shetland.

Catfirth is, at first glance, an unremarkable area of land sloping gently down to the sea. It certainly had not figured prominently as a site of botanical interest until a routine survey was undertaken by the local Biological Records Centre staff in 2015 in response to a planning application to build a handful of new houses on the land. The surveyor in question, Rory Tallack, had long hoped to find a bog orchid in Shetland, and what he found at Catfirth was not one bog orchid, but several hundred, growing in the vicinity of the boggy flushes and seeps that threaded the land and drained groundwater slowly to the shore. Previously bog orchid was known in Shetland from just a handful of sites, numbering a few dozen plants in all. Catfirth was not only now the best site in Shetland for the species, but it was also notable in a British context. In the New Forest of Hampshire only two hundred flower spikes appear at the very largest two or three colonies in a good year for the species.

I visited Catfirth shortly after Rory had discovered the orchids there – time limits had constrained his initial survey and he had been compelled to stop counting when he reached the low hundreds. Blessed with a little more time and knowing where in the large site to begin searching, I found approximately eight hundred flowering plants – and knew I had certainly missed many more. Bog orchids are easily overlooked – they are tiny, the smallest of all our native orchids, usually measuring a mere five centimetres tall. The flower stem is as slender as a stalk of grass, and the flower itself is the very antithesis of our preconceived notions of orchid blooms. With minute, jade-green flowers that verge on the translucent, this is no brash hothouse blossom – bog orchids are the shy *ingénues* of the British orchid flora.

Unsurprisingly, they are notoriously hard to find. Orchid field guides and textbooks are peppered with words of discouragement for the orchid hunter – bog orchids are elusive, tantalising and very difficult. They are seen sporadically, erratically, and are thought to be uncommon or even rare. 'Inconspicuous' is an often-used description, as is 'daunting'. Simon Harrap, author of the orchid hunter's bible *Orchids of Britain and Ireland*, concluded, 'All in all, it is best not to look for it until you are an experienced orchid hunter.'

This was a sentiment that Sally Huband, a local naturalist, could sympathise with. She had been looking for bog orchids in Shetland without success for some time, and had asked if I could show her some. We met at Catfirth and, with her young children Hector and Teal armed with magnifying glasses and eager to find some tiny green orchids, we walked out onto the wet flushes, where I hoped the orchids would by now be in flower.

The planned houses that had sparked the initial discovery of these orchids had still not been built. I wondered if this was in response to the orchids' presence – they were front-page news in the local newspaper at the time with the telling headline 'Discovery of rare orchid could delay houses plan'. I had been disappointed to see the *Shetland Times* focusing on the inconvenience the orchids might cause a property developer – I would have preferred that they celebrated the discovery of a nationally significant colony of an orchid that was threatened and in decline across Europe. In Britain and Ireland alone they have vanished from two thirds of their former range and are almost extinct in England alone.

Perhaps I was being unduly biased. The developer had stated that they were hopeful a solution could be found. I did not know what had subsequently happened – in theory, some of the houses could be built in an area of the site that did not appear to contain any bog orchids, but I worried about the potential impact of any human activity nearby on the hydrology of the site. Bog orchids are extremely sensitive to change, needing just the right amount of water of the correct acidity flowing past them year-round if they are to prosper. On this particular day, with Sally and her family walking by my side across the field, I was simply happy to see the site was, as yet untouched and unchanged.

Shetland fishermen, in the days before satellite navigation, used landmarks on the islands known as *medes* to orientate themselves when fishing inshore. Prominent rocks, houses, or features in the land were used to triangulate their position on the water and guide them to particularly favourable fishing spots. Lacking a GPS in 2015, and wanting to ensure I could refind the bog orchids in future, I had made a note of my own set of medes – a number of derelict brick buildings at the edges of the field that were all that remained of RAF Catfirth, a seaplane base that had been briefly operational here in the closing years of the First World War. The sheltered waters of the Catfirth Voe below the field would have provided the cumbersome and unloved Felixstowe F.3 seaplanes with as dependable a base as Shetland's fickle seas could muster. The relics of that brief military presence gave me the reliable directions I needed; aligning my medes according to my notes, I relocated the wet flush at which, the previous year, I had seen over a hundred flowering bog orchids.

Our visit was earlier this year, but the first of the bog orchids were already well under way. I cautioned Sally and the kids to be careful, showing them their very first bog orchid and stressing how easily one could miss seeing them at one's very feet – we would need to be careful to avoid stepping on any of these delicate flowers. Happily, there were drier tussocks of brown heather that, once checked for any unseen plants, we could kneel upon to get a closer view of the orchids themselves.

While tiny, each bog orchid flower was a masterpiece of understated beauty, as delicate and refined as early Lalique glass. They are unique amongst our orchids for being hyper-resupinate – the ovary on which the flower is offered is twisted a full 360 degrees around. Most orchids are resupinate – that is, their ovaries twist 180 degrees to present the flower upside down. The labellum, the petal that is often strikingly different from the other two petals on each flower, forms a lip that is on the lower half of the resupinate flower. On bog orchids the ovary, having twisted in a full 360-degree circle, presents the labellum on the upper half of the hyper-resupinate flower. I spared young Hector and Teal this delightfully nerdy detail – I did not want to scare them off – but did point out how each flower resembled a small green angel.

What would normally be the upper sepal formed the shield-shaped, jade-green lower half of the flower and the angel's body. Her petals were her arms, her darker green-streaked labellum her head and halo, while her lateral sepals formed arching pellucid wings held high above her. Each flower spike held a host of angels, some dozen or more perfect heavenly bodies presiding over a few square centimetres of saturated sphagnum moss from which the orchid emerged as two small, fleshy green leaves. Looking through my hand lens at the tip of the larger of the two leaves, I could see a fringe of miniscule bulbils forming. Bog orchids can reproduce vegetatively, so in time these tiny bulbils would fall off the leaf and, if lodged by the slow-moving water in the moss downstream, and infected by a suitable mycorrhizal fungus, they could form new plants without the need for fertilisation or the subsequent bother of forming seeds.

Many orchids rely on this intimate association with a fungal partner, but few rely on it quite as heavily as bog orchids appear to do. They have no roots to speak of, making do with fine root hairs instead. Living in extremely acidic conditions, surrounded by nutrient-poor, slowly flowing water, and with just two small leaves with which to photosynthesise, the orchids draw much of their sustenance from the fungal activity in their heavily infected rhizome, root hairs and leaf bases. Looking around us at Catfirth, I wondered just how many bog orchid colonies go overlooked in Shetland, and further afield in Scotland. While they are undoubt-edly in decline across their European range, there must still be many more unknown populations of them quietly going about their business unheeded by man.

When, later that afternoon, Peter collected me from Inverness air-port, I should have been feeling upbeat about the forthcoming day in the Highlands, not least in the certainty that I would, at long last, see my first ever small white orchids. However, a disturbing experience when hunting for the flower in Cumbria was on my mind, dampening my excitement.

On my way back north from Gloucestershire's single flowering red helleborine I had been convinced I would see small white orchids in Cumbria – a friend had visited a well-known colony at Little Asby Outrakes two days before my arrival, and had sent me photographs taken of a flowering plant in lovingly close proximity. Better yet, he reassured me that the few plants there were safe from predation by deer or rabbits, as they were cocooned inside small, protective cages. I had absolutely nothing to worry about – these small white orchids were a dead cert.

I was confused, upon my arrival at Little Asby Outrakes, to find no sign of any cages visible from the road. The field in which the orchids grow is a long piece of common ground, unfenced and running parallel to the narrow lane that leads off the moors of the Orton Fells and into the village of Little Asby itself. I had parked in a field gateway then walked the length of the Outrakes, at first on the road and finally down the centre of the field. The complete absence of any cages had me doubting myself – perhaps I was in the wrong field altogether? I worked my way up and down the road but could see no other land that matched the description of the field I had parked beside initially. There were a handful of orchids to be seen in the field, most notably heath fragrant orchids, small, long-spurred pink consolation prizes of a sort. But there were no cages, and certainly no small white orchids. Searching for them blind, without the cages to guide me to them, reminded me of my many fruitless hours searching for them in Shetland – a thankless task.

Scattered all around the Outrakes were signs of recent cattle presence, although no cows now remained – I picked my way around many fresh cowpats and large flattened areas of grass where the beasts had laid themselves down to sleep and chew the cud. It was in one such cow bed that I finally found the first of several flattened netting cages. While they were sufficient to keep rabbits and deer at bay, the cows had probably barely felt a thing as they crushed them beneath their bodies. I took some heart from finding the remains of the cages, as at least I could now focus my search in the immediate vicinity. There had only been one flowering plant, so narrowing my search area meant the haystack had just got a lot more manageable, even if the needle remained hopelessly small.

When I found it, my first small white orchid was a sad affair – a bitten off flower-spike and three cropped leaves. The surrounding vegetation exactly matched that in one of my friend's photographs. There was no doubt this was it – the sole flowering plant in the field two days previously was now half-eaten and no longer fit to be counted for my quest, let alone to set seed and reproduce itself. Dusk was falling on the fells as I systematically worked my way up and down Little Asby Outrakes, searching with mounting desperation for another small white orchid that might, perhaps, have been spared by the cows and come into bloom in the past days. I could find nothing but heath fragrant and heath spotted orchids. I tried to find some solace taking photos of a particularly fine heath fragrant orchid, but soon discovered the light levels had fallen too far for useful photography.

'You fucking faggot!'

The shout came from nearby. Looking up from where I knelt in the grass, camera set up in front of an orchid, I saw a red four-wheel-drive pick-up that stopped in the lane level with me. I looked around me, confused, slowly perceiving that the abuse was aimed at me.

'Come here, you gay fuck!'

Three men in their early twenties continued to shout homophobic taunts from the pick-up while I got to my feet, gathering camera and tripod in my arms, and tried to decide what to do. My car was on the lane nearby but, with my heart hammering with fear, I judged it imprudent to go anywhere near the road where my red-faced abusers sat, alternately screaming insults at me, laughing, and drinking from beer cans. I started to walk away from them, heading towards the wall that skirted the far side of the field. If needs be, I was ready to take off across country and abandon my car for the meantime. Turning my back on them caused them to redouble their efforts but, before I had reached the wall, they had grown bored and accelerated away. I ran for my car.

Afterwards, having driven a few miles away from Little Asby, my legs began shaking uncontrollably. This, I supposed, was the effect of adrenaline coursing through me. It had been a terrifying encounter. No violence had taken place, but the threat of it had been implicit. I'm not gay, but in that moment I understood what it must feel like to be persecuted as such. That this had happened in the open countryside, surrounded by rolling fields, dry-stone walls, with a song thrush singing somewhere unseen nearby, was utterly incongruous. I realised, with hindsight, that intolerance and prejudice recognised no such distinctions or boundaries. It could have happened anywhere. I had just been unfortunate to be a man looking at wildflowers whose path had happened to cross that of three young Cumbrian rednecks.

It was an experience that has come to haunt me afterwards. I have spent so much of my life alone in the countryside without any consequence apart from enjoyment of the places I have visited and the wildlife I have found in them. It had never occurred to me that I might, inadvertently, be vulnerable. That innocence, once lost, is gone for ever. I have felt more guarded, more cautious, in the countryside ever since.

The prospect of orchid hunting with Peter Stronach in the Highlands was a welcome antidote to that recent unsettling encounter. Besides the keenly awaited small white orchid, which we would see near to Peter's home in the evening, I also wanted to see my first creeping lady's-tresses of the summer. Peter took me to Curr Wood, famous amongst dipterists, or fly enthusiasts, for being one of only two sites in Scotland known to support the rare pine hoverfly – a fly notable as, like the orchids I sought, it depended heavily on a particular species of fungus if it was to prosper. As Peter explained the life cycle of the pine hoverfly, I struggled to maintain an appropriately impassive composure – the larvae of the hoverfly live in the soft, decaying material gathered in the rotten centres of pine stumps, a state of decay caused in the first instance by the unfortunately named pine butt-rot fungus.

The afternoon was cool and grey, and any hopes I entertained of seeing pine hoverfly were dashed by a marked lack of insect activity. Above us, as we walked into the Scots pine woodland, family parties of crested tits called incessantly, their high silvery voices filtering down to us on the thickly needle-strewn forest floor. Tree trunks as gnarled as crocodile skin rose high above our heads as we began to search for orchids.

'They flower in the wood beside my house,' Peter said, 'but I checked this morning and those ones aren't open yet. They're usually a bit behind all the others – it's colder there than almost anywhere.'

Peter lived on the outskirts of Aviemore, in an area of the Cairngorms that was, even by Scottish Highland standards, particularly chilly.

'I'm hoping these ones will be ahead of mine.'

We searched for a little while longer before finding the first creeping lady's-tresses. All had swollen flower buds, but none as yet had opened. The familiar sense of apprehension began mounting before we both, simultaneously, found fully flowering plants on the damp, spongy forest floor.

Almost all of the British population of creeping lady's-tresses are found in the cool pine woodlands of Scotland. For the most part they prefer the ancient Caledonian woodland habitat comprised largely of Scots pines, though in more recent times they have also been found in mature commercial pine plantations. They are also present at a handful of sites in Norfolk, and botanists have long speculated as to the origin of these anomalous colonies so far from the Scottish heartland. Three theories, all of them equally plausible and without any firm substantive evidence, attempt to explain their Norfolk presence: they were unwittingly introduced with pine seedlings brought from Scotland; they colonised via wind-blown seed either from Scotland or the Continent; or they were always present in low densities on Norfolk's heaths. In what I was learning to accept as *de facto* where orchids were concerned, there was at least as much uncertainty surrounding creeping lady's-tresses as there was certainty.

Their very name misleads – unlike our other two lady's-tresses, they do not belong to the *Spiranthes* genus. In appearance they are superficially similar, but there the relationship founders. Their genus is *Goodyera*, named after the seventeenth-century English botanist John Goodyer. Goodyer was a talented botanist with a keen eye for detail yet, despite adding new species to the British flora and producing a revised and corrected edition of John Gerard's seminal *Herball* that featured a number of British orchids for the first time in print, he languished in obscurity after his death. Botanist and cleric Canon John Vaughan wrote of him as the 'forgotten botanist'. Goodyer was, at least, commemorated by the Scottish botanist Robert Brown – a genus of orchids would, for ever, bear his name.

Of the approximately forty species that comprise *Goodyera*, only creeping lady's-tresses is found in Britain. It has an extensive global range, extending as far east as Afghanistan and Japan, and west of us in the United States. There it goes by the name lesser rattlesnake plantain – said to be either a reference to the snakeskin-like veining of the evergreen leaves or, more fancifully, due to an early belief that the orchid was an effective antidote for a rattlesnake bite. The latter explanation seemed like a dangerous mutation of the old European contention that dock leaves provide effective relief for nettle stings and, while I was enjoying immersing myself in orchid folklore, I was happy not to have a chance to experiment with creeping lady's-tresses' healing properties in the event of snake bite.

When planning my summer itinerary I knew that I wanted to see my creeping lady's-tresses in ancient woodland such as this, where punk crested tits called and rufous red squirrels skittered around tree trunks. Not for me the tamer surroundings of the north Norfolk coast, nor unanswerable questions about the origins of the *Goodyera* found there.

At close quarters, each plant's stem and its flowers were magnificently hairy, covered in thousands of short, fine white glandular hairs a bearded ghillie would be proud to sport. Each flower itself was a crisp, icy white, the hirsute sepals and petals forming a compactly hooded cowl around the drooping short labellum. Lying beside them, my nostrils filled with the sweet rotting, resinous smell of a pine woodland floor, I could feel my clothes growing damp at the elbows and knees, but I did not care. While I lost myself in orchid reverie, Peter was searching for something even more obscure than the unseen pine hoverflies – creeping lady's-tresses has the distinction of having a fungus that occurs on it alone. *Pucciniastrum goodyerae*, or creeping ladies-tresses rust, has been recorded in Scotland on a mere handful of occasions – and notwithstanding Peter's efforts, we were unable to add a new record that afternoon.

We passed a large drift of twinflower as we followed a narrow path back to the road. This was a new flowering plant for me – the county flower of Inverness-shire, they are improbably bifurcated, their red stems diverging like French electricity pylons to support two pale pink bell-like flowers. Given Peter's enthusiasm for pine hoverfly – an enthusiasm that befitted him as a professional ecologist – I did not like to say that I was far more pleased to see this delicate Arctic-Alpine survivor of the last Ice Age than a bristly black and orange fly or its pine-butt-rot-infested nurseries.

As evening approached, Peter brought me to the meadow in which I would, at last, lay the ghost of the small white orchid to rest. The location of this private meadow in the heart of the Cairngorms is an open, if closely guarded, secret amongst botanists, owing to the sheer numbers of small white and lesser butterfly orchids to be found there. It contains easily the largest population of the latter at any single site in Britain, while almost certainly hosting one of the most prolific colonies of small white orchid.

Peter had forewarned me that the meadow was looking particularly good this year, with estimates of over 5,500 lesser butterfly and 2,500 small white orchids. I could barely contain my excitement as we drew near and I began to see a haze of white and pink flowers staining the grass. The meadow slopes down to a quiet road and from the near boundary fence to the hilltop above, the entire field was a cloud of diffuse colour. When I realised this was entirely due to the orchids that carpeted the ground I found the hairs on my arms standing on end. The sheer density of orchids was having a physical effect on me: I could not stop smiling.

Most of the whiteness owed itself to the stately lesser butterfly orchids, their large, waxy ivory blooms glowing *en masse*, but a distinct swathe of finer, smaller white flower spikes nearby were something else – my first ever small white orchids. If I had been braced to be a little underwhelmed by this subtle orchid, all my doubts were dispelled in an instant once I settled carefully down beside them – they had a charm out of all proportion to the sum of their parts. They made a sad mockery of the single, ravaged plant I had seen in Cumbria – here they grew exuberantly, in profusion, hosts of single flower spikes interspersed with denser clumps of flowers, sometimes as many as ten flowering plants all clustered tightly together. Each flower spike, while not as tall as the grandest lesser butterfly orchids nearby, nonetheless rose impressively above the surrounding greenery. Their name described the flowers themselves rather than the sturdy orchid as a whole: the flower spike was comprised of a dense constellation of barely open green and white blooms, each drooping demurely. The white sepals hooded the remainder of each flower, and when I looked closely within them, I saw the petals and sepals were pale apple green.

The small white orchid is, like so many of its tribe, sensitive to the assorted vagaries of intensified agriculture. While primarily an orchid of the cool, damp north and west of the British Isles, it was once also found further south, in the Weald – but habitat loss and overgrazing appear to have spelt the end for these outlying colonies, with no sightings since the early twentieth century. The signs are there to suggest it is as sensitive to climate change as it is to the application of artificial fertiliser, for their range is shrinking back into the north-west. The bald statistics uncomfortably echoed those for the bog orchids I had seen during the morning in Shetland – small white orchids have been lost from two thirds of their former British and Irish historical range. Here in this small hidden meadow, at least, they were still thriving.

In places here they grew side by side with lesser butterfly orchids and heath fragrant orchids, their leaves all touching one another. It was possible to compose a photograph featuring all three species in one happy portrait. We meandered slowly around the meadow, surrounded by thousands of orchids. The heath fragrant orchids seemed to proliferate on the slightly higher ground, providing the swathes of pink I had seen upon my arrival, and in this area we also found heath spotted orchids and a fine example of the inter-generic hybrid between the two species, known as *x Dactylodenia evansii*. Each flower on this rare hybrid was a perfect blend of the parents, having the faint cerise spotting and blousy, broad labellum of the heath spotted while retaining the solid pink colouration and long spur of the heath fragrant. The flower spike stood out like a beacon in the field as it displayed strong hybrid vigour, being taller, denser and lusher than either surrounding parent.

With this plant in mind, I paid closer attention to the heath fragrant orchids – in such a dense population of flowers, there had to be a reasonable chance of further hybrids, if only I could find them. At this time of day there was a changing of the guard amongst flying insects, with many gaudy day-flying six-spot burnet moths seeking roosting sites in and amongst the orchids while the first of the night-flying moths were preparing to take to the wing. One of the night watch, a beautiful golden Y, rested on a heath fragrant orchid spike, vibrating its wings to drive heat into the muscles. I could see a small primrose-yellow cluster of, presumably, orchid pollinia stuck about its head.

Returning to the small white orchids for one last sojourn, I paused to smell the intensifying scent of nearby lesser butterfly orchids. They release their heady perfume in the gathering darkness to attract night-flying moths to pollinate them – an act I would have dearly loved to see had time and good fortune only allowed. My luck had not quite run out, though – nearby I noticed an unusually pale heath fragrant orchid. Looking more closely at it, my suspicions were aroused; could this pallid pink, fat and truncated-spurred flower be the hybrid between small white and heath fragrant orchids, *x Pseudadenia schweinfurthii*? It certainly looked the part. With night falling rapidly, and my time in the meadow at an end, I regretted not having a chance to spend longer here. I was certain there must be further intriguing plants to uncover – a hunch that, with hindsight, would prove to be well founded, as just days later a local naturalist discovered two flowering plants of the even rarer hybrid combination of small white and heath spotted orchids, x *Pseudorhiza bruniana*.

I realised this gathering interest in hybrids and the varieties within orchid species marked a change in me. My obsession with these intriguing flowers had moved up a gear, taking me from merely wanting to see all the British and Irish species to somewhere else more rarefied altogether. The delight and thrill of seeing a new species was still there, but like an addict growing habituated to his drug of choice, I was now actively seeking more novel, intense thrills still. Already I regretted not making time to visit Glamorgan to see the newly described *var. cambrensis* of bee orchid. That would have to wait another year. My dismay when I learned of the x *Pseudorhiza bruniana* this summer, too late to return to see them in bloom, had the acute stab of a lover's rejection.

I could console myself that these missed esoteric aberrations and hybrid combinations offered future opportunities to return to wonderful locations to look anew for them, but like a petulant child I wanted it all, and I wanted it now. I had caught a bad case of orchid fever.

13

Holy helleborines and heavy metal

Pilgrims have been making their way to the small island of Lindisfarne off England's north-east coast for centuries. Christianity first put roots down there at the behest of Oswald, king of Northumberland, in the mid-seventh century. Oswald, a Christian, asked the Irish of Dál Riata to send him a bishop to facilitate the conversion of his people to his faith. The Irish sent Aidan, a missionary monk, to help Oswald – and it was on Lindisfarne, known latterly as Holy Island, that Aidan founded a monastic cathedral, the base from which he travelled through the Northumbrian countryside preaching the word of God to nobles and peasants alike.

Aidan was to be the first of a succession of saints – Cuthbert, Eadfrith and Eadberht – associated with the island, so it was entirely fitting that, when genetic studies in the early years of the twenty-first century revealed a small population of helleborines found on the island to be an entirely unique species in their own right, this orchid should be given the Latin name *Epipactis sancta*, or holy Epipactis. The colloquial name is more descriptive – Lindisfarne helleborine describes perfectly the true nature of this most hermit-like of British helleborines. It is found only on Lindisfarne, and nowhere else in the entire world. Even on Lindisfarne it is rare, restricted to a small area of dune slacks on the peninsula known as the Snook at the western end of the island. The entire population of this Robinson Crusoe orchid numbers in the low hundreds; three hundred flower in a good year, and around a third of that when conditions are less favourable.

Judging when to visit Lindisfarne to see these endemic orchids was not easy. Their flowering period varies from year to year, depending on the weather in the preceding weeks and months. Orchid field guides say late June to late July, but this vague window was not helpful for my purposes – once the self-pollinating flowers open, they are infamous for being over very quickly. I did not dare visit Lindisfarne in mid-July, as I feared the flowers would have been and gone before me. Their coastal location only added to the potential for disaster. As I knew all too well from botanising at home in Shetland, one unexpected day of scouring, salt-laden wind pouring off the sea could scorch flowers beyond all useful recognition.

Early one morning in mid-July found me pausing to reflect at the end of the causeway that links the island to the Northumbrian mainland. This would be my third visit in as many weeks to Lindisfarne. On each previous occasion the helleborines had not yet been in flower and I had, instead, wandered the dune slacks with many hundreds of early marsh orchids for company. I had, at first, felt relieved that I had not yet missed the helleborines, but after my second visit had not only failed to yield any flowering plants, but had also shown little progress in the development of the many as yet budding marsh helleborines that carpeted areas of the same habitat in which the Lindisfarne helleborines lurked, I was concerned that this latest visit would also prove fruitless.

The tide had been out since before dawn, meaning the window of opportunity to botanise from first light was relatively limited before the rising sea rendered the causeway unsafe to cross once more. If I failed to leave Lindisfarne by midday I would find myself stranded on the island until late afternoon. This would not, usually, be such a hardship, for the scenery and wildlife of Lindisfarne makes it a wonderful place to pass the time, but this weekend would be devoted to helleborines on both east and west coasts of northern England; I could not afford to lose valuable hours of daylight on Lindisfarne when the siren calls of further, as yet unseen, orchids were taunting me from the mainland.

The causeway stretched ahead of me, the road shining wet with large puddles of seawater. Strands of olive bladderwrack were scattered on the road, abandoned there by the falling tide. Piebald ringed plovers and nervous, piping redshanks skittered on the exposed mud and sand, making the most of this twice-daily feeding bonanza. Halfway across the causeway stood a small white hut, raised high on thick pilings and made accessible by a steep, wooden slatted staircase – this was the causeway's refuge hut, barely big enough to house four standing people at once. A sign at the start of the causeway graphically showed the perils of attempting a misjudged crossing when the waters had not fully parted – a photo of a half-submerged car abandoned by the refuge bore the stark legend: *This could be you.*

In the past, pilgrims made their way to Lindisfarne across the exposed sands by a traditional pathway. This is still in use today, though visitors are cautioned to only attempt a crossing on foot when accompanied by an experienced local. I had no time to spare, although I would have loved to make my pilgrimage on foot. Romance had no place in my plans – I simply hoped that the fickle Lindisfarne helleborines would, finally, have deigned to open their flowers.

Having crossed the causeway, I left my car at the roadside at the edge of the Snook. Sandy pathways led through the circling fringe of dunes smothered with marram grass into the heart of the slacks beyond. I had not walked far before the laces of my boots were choked with thick red clots of hook-clad pirri-pirri burs. Lindisfarne had, simultaneous with the blossoming of Christianity on the island, been subject to sporadic incursions by marauding Viking raiders from Scandinavia, incursions which began in June AD 793 when, as the Anglo-Saxon Chronicle recounts, 'Heathen men came and miserably destroyed God's church on Lindisfarne, with plunder and slaughter.'

Centuries later, Lindisfarne was invaded once more, but this time by a more insidious foe – the snaggly seedheads of pirri-pirri, a plant native to New Zealand and Australia, believed to have been washed down the River Tweed on waste water used in the cleaning of imported Antipodean fleeces, made landfall on the shores of Lindisfarne. This was in the 1930s, and by the late twentieth century swathes of Lindisfarne's dune slacks were smothered in this tough invasive plant, to the detriment of the native plants, orchids included. An ongoing campaign to, if not eradicate the invader, at least manage its presence has seen cattle and sheep released to graze it, herbicides sprayed to kill it, and mechanical devices deployed to suck up the burs before they can spread seeds further afield. Visitors are cautioned not to carry any burs away with them inadvertently, so before leaving Lindisfarne I would spend twenty minutes scrupulously removing every trace of the invasive, clinging burs from my clothes.

It was the orchids that this alien plant threatened that I so dearly wanted to see. I had no sooner entered the outskirts of the dune slacks than I encountered both a new flowering orchid for the year and, by its very flowering, a good portent – carpets of low-growing marsh helleborines, at last, studded here and there by the pink and purple counterpoints of the last of the early marsh orchids.

If the early marsh orchids were the fading stars of a bygone moment this summer, these flamboyant marsh helleborines were supernovae in the orchid firmament. No British orchid can match them for extravagant, overdressed opulence. They are the Liberaces of our orchids, the queens of the desert, their large flowers abandoning any pretence at subtlety. Their large, frilly white epichiles, or outer lips, have the grace of a bridal meringue, while the sides of their blushing pink hypochiles, or inner lips, are heavily veined with purple. Their long oval sepals are confections of green and purple with a white tracery about their edges, and their two lateral petals intensify the rosy blush of the hypochile they shield. At the juncture of the hypochile and the frou-frou epichile is a deeply grooved lemon-yellow boss, or swelling. Each flower is held on a slender, finely hairy, aubergine-washed green ovary.

These are orchids that are easily the rivals of any of their tropical counterparts. Seen at close quarters they are almost overpowering in their colouration and structural complexity, appearing as if they would be more at home in a humid, heavily misted hothouse than in a cool, damp British coastal dune slack. I was surrounded by thousands of them, all coming into flower at once. Their hypochiles are curiously hinged and bend downwards under the slightest pressure. Charles Darwin hypothesised that this hinged mechanism would allow easy ingress for a visiting insect, permitting it to enter a flower without removing the hanging pollinia. The hypochile would spring back upwards once the insect was deep within the heart of the flower, forcing the insect upwards as it reversed out of the flower, and thereby removing the pollinia – to be carried on to another flower rather than self-fertilising the original flower.

Subsequent scientists offered alternative theories for the function of the hinged hypochile, and there is to this day no consensus. Later hypotheses suggest that the hinge mechanism may be important in determining where on the insect's body the pollinia are deposited – perhaps not attaching them to the head, as is often the case with orchid pollination, but instead adhering them to the thorax – a position that more effectively denies the insect the ability to remove them by grooming with its legs. Having seen a digger wasp in Kent fastidiously attempting to comb off the adhered pollinia of a fly orchid from his head, I could imagine that such a refinement in the pollination mechanism might prove advantageous for the marsh helleborines.

What is certain is that they are in decline as a British and Irish native orchid, having been lost from approximately 60 per cent of their British and 40 per cent of their former Irish ranges. As their name suggests, they are happiest in damp places, and this offers a clue to their downfall, as much of their former fen and marsh habitat was drained in the nineteenth century to reclaim land for agriculture. Agriculture may have struck a further nail in their coffin, because fertiliser run-off from fields creates high levels of nutrients in ground water, encouraging the growth of some plants to the detriment of others. Marsh helleborines are sensitive to such eutrophication, as it causes the places in which they grow to become choked with vegetation that out-competes the orchids. Similarly, when grazing is abandoned in these damp places, the subsequent invasion of encroaching scrub soon overpowers the more delicate flowering plants.

They seem to have survived better in their coastal stations, where the ill effects of intensifying and careless agriculture have been less pronounced. Certainly here in the dunes of Lindisfarne and, despite the best efforts of the encroaching pirri-pirri, they were still enduring.

Moving beyond the first flush of marsh helleborines I headed deeper into the Snook, to where the encircling dunes form an amphitheatre around a large, slightly undulating slack. The clouds that had shrouded the early morning sky were thinning now, and with the rise in air temperature, there came more insect activity – there had been an enormous, simultaneous emergence of six-spot burnets that rose in a blur of iridescent black-and-scarlet-blotched wings from the grass and low creeping willow at my feet with every step. Tawny streaks seen from the corner of my eye resolved themselves into rust-and-black-chequered dark green fritillaries waging territorial duels – or was it courtship? – in the open spaces at the edges of the dunes.

Here were more orchids, though nothing new for me. Amongst drifts of nodding, fluffy white cotton grass were many more marsh helleborines and scattered drifts of common spotted and northern marsh orchids with, inevitably, their vigorous hybrid offspring bearing tell-tale signs of both parents. Many superficially 'good' northern marsh orchids here had profusely spotted leaves – some orchid field guides allowed that they might have fine leaf-spotting, but given their propensity to hybridise, I preferred to discount all putative northern marsh orchids that had any spotting on their leaves. Had I strictly applied this personal rule here on Lindisfarne, I would not have been happy to call many, if any, of these *Dactylorhiza* orchids as unequivocal northern marshes, so it was fortunate that I had seen pure, uncontentious plants in the Hebrides and Shetland.

None of these, however, were the object of this morning's quest – I had eyes only for one orchid on Lindisfarne, the eponymous helleborine. I retraced my steps to the now familiar area in which I had seen immature plants previously. I could not, at first, find them on the shallow declivity upon which I had seen them before, and I began to doubt myself – perhaps I was in the wrong spot? One indistinct crater looked much like another here. I checked my location against the grid references I had noted beforehand. This was definitely the right place. Telling myself to calm down, and not begin to worry about the prospect of finding further Lindisfarne helleborines in the vastness of the Snook, I looked carefully around the edges of the small clearing in which I found myself.

Suddenly the creeping willow and grass resolved itself before my eyes and, there before me, I could see two small, sallow green forms rising up. Unmistakeably orchids, and certainly not of the *Dactylorhiza* tribe. These were *Epipactis*, but not the gaudy, flamboyant marsh helleborines – these were my Lindisfarne helleborines, and they were flowering at last. I felt the familiar surge of relief washing over me; another potential stumbling block in my summer-long quest had been overcome.

I knelt carefully beside them to examine them closely – this was the first time I had seen Lindisfarne helleborine in the flesh. They had only been formally described as a species in their own right at the time I was moving to live in Shetland. Hitherto, since their discovery on Lindisfarne in 1958, they had been considered to be merely an outlying population of dune helleborine. Doubts began to be raised about this identification in the 1980s as botanists noticed subtle differences between these Lindisfarne orchids and the dune helleborines found on the north-west coast of England, but it was not until 2002 that, on the basis of genetic analysis of the plants, the formal name of *Epipactis sancta* came to be adopted for them.

The visual differences between dune and Lindisfarne helleborines are relatively subtle and I had, to an extent, to accept these plants' identity on trust due to their location alone. Crucially, the base of the flower stem on each of these orchids was the same uniform, sickly yellowish-green of the rest of the stem and leaves – the base of the flower stem of typical dune helleborines is washed with violet – and the flowers lacked the faint hint of mauve usually associated with a dune helleborine's epichile.

The flowers were, if I was honest with myself, rather uninspiring and bland. The spice of their extreme rarity helped to season my appreciation of them, but from a strictly aesthetic perspective they were underwhelming. The pale chartreuse tones of the plants' stems and leaves extended into their flowers, with the petals and sepals sharing the same insipid hue. Each looked faintly nutrient deficient, as if they were struggling to extract much goodness from the sand from which they grew. The heart-shaped lip of each flower was somewhat whiter at the very edges, while the inner walls of the cupped hypochile had a dirty smear of chocolate brown. They were not much to look at, but I could not have loved them more; that an orchid had evolved to call this tiny, sacred scrap of land and nowhere else in the world home seemed miraculous to me.

Even on the Snook they are rare, and are absent from areas of habitat that appear identical to those nearby in which they are found. From my vantage point at ground level I could see a further six flowering plants, one of which, to confirm my previous fears, had almost finished flowering for another year. I was struck by the sobering realisation that these nine plants could represent as much as 3 per cent of the entire global population of flowering Lindisfarne helleborines. *Epipactis sancta*, the holy helleborine, has such a precarious existence. While Christianity spread across Britain from the cradle of Lindisfarne, this stubborn, special orchid poignantly struggles to spread across just one corner of the island it calls home.

As the afternoon drew on, I came to my final destination of this first day of helleborine hunting. There had been, in the course of this summer, certain locations I had never visited before that I had looked forward to becoming acquainted with more than others – places that fired my imagination in a way that others simply did not. The saturated, teeming Norfolk fens had been one such, as had the rich tapestry of the flower-rich machair of North Uist. This, Bishop Middleton Quarry in County Durham, was another place I had dreamed of coming to for years, particularly keenly once I began to plan this summer's great orchid quest. I had been delighted to finally have an excuse to leave Shetland and come here in the late summer.

My targets were two orchids in particular, but almost as much as them I anticipated seeing a tiny brown butterfly for the first time in decades. It had been years since I last saw a northern brown argus, a rich chocolate-brown-coloured member of the *Lycaenidae*, a family of butterflies that predominantly have metallic blue wings. I knew the orchids were in bloom, but seeing the butterflies actively on the wing demanded warm sunshine. In my imagination I had pictured an afternoon just like this one – sun-drenched and still, rich with orchids on the ground and butterflies in flight all around me.

Walking into this Durham Wildlife Trust reserve, one passes through a short, dense area of woodland. Nothing then prepares the visitor for the dramatic moment when the trees part and the quarry is revealed – a sheltered expanse of flower-studded, grassy quarry floor with low, honey-coloured, tree-topped limestone cliffs on either side. Abandoned as a working quarry in the 1930s it has been, over time, recolonised by an impressive range of limestone flora, not least of which are the orchid for which the quarry is particularly famous – dark-red helleborine. Around two thousand plants are found here, a total population that is estimated to number more than those of all the other British sites combined.

Only a few paces across the quarry floor brought me to my first dark-red helleborines – small, rather stunted examples, but ones that simply served as hors d'oeuvres for what lay beyond on the slopes at the foot of the quarry's low cliffs. Here were swathes of dark-red helleborines, thick clusters of burgundy flower spikes in vast profusion growing where the warmth of the late afternoon sunlight radiated from the stones all around them. I felt disloyal in my cursory treatment of the other new orchid for the year that I stopped, all too briefly, to examine as I made my way to the helleborines. Scattered around the quarry floor were dozens of dark pink marsh fragrant orchids, flowering later in the summer than either of their similar chalk or heath fragrant counterparts, and structurally distinctive from both. I paused for them, taking time to register their densely packed, columnar flower spikes like the spires of fenland churches, and to examine carefully the structure of individual flowers, but the compelling, magnetic beauty of the helleborines was always going to draw me away.

I scrambled up to the dark-red helleborines at the foot of the cliffs – and discovered they were everything I had hoped they would be. Each flower spike lived up perfectly to the *atrorubens* of their Latin name, with a stalk the deep colour of aged burgundy and flowers of a more vivid, younger red-wine tone. I felt intoxicated, drunk on orchids as I moved from plant to plant. Each flower spike bore many flowers, with some carrying in excess of twenty blooms apiece. With the exception of a rich, buttery yellow anther cap in the very centre of each flower, the rest of the bloom was that contiguous clear, deep red, glowing in the late afternoon light as sumptuous as a maharajah's rubies.

They grew all around me, at the base of the cliffs, and further up the sloping sides of the quarry. Here and there, high overhead, I could even see plants growing from the merest crevices of the rock face itself. Amongst the more accessible plants were clumps of primrose-yellow-flowered common rock rose, a food plant for northern brown argus caterpillars. With butterflies in mind, I climbed steps carved into one corner of the quarry up to a broad gallery halfway up the quarry sides, a wide grassy area that ran parallel to the quarry floor below. A small cutting at one end led into an enclosed, scrub-choked area with steeply banked sides. A male bullfinch sang from the depths of the bushes and, when I answered his call with a matching fluted whistle, emerged into the open to exchange calls with me.

I was soon distracted, for on the banks I found male northern brown arguses engaged in vehement aerial disputes with one another. The reason for this territorial intensity became clear when I discovered a pair of northern brown argus unobtrusively mating with one another, both hanging tightly to a grass stem. One male, tired of his fruitless display flights, settled nearby to bask on a bare patch of soil, his wings spread widely to absorb the fading heat of the afternoon sun. One hindwing had a small chip missing, perhaps evidence of a close encounter with a bird, but otherwise he was still in pristine condition, his rich cocoa forewings sporting tiny, immaculate, snow-white counterpoints in their centres.

Yet it was the dark-red helleborines that drew me helplessly back to them. As the sinking sun's light grew more golden and mellow, their luminosity only increased still further. I was mesmerised by them – in the still, warm air a faint cloud of vanilla scent hung around the densest patches of them, the subtle perfume enhancing their charm.

The following morning I planned to see more dark-red helleborines in their classic British habitat, on upland limestone pavements in Cumbria. With them, I hoped, I would also have a chance to see their rare hybrid with broad-leaved helleborine, known as *Epipactis x schmalhausenii*, named after Johannes Schmalhausen, a nineteenth-century Russian botanist who first recorded the hybrid in his homeland in 1874.

My guide through the complex landscape of Hutton Roof and the intricacies of *Epipactis* hybridisation and variation would be Bryan Yorke, a dedicated and amiable naturalist who in recent years had made a particular study of the orchids of Hutton Roof, visiting almost daily throughout the flowering season and charting the lives and loves of the helleborines he found there.

Bryan led me through the fields and woods that cloaked the flanks of Hutton Roof as it rose above the small Cumbrian hamlet of Clawthorpe. The woods began to provide clues to what lay unseen above us – we threaded our way through large, jagged moss-smothered limestone boulders before rising above the tree line and out onto the rocky immensity of the limestone pavement of Hutton Roof itself.

'The locals used to quarry the rock from here in the past,' Bryan explained. 'You'll see plenty of walls in Clawthorpe and

Burton-in-Kendal made of the local stone. It's always been a special place – this was one of the original Rothschild Reserves, and the only one of them to feature limestone pavement.'

In 1912 Charles Rothschild, banker and entomologist, founded the Society for the Promotion of Nature Reserves (SPNR). In terms of recognising the need to conserve beleaguered, special habitats in Britain and Ireland, the SPNR was decades ahead of its time, borne of the 'desirability of preserving in perpetuity sites suitable for nature reserves'. With the help of local societies and individual naturalists, the SPNR's first act was to compile a list of special sites for potential purchase as nature reserves. After three years of surveying, Rothschild and his colleagues had found 284 sites deemed 'worthy of conservation'. These were the Rothschild Reserves, chosen for being 'the breeding places of scarce creatures', 'the localities of scarce plants', and of 'geological interest'. Hutton Roof was number 193 on Rothschild's list.

Charles Rothschild died young in 1923, aged just forty-six, and never lived to see his vision of practical nature conservation fully realised. His dream, however, endured – in the 1940s legislation was drafted to protect most of the sites identified in the list drawn up by Rothschild and, in time, the SPNR went on to evolve into the organisation now known as the Wildlife Trusts, custodians of many special areas of natural history interest that I visited in the course of my orchid summer.

Bryan, armed with a walking stick, made rapid progress across the uneven terrain, navigating his way unerringly across what, at first glance, appeared to be a featureless, grey, rocky moonscape interspersed with hazel and juniper bushes that had somehow found a toehold in the grykes and crevices of the pavement. The limestone pavement was rarely easy going – comparatively little of it formed flat slabs, and the parts that did were interspersed with deep clefts and fissures. Elsewhere, much jagged limestone rubble and shards of stone littered the ground. This was a harsh, beautiful place, one that demanded much of those who would enter it, and rewarded their devotion richly but sparingly. This was W.H. Auden's region of 'short distances and definite places', a geology that inspired 'In Praise of Limestone', in which Auden concluded,

when I try to imagine a faultless love
Or the life to come, what I hear is the murmur
Of underground streams, what I see is a limestone landscape.[1]

It soon became clear that Bryan not only loved this place, but he also knew each and every plant here personally, and carried with him a ring binder containing each plant's history. While he had not quite gone as far as naming them all – though some rejoiced in personal names like Bracty and Stripy – each plant had a number and a record of how it had fared from year to year. He led me from one to another, joyfully telling me, 'This is a special place for *Epipactis*. It's a place where the straightforward has become the rarity, and the rarity has become the norm!'

I soon understood what Bryan meant, as he showed me a plethora of *E. x schmalhausenii* hybrids, plants with characteristics suggestive of both broad-leaved and dark-red helleborine parents.

'It's getting to be hard to find classic dark-red helleborines up here!' Bryan said gleefully. He began to show me plants that, morphologically at least, seemed to be dark-red helleborines, yet had flowers that were very different from those rich, wine-red flowers I had drunk my fill of the previous day in County Durham. Some plants had flowers that were typically deep red apart from striking lemon-yellow petals; others had those unusual lemon-petalled blooms borne on green flower stems rather than the usual dark burgundy. Finally, Bryan took me to see a dark-red helleborine with entirely cream-coloured flowers; this was the extremely unusual variety var. *lutescens*, a pallid shadow compared to her conventionally coloured brethren.

'Since coming to live up here, it's been like being on holiday every day – it's just like a beautiful dream I want to go on forever!'

Bryan exuded happiness from every pore as he scampered from rock to rock, and orchid to orchid. He shared the same deep connection with place I felt in Shetland, and that I had seen earlier in the summer in Richard Mason, the manager of the RSPB's spectacular marshy reserve at Sutton Fen.

'I know you've probably not got much time, but I could spend all day showing you round up here. There's so much to see! And there's always something new to find...'

Pausing briefly, Bryan shared his ring-bound notes with me. Interspersed with his observations and notes on each plant were hand-drawn and coloured illustrations. Bryan attempted to pass modestly over these, but each was a masterpiece that deserved close examination. Bryan was attempting, in these pages, to analyse and understand the lineage of every plant – its specific identity as either pure dark-red or broad-leaved helleborine, a variation within either species, or a hybrid between the two. I understood this very human urge to label and be certain, but given the enormous variety these plants exhibited I began wondering whether they defied categorisation. Certainly, relatively few plants seemed to be classic examples of either species and, given that *E. x schmalhausenii* is a fertile hybrid and could, in its own right, hybridise either with other hybrids or both parent species, I wondered how many of these plants on Hutton Roof carried genes of both broad-leaved and dark-red helleborines. I imagined that most of them were hybrids of one generation or another.

This hybrid swarming was something I was familiar with at home, where northern marsh and heath spotted orchids – and their hybrid offspring – all blithely interbreed given half a chance, but it was not something I had expected to encounter so dramatically amongst *Epipactis* orchids. I had considered them elevated above such sordid behaviour. I could prove nothing, of course, of these plants' lineage, but I realised that was not really the point – I was simply enjoying immersing myself in the harmless speculation a host of variable orchids engendered, and better yet in such spectacular surroundings. This was the area that nineteenth-century art critic John Ruskin proclaimed offered the 'finest view in England, and therefore the world'. While he may have liked the landscape, given his prudery where orchids were concerned, I suspected he would not have approved of all the orchidaceous promiscuity that was going on here. Ruskin's marriage to Effie Gray was never consummated, but the orchids in the landscape he loved had displayed no such qualms about one another's charms.

It was time to take my reluctant leave of the burgundy, dusky pink and primrose-yellow harlequin hybrids of the shattered rocky pavements of Hutton Roof. This weekend promised two further helleborines, dune and green-flowered. While neither would compete with the beauty of dark-red helleborine in any of its myriad manifestations, I would get to enjoy orchid-hunting in the company of one of the most intriguing and colourful characters I had encountered this year: Richard Bate, an orchid enthusiast I had met with his wife and daughter while photographing lady's slipper orchids in Cumbria.

Richard had offered to show me the helleborines found on the north-west Sefton coast near to his home in Preston, an offer I could not resist. Richard was a compelling enigma, unlike any botanist I had ever come across – a cross between Victorian scientist Gregor Mendel and rally driver Colin McRae, obsessed in equal measure with the genetics of *Epipactis* helleborines and lightning-fast Subaru Imprezas. He was a skilled dental surgeon by trade, but did not suffer fools gladly and was prone to vehement condemnation of those with whom he disagreed. Botanists, I had found, tended to be older, with polite and diffident characters. Richard was, exuberantly and unashamedly, none of these things.

The journey from Preston to Ainsdale-on-Sea was alternately exhilarating and terrifying. Strapped into the passenger seat of Richard's car, I tried to maintain a coherent conversation about the intricacies of species formation in *Epipactis* helleborines. Richard's breadth and depth of orchid knowledge seemed boundless, and he scathingly dismissed those hypotheses he found wanting with the same peremptory, clinical abandon with which he despatched the miles to the Sefton Coast. My legs were shaking as I clambered out of his Subaru into a baking July afternoon. Orchid hunting had never been as high octane nor as profane as this.

Our target here was green-flowered helleborine. An unassuming wallflower of an orchid that is found scattered around the British Isles, it's sometimes easily overlooked in the very depths of woodland or the barely vegetated hollows of old sand dunes. It was this dune slack habitat that we were to search, home to two species of helleborine, an abundance of natterjack toads and, on this sunny afternoon, many families with young children enjoying a day at the seaside. A heavily tattooed father looked us slowly up and down as we passed him at the gateway that led from the small beach car park into the dunes, suspicion writ large on his face. I was acutely aware that two men carrying cameras with large lenses attached to them presented a picture ripe for misinterpretation.

Leading the way into the dune slacks, Richard began dampening my expectations. Passing a small colony of marsh helleborines he noted, 'They're looking pretty knackered, aren't they? It's been so hot here in the last few days, it's finished them off.'

This succinct assessment of the orchids was an accurate one – the flowers had none of the tropical, frilly flamboyance of the fresh swathes I had seen on Holy Island. Here the pink, white and yellow blooms had shrivelled, reduced to crisp brown curls like shredded tobacco. Richard's next pronouncement was more ominous. Stopping by a knee-high patch of creeping willow he paused, scanning the vegetation at his feet, then remarked,

'Well, that's not so good. This was where the big one flowered last year – the biggest *phyllanthes* I've ever seen. I'm worried this dry spell might have done for all the *phyllanthes*.'

Richard habitually referred to each orchid by its scientific name and clearly read a lot of technical papers, which only use Latin binomials when referring to species, in the interests of strict accuracy. In his easy familiarity with his beloved orchids, he dropped the prefix of the Latin binomial so that green-flowered helleborine, *Epipactis phyllanthes*, became simply *phyllanthes*.

We continued to pick our way along the narrow, sandy paths that meandered through the dunes unfolding before us. The sound of playing children receded, and just as I began treacherously to wonder if we were going to find a green-flowered helleborine in the shimmering sand, Richard stopped abruptly.

'I'm pretty sure that's one. Over there...'

He was pointing at a sand dune some thirty metres away. Rising from a slack at a forty-five-degree angle, the dune's sides were dotted with tufts of greyish-green marram grass. Squinting in the direction Richard indicated, I could see nothing remotely resembling an orchid, and asked whereabouts on the dune it was. Richard directed me towards a bare area of sand a third of the way up the dune. There appeared to be nothing there. We walked towards the dune and, having halved the distance between the point of our initial sighting and the dune, Richard paused, looking carefully again at whatever he thought he had seen.

'Yep. I reckon that's one.'

I could now barely discern a short stalk. There was a plant there, certainly, but I still had no confidence that it was an orchid, let alone a green-flowered helleborine. We moved on and clambered up the shifting sides of the dune where, to Richard's quiet satisfaction and my immense relief, there was my first green-flowered helleborine of the year. But what a small, denuded orchid this was. Scraping six inches tall, growing out of the bare unruffled sand with no nearby vegetation for shelter or succour, this sallow, yellowish-leafed plant was a shadow of the specimens I had seen in the past.

Still, the pendulous flowers brooked no argument – at the end of long, ribbed green ovaries, pale jade-green sepals and petals tapering like Norman kite shields framed a heart-shaped white epichile with the barest hint of apple green. The hypochile behind it was a similar unsullied milky green. The only other helleborine that might grow in habitat such as this is the aptly named dune helleborine, but a glance at the hypochile alone was enough to dispel any thoughts that this individual might belong to that species – the interior of the hypochile of dune helleborine is washed with a sullied brown, like the dregs of a mug of hot chocolate.

Kneeling beside it, I examined the helleborine carefully, establishing the identity for myself with a thoroughness these *Epipactis* deserved. The path to identity for green-flowered helleborine had been a twisting and uncertain one, a taxonomic maze with misleading dead ends and more than a few false turns. It was first found in Phillis Wood in West Sussex in the 1830s, leading some to speculate that the Latin name for the species, *phyllanthes*, might commemorate the place of its discovery. It is far more likely that *phyllanthes'* etymology is from the Greek *fyllon* – a leaf, or blade – and *anthos*, or flower, giving us a compound translating as 'leaf-like flower'. The first formal description of the species was made in 1852 in the pages of the *Gardener's Chronicle*, but thereafter the waters muddied as further varieties were described as either species in their own right or, in the case of one particular variety, as a variety of another species altogether.

Var. *vectensis* spent twenty-two years ascribed to narrow-lipped helleborine before, in 1940, it was elevated to full species status in its own right – a promotion that was to prove short-lived for, in 1952, both it and var. *pendula* (another variety that was enjoying full species status at the time) were demonstrated by the botanist Donald Young to belong to the same species as *Epipactis phyllanthes*, the variety of green-flowered helleborine that is commonest in southern England. Botanists tussled with this variable helleborine for many decades, as each of the four named varieties found in Britain is physically distinctive from the others. To this day, there remain some who contend that at least some of the varieties may yet warrant species status in their own right. I was happy to conclude that this dwarf plant was indeed a green-flowered helleborine, and that it belonged to the *pendula* variety.

The sand was almost too hot to touch, and the air smelled biscuity and mineral. Small wonder this plant was not looking at its best, and I did not give much for its chances of enduring for long in such unforgiving surroundings. I looked back to where Richard had first spotted the plant. I wondered at his ability to pick out an orchid this small, this plain and unassuming, from such a distance in such bright, glaring light. Yet the only footprints crossing the sand and ascending the dune were ours.

Richard had moved on while I was contemplating this first green-flowered helleborine of the year. He scoured the dune slacks beyond me, moving restlessly through the low vegetation, searching for further specimens. His persistence was shortly rewarded with three further, more typical examples of var. *pendula*. Growing up through the blankets of creeping willow, these plants were taller, lusher and more vigorous than our first individual had been. Each stem bore more jade-green flowers, and the leaves and stem lacked the faint yellow cast of the depauperate plant. These orchids were textbook var. *pendula* green-flowered helleborines worthy of some appreciative attention.

We walked slowly back to Richard's car, picking our way carefully along the narrow pathways that threaded the dune slacks.

Every step was a challenge as, suddenly, there were hundreds of young natterjack toads making their first tentative steps on land all around us. Each was a tiny simulacrum of an adult toad, a fingertip-small, almost black-skinned warty homunculus crawling wide-eyed across the paths, oblivious to all as they explored this new, dry world into which they had finally emerged *en masse*. They are known locally as the Birkdale nightingale, an allusion to the adult toads' surprisingly beautiful, alien and carrying mating calls. Poet Jean Sprackland recalls:

On Spring nights you can hear them
two miles away, calling their mates
to the breeding place, a wet slack in the dunes.
Lovers hiding nearby are surprised
by desperate music. One man searched all night
for a crashed spaceship. [2]

The mute arrival of these dilettante toads had not gone entirely unnoticed – in one slack an elegant, snow-white little egret was hungrily feeding on them, thin neck stabbing rhythmically at the ground like a sewing machine. It rose in an indignant flurry of wings at our approach, arcing overhead in a low trajectory that spoke of an interrupted but merely delayed meal.

A further short, blurring drive brought us to the edge of a large stand of pine trees. We had swapped damp dune slacks for an entirely different, drier sandy habitat, and were now looking for a different helleborine altogether – here Richard was confident we would find dune helleborines. If our green-flowered helleborines had been where local families went to play, our dune helleborines would be on the doorsteps of their homes – a main road and a railway line were all that stood between the plants' habitat and the sprawling housing estates of Merseyside. A wide sandy path led from the roadside into the trees, a mercifully shaded and resinous haven from the sun's zenith.

Where some orchids had proved coy and played hard to get this summer, dune helleborine was to give itself up easily to me. Within only a few minutes we had found our first flowering plants, knee-high, densely flowered orchids growing in the scattered shady margins of the trees. Their character was immediately, profoundly different from that of the green-flowered helleborines. If green-flowered helleborines had been the shy, demure girl who avoided eye contact at a party, dune helleborines were the confident woman who greeted you at the door, kissed you warmly and pressed a drink upon you. They were everything the green-flowered helleborines had not been – growing proudly in the open for all to see, and thick with flowers.

I had never seen dune helleborines before and, if I was honest with myself, I had not been particularly looking forward to encountering my first examples of their kind. Nothing I had read about them had served to heighten any sense of anticipation – field guides referred to their flowers as 'dull', 'plain' and 'small', epithets that did them scant service. Richard, meanwhile, was characteristically enthusiastic, extolling their qualities with the exuberance of a young dog working a particularly juicy bone.

'They're just brilliant!' he exclaimed, leading me from our first plants at the wood's edge towards further plants growing from creeping willow and bare sand in the open. 'Look, you can see where they're coming from one rhizome!'

Sure enough, the plants emerging in the sandy, exposed areas were growing in clearly visible meandering lines, in some cases almost six feet long. Richard continued, 'And look – there's two forms growing here, almost side by side – you've got the woodland form and the dune form right here.'

Those under the trees had apple-green leaves, while those growing in the open had yellowish-green, sickly leaves the colour of a cooking apple left too long in a fruit bowl. On both forms, however, it was the flowers that confounded my expectations. Far from being dull or plain, each flower was surprisingly colourful when examined closely. Borne on a fat, faintly hairy, and thickly ribbed green ovary, three chartreuse sepals and two crystalline rose-quartz petals framed a bulbous, capacious, ruby-hearted hypochile fronted by an amaranth-bruised, green-tipped white epichile. Each flower seemed to sparkle like a jewel in the sunlight, an illusion reinforced by a network of gossamer spider silk that lanced and shimmered geometrically around every flower spike I examined.

I had not expected to find dune helleborines this beguiling, and the spell was served further by a proliferation of shiny red soldier beetles that studded the orchids' flower spikes, gorging themselves on the nectar within the hypochiles, their black-tipped, rusty wing-cases glittering as they thrust their forequarters into the heart of each flower. Dune helleborines are naturally self-pollinating, but these beetles were helping to ensure a healthy cross-pollination – each beetle invariably sported a fat cluster of crumbling pollinia stuck upon its thorax, as potently yellow and textured as a forkful of scrambled eggs.

Dune helleborines are endemic to Britain, with a world population that may number as few as ten thousand plants, but like the green-flowered helleborines I had seen earlier in the day, they too had caused taxonomists some headaches in the early twentieth century. Echoing the genesis of var. *vectensis* green-flowered helleborine, in 1921 they were described as a subspecies of narrow-lipped helleborine. Five years later they assumed their rightful place as an endemic British species in their own right, known only from populations here on the north-west coast of England and across the water on nearby Anglesey. Until the late 1960s and into the 1970s this seemed relatively uncomplicated and, even then, the discovery of populations of what appeared to be narrow-lipped helleborines at inland sites in the north of England did not appear to have any bearing upon what botanists knew of dune helleborines. (Though, with hindsight, the discovery of a reclusive species of helleborine best known from southern English beechwoods in entirely different habitat in the north of England – habitat that featured sites heavily contaminated with industrial waste – might have caused some botanists to feel a little perturbed.)

The situation became more clouded still when, from the late 1970s, botanists began discovering populations of helleborines in the north of England that were intermediate in form between dune and narrow-lipped helleborines. It seemed then as if dune helleborines had gone full circle when they were re-ascribed to narrow-lipped helleborine, though this time demoted from being a subspecies to a mere variety instead. It was only with the benefit of genetic analysis in the early twenty-first century that botanists finally understood the complexities of what grew in our midst – narrow-lipped helleborine was, after all, confined to the south of the British Isles, while dune helleborine was, once more, a species in its own right. What of those strange, narrow-lipped lookalikes, and their seemingly intermediate forms with dune helleborine? Those were a distinct subspecies of dune helleborine, known as *tynensis* or, colloquially, Tyne helleborine.

Naturally, this being a helleborine story, there remains mild controversy and unfinished business. Like fretfully picking at a loose thread, the more one pulls, the more the whole unravels where these complicated orchids are concerned. Those *tynensis* helleborines, predominantly found growing inland along the River South Tyne on gravelly soil contaminated with lead and zinc tailings, but also on similarly contaminated land elsewhere in northern England and southern Scotland, have been subject to subsequent close genetic scrutiny. While the human eye can discern physiological differences between them and 'normal' dune helleborines, the unflinching genetic perspective is far more discriminating – it appears as if dune and Tyne helleborines are extremely closely related and have only comparatively recently separated into two slightly different entities. Perhaps the tolerance to extreme conditions that allows dune helleborines to prosper in the salty, dry coastal conditions of the northwest coastline has conferred it with qualities that have enabled it to find a niche in free-draining, heavy-metal-contaminated conditions inland. Tyne helleborine might not be a species yet, but it could be a species in the making – for now it is dune helleborine's bridesmaid, but one day it may be the bride herself.

I needed to make what birdwatchers call an 'insurance tick' – for the purposes of completeness, should taxonomists move the goalposts in the future, I needed to see some var. *tynensis* dune helleborines. Taking my leave of Richard, I went inland, travelling east to the former industrial heartlands of the Tyne Valley where, at Wylam in 1781, one of England's greatest engineers was born.

George Stephenson was both the product and the engine of the Industrial Revolution – known as the Father of the Railways, he designed steam engines that formed the backbone upon which much of Britain's industrial growth relied and, with it, the incidental pollution that created the conditions in which dune helleborines began to transform into Tyne helleborines.

The house in which Stephenson was born is made of whitewashed natural stone, and sits on the north banks of the River Tyne. I felt a little homesick as I walked past it to the narrow strip of meadow and woodland that flanks the river itself – it looked very much like my home in Shetland, a place I had been away from more this summer than in the entire preceding dozen years in which I had lived there. On this soporific, sunny July afternoon I would be able to hear the mournful calls of curlews and golden plovers in my fields. Here, just a few miles west of Newcastle upon Tyne, I could hear only the sounds of human life passing around me – the faint hum of traffic in the distance and, nearby, conversation from the outdoor tables of the small National Trust tea shop beside Stephenson's birthplace. I promised myself a cold ginger beer, but only when I had seen my orchids.

I found my first Tyne helleborines growing in the long grass at the very edge of the meadow that runs parallel to the River Tyne, spilling over from the main population and hidden beneath the sparse trees that separate grassland from river. In that shaded hinterland I found many more; not much grew here at the foot of the trees but, picking my way around tangles of fallen branches, I discovered the Tyne helleborines unobtrusively thriving, broken flickers of colour through the screen of trees and leaves from where I knelt amidst the flowers, and hidden from the gaze of the few walkers who passed through the meadow.

Each floppy-leaved flower spike was as deceptive as a ballerina. Seemingly too delicate and spindly to endure, yet evidently strong enough not only to survive but to cover their stage with ease. My estimate of dozens of plants rose as I picked my way through the trees to hundreds. Their flowers were muted versions of the dune helleborines I had seen on the Lancashire coast, cold green blooms with long, pointed epichiles. I could understand why the botanists who found these strange helleborines in the late 1960s and early 1970s had thought, though the habitat was so very wrong for them, that these must be narrow-lipped helleborines. In the intervening years they would prove not to be the latter and might, in the distant future, prove to be more than the subspecies of dune helleborine they were currently considered to be.

I could now enjoy that longed-for cold drink, safe in the knowledge that I had seen both dune helleborine and its heavy metal-loving daughter. Meanwhile, narrow-lipped helleborine would have, for now, to, wait a while longer.

14

To helleborine and back

The first of the autumn's helleborines seemed to have exacted a heavy toll from me both physically and emotionally. I was tired and I felt somehow jaded. I looked back and realised that I had, until this point, been fortunate that my detailed planning had not been derailed by circumstance. Granted, there had been moments when my journey through Britain and Ireland's botanical wonderland had threatened to falter – my troubles finding dense-flowered orchids on the Burren still haunted me, while my cold and inconclusive search for Pugsley's marsh orchids on Rum remained a particularly miserable memory.

Yet for the most part everything had worked out remarkably smoothly so far and I had been especially lucky in some vital regards. I had been in the right place at the right time to see the contentious, exotic sawfly orchid before it succumbed to Storm Katie's ravages, and the beautiful 'missing link' orchid, the hybrid between man and monkey orchids, had flowered in Kent for the first time in almost thirty years.

In hindsight, I had enjoyed a relatively easy ride. Why, then, had seeing the first autumn helleborines left me feeling, in the aftermath, so very different? I wondered if I was suffering from orchid fatigue, an overload of my senses. I had spent every weekend since April away with the orchids in all corners of the British Isles. Home was becoming a stranger to me, while my every waking thought was consumed with flowers – what I had seen, what I had yet to see, where I would find them, and what they all meant. Such unceasing concentration was exhausting and, even when I was not consciously looking for orchids, I was now unthinkingly finding them. The moment when, while driving in the outside lane of the M5 motorway, I saw a stand of purple orchids on the embankment and caught myself thinking, *Probably southern marsh orchid – maybe I could stop on the hard shoulder and have a look*, I knew that I had, if not a problem, then certainly a bad case of orchid fever.

Seeing the first of the autumn helleborines had not entailed any particular effort compared to what had gone before. Perhaps I had reached a tipping point where the prospect of still more time spent away from home, searching for relatively drab and unspectacular *Epipactis* helleborines, simply did not fire my imagination in the same way that the showy *Ophrys* and *Orchis* species had. Was I really that shallow?

One of the benefits of being based in Shetland was the amount of time spent travelling back and forth between the islands. I had the daily luxury of time to think while absently watching for birds or cetaceans from the ferry, and this year, 2016, Shetland was enjoying a good summer for killer whales, with hunting pods seen almost daily. I came to realise that it was not the orchids that were the problem – my love for them remained undiminished and, as they now appeared even in my dreams at night, it was, if anything, stronger than ever after this glorious summer. My malaise stemmed from what I was seeing while looking for the orchids or, rather, both what I was seeing and *not* seeing.

Thirteen years living in Shetland had, without me realising, allowed me a clarity of vision that might not have been possible had I remained living on the British mainland. Had I stayed there, incremental change would have passed me by, accruing slowly like dripping cave water until, in time, a stalactite had formed unheeded by me. As it was, I had travelled through the British countryside with the scales fallen from my eyes. Yes, I had seen all the orchids I had hoped to see. But I had also witnessed towns and villages enlarging where fields and woods I once loved had stood. I had travelled roads that had not existed before – convenient, yes, but at what cost? And while I had seen much wildlife besides the orchids that had given me joy and lifted my heart, I had noticed time and again the absence of other creatures I had once taken for granted. Where were the purring, shuffling turtle doves that had been a fix-ture of my days living in Kent? They were nowhere to be seen or heard and, in their absence, they were not alone. Some birds were strikingly less abundant, and what of the butterflies?

In places where the land was receiving particular attention and being managed thoughtfully, I had seen scarcer species in good numbers – my encounters with freshly emerged, tawny Duke of Burgundies had been one of the most uplifting moments of the summer – but of the less iconic species, the habitat generalists, I had seen far fewer individuals than once I might have hoped or expected to. Fewer small coppers, common blues, or gatekeepers – butterflies I had grown up with and taken for granted as a child were now, I realised with a start, simply … absent.

I knew I needed to put these thoughts to one side for the time being, and concentrate on the remaining orchids I had yet to see. I now felt I ought to have a fairly straightforward run towards my goal of seeing all of Britain and Ireland's orchid species in the course of one year. Lindisfarne helleborine was the last of the strictly site-specific species that might have proved a stumbling block. If I had failed to see it on Holy Island there was nowhere else I would have been able to find an alternative flowering plant or two. With the obvious exception of the elusive ghost orchid, my remaining unseen orchids all occurred at multiple locations. If one site let me down, I would at least have a fighting chance elsewhere.

One of the scarcer species concerned me more than the others put together. This orchid had, above all others, played a pivotal, albeit confusing, role in the unravelling story of Britain's helleborines in the past century. Narrow-lipped helleborine had, at various points, muddied the waters of both dune and green-flowered helleborine identification. Inevitably the recognition of narrow-lipped helleborine in its own right was far from straightforward. Initially believed to be a variation of broad-leaved helleborine, the first claimed British record dates to 1841. William Leighton, a childhood friend of Charles Darwin, who was said to have inspired in him an interest in botany, described it in his *Flora of Shropshire* as being present in 'woods at Bomere pool', though it was only identified as narrow-lipped helleborine retrospectively, in 1919. Subsequent investigations revealed only broad-leaved helleborines in the woods at Bomere Pool, and a herbarium specimen collected there by Leighton proved also to be the latter, common species. It was not, therefore, until 1921 that narrow-lipped helleborine was formally described as a species all of its own on the basis of a colony studied in deep beech woodland in Surrey.

This habitat is typical of that beloved of this most reclusive of all our native *Epipactis* helleborines – dense woodland, predominantly beneath beech trees, on strongly calcareous soil derived from chalk or limestone, and always in the deepest shade where few other plants can thrive. This is an orchid loves the lime but shuns the limelight.

I planned to see narrow-lipped helleborines in their 'type locality', the location from which they were first formally described as a species. This meant a return to Surrey, the county that had supplied such a memorable encounter earlier in the summer with that other lover of heavily shaded beech woodland, the bird's-nest orchid. In most normal years one can find narrow-lipped helleborines within a few yards of the public car park at the edge of the Sheepleas Nature Reserve, but this particular late summer had been no normal year in the south-east of England, and weeks of high temperatures and low rainfall had wrought a devastating effect on Sheepleas' helleborines. Days before I was due to visit the reserve I heard worrying news from a friend who had already made a preliminary investigation there on my behalf – the helleborines were in a parlous state, with little sign that any of them would be flowering this year.

This was cause for grave concern. Narrow-lipped helleborine is not only a delicate and retiring orchid, but is also a species that has declined markedly in the decades since it was first discovered in Britain. Loss of suitable habitat has certainly contributed, with some former outposts converted into unsuitable conifer plantations, but as is often the case with conservation, the rise or fall of a species is rarely attributable to one factor alone. It is likely that climate change has played a part, with increasingly frequent severe storms felling deciduous trees and thereby allowing more light into previously dark understoreys.

The burgeoning populations of deer in the British countryside are far from benign as, in woodlands, they heavily graze the understorey. Declines in the population of birds dependent on thick understorey habitat, such as nightingales, may at least in part be due to this loss of habitat – and browsing by deer is also a known and significant hazard for monitored populations of narrow-lipped helleborines. Human pressure probably does not help either – the use of heavy machinery in woodlands and activities such as mountain biking, dog walking and horse riding may all be playing a part in the species' decline – a decline that can be measured as a loss from over 50 per cent of the helleborine's former range.

I feared that seeing narrow-lipped helleborine might not be as much of a formality as once I had assumed it would be. Failure to see them at Sheepleas would mean I needed to find them elsewhere, so I began to research fallback locations on the escarpments of the Chilterns and the Cotswolds.

My luck took a change for the better the day before I was due to travel to Surrey – Mike Waller, a fellow orchid enthusiast, posted photos online of narrow-lipped helleborines flowering in peak condition in Surrey. He kindly shared their whereabouts with me – and it proved to be that they were at Sheepleas, but not in the area of the reserve where I had anticipated seeing them. Armed with this vital information I could travel in an easier state of mind – although I could not help worrying about the damage just one peckish deer could do in the space of a single grazing session to the dozen plants Mike had reported.

I arrived at Sheepleas after a fretful night's sleep in which deer had figured prominently. The sun was on the cusp of rising as I made my way into the flower-rich meadows that fringed the area of woodland I would be searching. Long grass clotted with mauve clustered bellflowers brushed at my knees as I walked towards a dark bastion of beech trees. Pushing my way through the thick hedge that bounded the woods, I entered a darkness that was almost total – the dense canopy of beech trees above me stole what little light there was from the sky. Somewhere nearby a large animal crashed away through the undergrowth, startled by my clumsy entry to this place in which I emphatically should not be. Woodlands tolerate our presence by day, but after darkness falls they are the realm of those more at ease in their impenetrable vastness. We do not belong in these dark, owly places. My heart hammered in my chest. In an instant I was transported back to childhood, terrified by the sudden clatter of woodpigeons in conifer plantations. It was hard not to feel like prey.

Presently the rising sun threw long, horizontal golden shafts into the wood, illuminating a soft carpet of dead beech leaves as russet as fox fur. Straggles of holly gleamed blackly in the darkness at the base of beech trunks that rose smoothly into what remained of the night. The metronomic alarm calls of nervous blackbirds subsided in the near distance. The wood breathed again and, with it, I did too. The beech leaves smothered the ground before me, a shroud of slow decay uninterrupted by all but a few slender, stately green forms that the gathering sun rendered luminously green before me. I had found my helleborines.

Their bracts and pale flowers drooped languorously above a mere few long, elegant leaves. They were aristocratic and somehow aloof in the gathering silence. Interrupting the sense of communion with something as base as photography would have felt sacrilegious – I sat instead in the comfortable curve where smooth beech trunk met ground and allowed myself the pleasure of watching the new day form around the patient orchids.

Time, sadly, was a luxury I could ill-afford this particular weekend, for my helleborine travels would take me the length of England and up into Scotland, and then further away still. I could not stay for long with the narrow-lipped helleborines, and I could allow myself only a few hours of daylight in which to enjoy them and to explore the woods more thoroughly. In all, I could only find a handful of their kind at Sheepleas, most of which were not in flower. Those that were, however, were as beautiful at close quarters in daylight as they had appeared from a distance at dawn.

Each flower echoed the elegance of the plant as a whole, with elongated, pointed apple-green sepals offset by paler green petals veined with the faintest of rosy pinks, and a long green and white epichile below, as sharply pointed as an arrowhead. This was the slender lip that gave the orchid the scientific name *leptochila*, from the Greek *leptos*, or narrow, and *kheilos*, or lip. The similarity of each flower to those of the *tynensis* dune helleborines I had seen earlier in the month was striking. These plants, however, were the real thing – direct descendants of the very first of their kind to be described almost a century before, in 1921.

It took years for botanists to unravel the Gordian taxonomic knot that are Britain's *Epipactis* helleborines, but even now they continue to spring surprises upon us. Julienne Schiebold has been studying the relationship between these enigmatic orchids and their mycorrhizal fungal partners for years, and has discovered that the narrow-lipped helleborine has the most refined and fastidious of palates. These helleborines shun common or garden woodland mushrooms for their fungal partners, and choose instead to draw their nutrients from the most exclusive and delicious of all subterranean fungi – truffles.

Julienne's field research has taken place in the dense, ancient beech woodlands of Nördliche Frankenalb in north-east Bavaria, an area described by mycorrhizal expert Professor Sir David Read as 'orchid heaven'. Here little light filters through the shadowy tree canopy. The conditions on the woodland floor are challenging for most plants, but not for *Epipactis* helleborines. The secret to their success, the truffles, lies hidden beneath the forest floor and, to find them, Julienne enlisted the help of a *Trüffelhund* called Snoopy with soft, curly fur the colour of cappuccino foam.

Snoopy is a Lagotto Romagnolo, an Italian breed of dog famed for their truffle-hunting prowess; Lagotto Romagnolo puppies destined to be truffle hunters are fed truffles before they are weaned in order to develop a lifelong taste for the distinctive, earthy fungi. Julienne, accompanied by Snoopy and his mycologist owner Peter Karasch, searched for truffles in the winter at sites where they knew narrow-lipped helleborines grew.

'You cannot imagine how much fun it was to revisit the orchid sites and search for the truffle fruiting bodies with a truffle-hunting dog!' Julienne told me. 'Snoopy was not very interested in truffles to begin with – he was more interested in looking for traces of deer or wild boar – but later he was really eager to find truffles and we found more than twenty-five fruiting bodies of four species in less than four hours.'

She added, 'It's a rumour that truffle-hunting dogs do not eat truffles. Snoopy would love to eat them, so we had to be quick after he indicated that he had found a truffle and started to dig it out with his paws. Instead he received a piece of liverwurst as a treat after he found a truffle.

'We think that truffles were actually really abundant there, and that *Epipactis* orchids in these woodlands might be a good indicator species for truffle occurrences as well.'

If Snoopy's truffle-detecting skills in Bavaria's beech woods were impressive, what Julienne found in her laboratory was even more so – narrow-lipped helleborines contained distinctive nitrogen stable isotopes found specifically in their neighbouring truffles, confirming that the orchids were drawing nutrients from the truffles themselves. I was enchanted by this revelation – it seemed wholly appropriate that one of our aloof, elusive and enigmatic orchids should be feeding upon the most exclusive fungi of all.

Julienne agreed with me. 'Of all of my research, this is the story I like and enjoy the most. Being an orchid nerd is such a great thing – you can certainly fall in love with their beautiful flowers, but they are also so very interesting underground.'

If some orchids have proven to have refined tastes, still others provide us with something that is very much to our taste – vanilla, second only to saffron in pound-for-pound value as a spice. In the course of my summer with the orchids I had smelt a number that were faintly vanilla-perfumed, but it is their tropical counterparts that produce the vanilla pods we are so familiar with. These long, aromatic black seedpods were first introduced to Europe in the sixteenth century by the Spanish conquistador Hernán Cortés, who was said to have been served it by the Aztec emperor Montezuma in 1520.

The Aztecs had been using *tlilxochitl*, or 'black flower', pods as a flavouring for years before the arrival of Cortés. Once the pods began to arrive in Europe they were immediately popular, at first as a delicious flavouring in hot chocolate but latterly, after Elizabeth I's pharmacist Hugh Morgan had popularised them, as an additive in alcoholic drinks, perfumes, and tobacco. Inevitably, given the long-standing reputation of orchids as an aid to 'stirre up Venerie', by the eighteenth century imported vanilla was widely perceived across Europe to have aphrodisiac qualities. German physician Casimir Medicus noted, 'No fewer than 342 impotent men by drinking vanilla decoctions, have changed into astonishing lovers of at least as many women.'

The next stop on my journey north was in the dark woods of Buckinghamshire, where I would find the first flowering violet helleborines of the year. While they share the narrow-lipped helleborine's predilection for darkness, violet helleborines are significantly less rare and much less fussy in their requirements. I hoped to see a particularly unusual example of their kind, known as var. *rosea* – one that lacked chlorophyll and, with no green tones whatsoever, luminously bubblegum pink all over.

I found normal violet helleborines in considerable numbers along the heavily shaded, tunnel-like roads that intersected the woods surrounding Princes Risborough. They grew in thick clumps by the roadside, thrusting out of damp verges with a vigour unseen in any other helleborine. Each flower spike had a strongly purple-flushed stem and an abundance of *eau de nil* blooms. I abandoned my car in a wet gateway to pick my way back along the road, finding more and more of them wherever I looked. From the very edge of the road itself, back as far as the eye could see in the woods beyond, there they were – rarely growing as single plants, more often they formed small bonsai bushes of orchids almost knee-high. Violet helleborines have famous longevity, with single-stemmed plants known to be decades old and particularly large clumps perhaps dating back centuries.

I had directions for five individual var. *rosea* plants in the area, and made my way from one to another in a kind of awed pilgrimage. All of them had small, low circles of dead branches set around them, decaying wooden henges erected by previous admirers in a subtle, mute attempt to protect the precious orchids from inadvertent harm. Each plant was formed of one, weedy flower spike alone, displaying none of the vigour of their normal, chlorophylled counterparts. Yet, despite lacking the ability to photosynthesize what little sunlight filtered through to the dark places in which they grew, each plant was acquiring enough nutrition to form flowers – testament once more to the efficacy of the orchids' association with underground fungi from which their rhizomes could draw sufficient sustenance to both emerge above ground and form flowers.

Set above hot-magenta leaves, the flowers themselves lacked the subtle tonal delicacy of normal violet helleborines – each was isabelline white with a shocking acid-pink area inside the hypochile. They exerted a compelling but faintly repellent albino fascination – I was reminded of white mice with their glittering ruby eyes and pale ham-coloured tails. My squeamishness was not shared by a host of small red flies that swarmed around the open flowers – the nectar of violet helleborines is said to be mildly narcotic, and certainly many of these flies seemed stupefied as they clung motionless to the pointed, lysergic pink bracts in which the flowers were set.

The final helleborine left to me was the commonest of all, a helleborine that defied all preconceptions of orchids' delicacy or rarity. Broad-leaved helleborine featured in the earliest English herbal, that written by William Turner in 1562, where he recorded it as seen 'in England in Soffock' – an understatement, for broad-leaved helleborine is both widespread across the British Isles and certainly overlooked. While happiest in deciduous woodland, it is made of stern and adaptable stuff, able to flourish in more demanding habitats still. It can cope with elevated limestone pavements and coastal dune slacks alike, and has proven itself a tenacious colonist of manmade habitats, as at home on the spoil heaps of former industrial sites as it is in the clean cathedrals of ancient beech woods.

I had seen broad-leaved helleborines already, albeit not yet with open flowers, when Bryan Yorke had shown me the hybrid swarm of *Epipactis x schmalhausenii* on his beloved Hutton Roof. There the resident populations of broad-leaved and dark-red helleborines freely hybridised with one another. I intended to see flowering broad-leaved helleborines in what is considered to be their British stronghold – not in the open countryside, as one might have expected, but instead in the gardens and streets of Glasgow. Fate, meanwhile, had intervened with my carefully laid plans.

Bryan had shown me one further non-flowering helleborine while I had last been on Hutton Roof – what he considered was a green-flowered helleborine, albeit one that had never flowered. I had paid this orchid scant attention, distracted instead by the cornucopia of forms of dark-red helleborine and its hybrid offspring all around me. In the intervening days this unassuming orchid, growing in a crack in the limestone pavement in the lee of a stunted hazel bush and the only one of its kind thought to be on Hutton Roof, had finally confounded all expectations and successfully flowered. What had emerged from those tight green buds was something quite unexpected – flowers that looked nothing like any recognised British species of helleborine.

Bryan's photos, posted online by him with characteristic modesty, had caused a quiet flurry of interest amongst his Twitter followers. Birdwatchers have subdivisions within their broad tribe – for example, those who have a particular interest in gulls are known, not always affectionately, as laridophiles. In the British orchid scene those with a passion for *Epipactis* helleborines go by the epithet of epipactophiles. Bryan's unusual helleborine had mobilised the epipactophiles, and he had received requests from a number of them to be shown the plant in question.

I had consulted my reference books and searched images online, only to find the nearest match to Bryan's helleborine were the flowers of a helleborine that appeared to occur only in southern Sweden, Denmark and the islands of the German Baltic. Once thought to be a species in its own right, *Epipactis confusa* had been shown by Danish researchers to be genetically indistinguishable from green-flowered helleborine and had, therefore, been relegated to a variety of that species. If I had learned one hard lesson from all the *Epipactis* that had gone before me, it was that certainty as to what constituted a species amongst them was a hard thing to come by, as elusive and nebulous as a ghost orchid in a British woodland. What had once been considered a species, and was now considered a sub-species, might yet one day be elevated back to being a species. I was making sure I saw all four of the recognised British green-flowered helleborine subspecies for that very reason, and there was no way I would countenance missing what might prove, at the very least, to be another. I needed to make a diversion to Hutton Roof.

On this occasion, Bryan was unable to accompany me onto the limestone pavement he knew like the back of his hand, an absence I was soon to feel keenly. As I emerged from the moss-laden, boulder-strewn wood that skirts the lower flanks of Hutton Roof, I began to wish I had paid better attention to the route Bryan had taken on my last visit, as dense thickets of impenetrable scrub lay between me and the limestone pavement beyond. Mindful of the many ticks I had found buried in my legs after I had last walked on Hutton Roof, I was loath to push through the chest-deep bracken that seemed to mark the clearest route – somewhere here there had to be the footpath that Bryan used on his daily visits. Unfortunately, I could not find it. I gritted my teeth and plunged into the bracken.

Finally scrambling onto the rough limestone slabs that mark the edge of the pavement area was a relief, but only a temporary one. Bryan had led me on a meandering, enormously enjoyable route around Hutton Roof, but with no ready landmarks to refer to, and no recollection of what path we had taken, I would have to rely on using my mobile phone to help me find the ten-digit grid reference I had for the helleborine. This felt like a treasure hunt, albeit a rather chastening one, as I had previously taken some pride in my ability to find my way in the open countryside. It was only in cities that I found navigation impossible.

Before I finally stumbled across the contentious helleborine I had, inadvertently, seen my first flowering broad-leaved helleborines of the year. For the most part I paid them little attention, as I knew I would see many more in due course and, besides, Bryan's frequent complaints about the ravages of deer and hares had lent urgency to my search. I made a brief exception for one unusual plant with leaves, bracts and even ovaries all humbug-striped with cream streaks. I had never seen any orchid of any species quite like this. The first flowering broad-leaved helleborine of my orchid summer closely resembled an intensively bred decorative garden *Hosta*.

My relief when I found the putative *var. confusa* green-flowered helleborine was considerable. At a glance I could see that it was not only still standing, unharmed by the local deer or slugs, but the flowers remained in good condition. A small wall of sharp-edged limestone shards and blocks had been erected around it to afford the orchid some protection. I carefully removed them, and could at last enjoy a close look at the flowers and the plant as a whole.

This was a more delicate, graceful plant than the broad-leaved helleborines and their various hybrid offspring across Hutton Roof, with a slender green stem laxly bearing just seven unusual, drooping flowers predominantly set to one side. The flower colouration was remarkable. Their petals and sepals were the clear, crisp green of unripe apples, but it was the heart of each flower that intrigued the most – the epichile, set to the fore, was heart-shaped, white at the edges with a green tip and, at the junction with the cup-shaped hypochile behind, were two violet-tinged, attenuated magenta bosses split by a more darkly stained central rib.

Curiously, each flower had a viscidium – the small white knob present in those species of *Epipactis* helleborine that are allogamous, or cross-pollinated. Some *Epipactis* are autogamous, or self-pollinating – in these species, the viscidium is either absent or does not persist long after the flower opens. Seeing this, I could understand why some epipactophiles had been quick to dismiss this plant as simply an unusual broad-leaved helleborine rather than a variety of green-flowered helleborine, as the latter is said to be autogamous and thus should not bear a flower with a functional viscidium. Yet everything else about these plants, viscidium aside, seemed still to suggest to me var. *confusa* green-flowered helleborine – a confusing situation worthy of that plant's varietal name, as I could not reconcile the persistent viscidium with what I knew of green-flowered helleborine.

I could draw no firm conclusions at this point. Having taken notes, measurements and photos, I now needed, in the fullness of time, to see where the data led me, and what opinions would emerge from orchid experts with far more knowledge than I possessed. Months later, I was forwarded an email from an epipactophile who had seen the putative var. *confusa* green-flowered helleborine. In the intervening months the handful of British botanists who had seen it had split their opinions as to what it actually was – but most, on the basis of the persistent functional viscidium, had decided it was an extremely aberrant broad-leaved helleborine.

My correspondent had sent his detailed notes and photographs to one of Europe's leading *Epipactis* orchid experts, Jean Claessens of the Naturalis Biodiversity Centre at Leiden in Holland. Jean's reply threw the debate over this unusual plant wide open again.

I saw the functional viscidium of *Epipactis phyllanthes* [on the] Ile d'Oleron in France myself. It shows how allogamous features can occur in autogamous species.

As to your *Epipactis*: the colouration of the lip is remarkable indeed. The photos clearly point towards *phyllanthes/confusa* …

Back on Hutton Roof, I was simply delighted to have not missed this intriguing plant – no matter what it represented from a taxonomic perspective, it was, all the same, a fascinating orchid that encapsulated all that was so wonderful about the *Epipactis* helleborines. Most of them eschewed brash and showy colours for a more subtle, understated beauty; less was somehow more where their looks were concerned. They were genetically complex, and did not give themselves up readily or easily. There was a lot to like about them once one took the time to savour their intricacies.

Replacing the protective shield of stones as I had found them, I took my reluctant leave of this unique orchid. The feeling was familiar to me now: the pang of loss when turning my back on a plant I may never see again unless I made a particular, concerted effort to return to it and it alone. This quest to see all of the orchids had given me so much but had leavened the pleasure with an awareness of how restricted and rare some of the objects of my desire really were. Their vulnerability concerned me. Whatever it proved to be, this orchid on Hutton Roof was, to the best of our knowledge, the only one of its kind in the British Isles. Lose this, either to simple mischance or wilful mischief, and that was it – gone, for ever.

Such a fate was unlikely to ever befall our broad-leaved helleborines, least of all in Glasgow. Here the orchids flourish like nowhere else in Britain, springing up on railway embankments and sidings, on traffic islands, in gardens and on patches of wasteland cheek by jowl with that perennial urban opportunist, *Buddleia*. I began my exploration of this unlikely habitat in the very heartland of orchid improbability, heavily developed Maryhill.

North Kelvin Meadow was, for a while, a Glasgow City Council-operated recreational area, the Clouston Street playing fields. Neglect by the local authority left the hard courts abandoned for a quarter of a century behind the chain-link fences, their few buildings the haunt of drug addicts and the homeless seeking brief shelter from the streets of Glasgow. Trees began to find the cracks at the edges of the site, springing up and shielding the deterioration within from the surrounding streets. Out of sight, and largely out of mind, the former Clouston Street playing fields were just another pocket of lost land in the heart of Glasgow.

In time, the community coalesced to make good the failure of the local authority that served them. While the land still belonged to Glasgow City Council, it was the residents of the surrounding area who formed a community group to develop what came to be known as the North Kelvin Meadow. Nature had already begun to reclaim the site, but now the community itself responded to a collective need for a green space in the city. Nurturing what was already there, the trees became a children's wood, replete with dens and treehouses, and residents created raised beds as miniature allotments, planted a fruit garden, created composting facilities, put up bat boxes, and began to hold community events on the open grassy areas. The outbuildings, once the haunt of the drug addicts, were made secure.

Glasgow City Council, meanwhile, had plans of its own for the North Kelvin Meadow area. Determined to sell the land to a property developer, the council served an eviction notice on the community group in 2009, taking them to court later that year in a move described as absurd by Patrick Garvie MSP. Even the sheriff hearing the case concluded that the group had 'done only good'.

This dispute rumbled on in the years that followed. By the time I came to visit North Kelvin Meadow, the community group had continued to cherish, develop and make good use of the green space in their midst, while maintaining their opposition to the Council's plans. I had spoken to Douglas Peacock, one of the group's long-serving stalwarts, and I was keen to see the orchids that Douglas told me had, unbidden, recolonised the area after Glasgow City Council abandoned it. The group made specific mention of the orchids in the evidence they had compiled to demonstrate the value of North Kelvin Meadow; I found it telling that, of all the species that had colonised the abandoned site, it was the orchids that captured their imagination. Orchids, whether or not they are actually uncommon, have a compelling and valuable allure. Their presence was a godsend for anyone opposing a property development. Douglas told me, 'I'm personally amazed just what support and interest we get every time our wild-flower meadows or orchids get a mention or a picture.'

He went on to describe where the community group was in their fight with Glasgow City Council. After years of legal wrangling, matters were finally reaching a conclusion in the coming months, and the Scottish government had appointed two Reporters to examine the case and decide whether or not the land should be sold for development or retained as a community asset. A few weeks before my visit, the first Reporter had concluded that the site was 'a highly valued open space which is well used and maintained by the local community, and which should continue to be safeguarded for that purpose'.

The community group was now waiting for a public hearing to be held in September by the second Reporter – this would determine whether the planning application submitted by the developers be approved or refused. The Scottish government would then make a final ruling that would determine the long-term future of North Kelvin Meadow. Eight years of a community resisting unwanted development and valuing a green space in their midst was coming to a long-awaited and tense conclusion.

Douglas arranged for me to meet two of North Kelvin Meadow's regular users at the site, Laura Murray and Daryl Philip. I arrived a little before them, walking up one of the streets that flanks the meadow. In many ways Kelbourne Street was like any other inner-city street – plastic bottles, discarded takeaway packaging and crisp packets lay in the gutters and on the pavements, while in the road itself an overflowing green wheelie bin huddled for shelter alongside an abandoned and enthusiastically vandalised caravan. Red brick and stone tenements stretched away into the near distance.

Along one side of the street, however, a thin line of young trees rose from behind a broken, low fence. Through them I could see something very different – a green space, but one without the awkward, stilted formality of a city centre park. Now I understood, at a glance, why the community group had chosen the meadow epithet. North Kelvin Meadow felt like a fragment of the open countryside dropped inside Glasgow by some benevolent, giant hand. An open grassy area, dotted with wildflowers and a scattering of trees, was bounded on one side by a small, dense area of woodland and on the other side by a collection of raised beds and fruit trees. Pathways meandered invitingly into the wood and through the meadow – an area with not a scrap of refuse to be seen in it. If I wanted to spend time exploring and enjoying an area like this, I could only imagine what the space would mean to the families who lived and worked nearby. North Kelvin Meadow spoke of a place appreciated, cared for and valued by the community in whose heart it sat, and where young and old alike could connect with nature.

Laura arrived shortly after me, with her two young sons at her side. Boisterous and irrepressible as puppies, they tore off into the meadow, chasing one another through the trees.

'That's the Children's Wood,' Laura explained. 'It's a great place for them. They can make dens, run around, and let off steam. It's a place where they can play and really *be* kids.'

Daryl arrived and hid his bicycle in the undergrowth behind the raised vegetable beds. We began making our way together slowly through the unfolding pathways that intersected the bushes and trees around the edges of the meadow, Laura's sons enthused by our quest – I explained that we were looking for orchids, a fairly rare sort of flower to see in a city.

'Is this one?' chorused the boys over and over.

We had a few false starts with other flowering plants at the meadow's fringes before we found our first orchids – and they were not, as I'd imagined they would be, broad-leaved helleborines. Instead, we discovered amongst the grass a trio of flowering common spotted orchids and, surrounding them, eight more non-flowering plants, their finely purple-flecked strap-like leaves distinctive amongst the surrounding vegetation. The flowers themselves were almost entirely gone over, with just a few browning pink and white blossoms left at the top of each flower spike, and swelling green ovaries beneath that augured well for many more of their kind in the meadow in the fullness of time. The advent of just one or two common spotted orchids had already, judging by the scatter of non-flowering plants nearby, proven fruitful where once only asphalt and, latterly, piles of rubbish had once been found. Daryl recounted, 'The community came together to clear up the site. People just turned up and lent a hand. The first clean-up was incredible – over sixty black bags of rubbish, and bigger stuff too. The place was just a dump – old tyres, mattresses … you name it, we found it here. Ever since, we've kept on top of the place – we put a door and shutters on the old brick building that the addicts used, made it secure. We made the raised beds, built compost bins, and organised community events here.'

Laura's sons crouched beside the orchids. I wished the flowers were in their prime as, even to my biased eyes, they were not the colourful, impressive plants I would have wished two youngsters' first wild orchids to be. These were a pale shadow of that first lush early purple orchid I had found when I was their age, and that had inspired a lifelong fascination with orchids in me – I rather doubted that these common spotted orchids would do the same. Even the 'common' part of their name did them a disservice.

Continuing to look for helleborines, we neared the edge of the site that bordered Clouston Street. Here, beneath large, mature lime trees, Douglas had assured me we should find orchids. Daryl continued, 'You can see we're still working on it when we can get people together to help. We've cleared the ground of ivy here in the past few weeks.'

The work party had done their job well – the ground was almost bare, with just a few scattered ivy leaves testament to what had, presumably, once grown here in some abundance. Unsurprisingly, given the workers' thoroughness, there were no broad-leaved helleborines to be seen. I reassured a plainly embarrassed Daryl and Laura that this did not spell the end of the orchids that had once been growing here – helleborines in the open countryside can fall foul of all manner of accidents, not least deer or slug damage. Failure to flower and produce seed in one year is not the disaster it might seem – each orchid rises from an underground rhizome, some of which may remain dormant for a number of years, so there was a good chance that some of North Kelvin Meadow's helleborines would emerge again next year. Both my hosts were visibly relieved.

We finished our circuit of the meadow, passing the raised vegetable beds and young fruit trees that comprised the community allotments. Laura stopped by a wooden half barrel, and picked some pea pods for her sons.

'They wouldn't have anything like this if it wasn't for the meadow,' she reflected. 'We've grown all kinds of things here, haven't we, boys? Lettuces, peas, beetroots … I'm no expert on the land, but I just love the meadow. It'd be such a shame if the council gets its way and the flats are built here.'

We said goodbye to one another at the entrance to the meadow, Daryl retrieving his bicycle from the bushes and Laura shepherding her reluctant sons away from their fun. I headed into the heart of the city, reflecting on a morning that, while it had not yielded any broad-leaved helleborines, had been an orchid hunt with a difference – one that had opened my eyes to just how valuable the natural world, however one appreciated it, was to us all.

As I walked through the streets I began to notice broad-leaved helleborines – indeed, it seemed as if they were suddenly everywhere. Growing in gardens cheek by jowl with bedding plants, on verges, even from the bare gravel on a traffic island; once my eye was attuned to them, I could not fail to find them at every turn. Glasgow's reputation for the species was well deserved. Many of the plants were robust and sturdy, and some were well over knee-high, and profusely laden with flowers. The flowers themselves varied greatly, some being richly suffused with wine-red tones and others being delicate confections of green and white – and many more of all shades of green, pink and purple in between those two extremes.

Several of them had sluggish wasps crawling amongst their blooms, as befuddled as those that feed later in the autumn on fermenting orchard windfalls. This impression of drugged intoxication was not entirely fanciful, as broad-leaved helleborines produce potent nectar within their capacious, cupped hypochiles. Scientists have analysed this nectar and discovered a remarkably complex cocktail of chemical compounds, varying from those that benignly release a compelling vanilla scent to others that form powerful narcotic agents. This is a well-known feature of a number of orchid species worldwide – in excess of 1,500 alkaloids with overpowering properties have been identified as present in members of the orchid family. Amongst several narcotic elements identified in broad-leaved helleborine nectar alone is the chemical 4.5a-epoxy-14-hydroxy-3-methoxy-17-methyl-morphinan-6-one or, to give it its common name, oxycodone.

This is a powerful semisynthetic opioid with a colourful and tragic history. First synthesised in 1916 in Germany by scientists looking for an alternative painkiller to heroin, by the advent of the Second World War oxycodone was in mass production. The notes of Dr Theodor Morell, Adolf Hitler's personal physician, indicate that the Führer received repeated injections of oxycodone. Göring nicknamed Morell *Der Reichsspritzenmeister* or Injection Master of the Reich, a bitchy reference to the doctor's preferred method of medical intervention.

Nowadays it is a widely abused pharmaceutical product, due to its tendency to induce feelings of euphoria, relaxation and reduced anxiety. In the USA alone the US Department of Health and Human Services estimates that around 11 million people use oxycodone recreationally every year. Its effects are far from entirely benign – worldwide, thousands of deaths annually are ascribed to oxycodone abuse. Risks notwithstanding, the presence of oxycodone, even in such minute quantities as would be found in broad-leaved helleborines, has led some opportunistic hedonists to wonder if it can be readily extracted from orchids for recreational purposes.

While oxycodone did not noticeably induce a state of relaxed euphoria in the late leader of the Third Reich, it appears to do so very effectively in the wasps that broad-leaved helleborines rely upon for pollination. Decades before we understood the narcotic effects of the orchids' nectar, stupefied wasps had been recorded crawling about their flower spikes. Botanists have speculated that the orchids have evolved their narcotic nectar as a means to improve the efficacy of their pollination – the stupefied wasps linger longer on the orchids' flowers, thereby improving the plants' chances of a higher proportion of their flowers being pollinated. Certainly the wasps I was seeing on helleborines in Glasgow showed every sign of intoxication, being sleepy enough to tolerate crawling groggily across an imprudently offered fingertip before plunging their heads back inside a waiting flower.

My walk through the city finished at the Necropolis, the Victorian cemetery that stands on a hillside in Glasgow beside St Mungo's Cathedral. Broad-leaved helleborine had been reported from within the cemetery grounds in 1986, but not subsequently. I rather hoped I might find the plant there again, but made a bee-line for one grave in particular – that of the nineteenth-century botanist Roger Hennedy. A former muslin print designer, Hennedy was an avid botanist within the Glasgow city bounds and beyond, often in the company of his friend, the renowned war artist William 'Crimea' Simpson, as recorded by Hugh MacDonald in *Rambles Around Glasgow*: 'Our flower-loving friend is now in all his glory poking and prying along the vegetable fringe that skirts the path. Every now and then we are startled by his exclamations of delight, as some specimen of more than ordinary beauty meets his gaze.'

This was, I thought, a very apt description of every botanist I had ever encountered, myself included. I poked and pried along the paths and fringes of the Necropolis, seeking both one tomb and one flower in particular. I found the flower first – and not just any broad-leaved helleborine, for this one was the entirely green-and-white-flowered variety known formally as var. *chlorantha*. This probably deserved an exclamation of delight, but I settled for kneeling beside it to take some photographs.

'What've you got there?'

I jumped, startled by this unexpected question. Looking up I found myself confronted by a pair of eyes as green as the sepals of the helleborine before me. A tall, blonde-haired woman stood beside me on the grass, looking down inquisitively at me.

'It's an orchid – a broad-leaved helleborine. But not just any broad-leaved helleborine – this one's an unusual variety – they're normally a little more colourful than this one ...'

I realised I was babbling. My explanation dried up. Judging by the laughter that hovered at the corners of those green eyes, my companion was not discouraged by my awkwardness. I stood up to introduce myself, to explain why I was looking for orchids in a graveyard, and to attempt to salvage some semblance of my former equanimity. Jenny, a teacher in the city, was intrigued by my quest.

'You came here just to see these plants? And you're going where next? How many orchids have you got left to see this year?'

So many questions, all but one of which were easily answered. I explained my next destination was an outpost of broad-leaved helleborines an ocean away from Scotland, and that a handful of orchid species remained to be seen on home shores – one of which, the ghost orchid, was far from a certain thing. The last flowering plant to be seen in Britain had been found in 2009.

'Do you think you'll find one?'

This was a hard question. I did not want to jinx my quest, but although history told me that ghost orchids were extraordinarily difficult to find in Britain, I had a good feeling about my chances. I knew the exact location of the last flowering plant, and would have time to devote to searching suitable habitat elsewhere in the orchid's historic range. While the last few weeks had been worryingly hot and dry in much of England, the weather had been wetter in the west, and warm, damp, humid conditions seemed to favour ghost orchid emergences. Broadly speaking, conditions in 2016 appeared to be mirroring those of 2009 in the area where the ghost orchid had last been seen. I played down my chances with Jenny, but secretly I was hoping this might be the year.

Having found Roger Hennedy's grave together, we parted company at the edge of the Necropolis, Jenny returning to her interrupted walk and me making my way to the airport. As we said goodbye, Jenny asked me to send her details of where she might see more orchids outside of town the following year. I may not have converted Laura's sons at North Kelvin Meadow into ardent orchidophiles, but perhaps I had made a favourable impression on one person that day.

At the time, Roger Hennedy was botanising in and around Glasgow, many of his countrymen were emigrating in search of better prospects in the New World. During the nineteenth century, many of those Scottish emigrants chose to settle in the United States. It seems unlikely that broad-leaved helleborines were knowingly taken with them – more plausible is that seeds travelled with emigrants in the soil of transplanted trees – but what is certain is that the first broad-leaved helleborines found in flower in America were discovered in 1879 at Syracuse in New York State by the Ladies' Botanical Club of Syracuse. After that initial discovery, they were found widely across the United States, having extended their range right down to California in the far south-west by 1961. Known in America as the weed helleborine, broad-leaved helleborine has proved itself to be an extremely adaptable and tenacious colonist.

While the orchid's success had earned it the weed helleborine sobriquet, it was regarded for the most part as a relatively harmless addition to the United States' flora. Only in Wisconsin was it declared an invasive weed and thus became the target of a programme of active eradication. However, my visit to New York to see broad-leaved helleborines in the context of an invasive alien in the State in which they were first discovered coincided with a presentation by Dr Eric Morgan, the professor of botany at Farmingdale State College. Eric suggested that broad-leaved helleborines were not as benign as they first appeared, and told me, '*Epipactis helleborine* has been an overlooked "cute" non-native plant in the New York region, often given a pass when considering its potential impact since it's an orchid.'

This reminded me of the reverence that Douglas Peacock had recalled was engendered whenever the North Kelvin Meadow community group mentioned their broad-leaved helleborines. Orchids inspire adulation like no other family of plants. Love is famously blind and, in the case of an invasive orchid in America, this appeared to be particularly true. Eric continued, 'Long Island has thirty-six historic native orchids, roughly one third of which are still present. Most of these are fed upon by a small weevil, *Stethobaris ovata*. This weevil is often in very small numbers, and my data seem to support my hypothesis that the populations are kept in check by the scarcity of their food source, the orchids. As *Epipactis helleborine* has expanded, increasing the food supply, the weevils are reaching significantly higher population levels.

'As *Epipactis helleborine* goes dormant months before our native orchids, the weevils are quickly seeking out the native orchids, damaging them in much higher levels than was previously done. I have a ton of data showing that where *Epipactis helleborine* is present, native orchids are always damaged more than when *Epipactis helleborine* is not present.'

While I would not expect to find native orchids growing within the cultured confines of New York's Central Park, what I did find there on a hot, siren-warbling August afternoon were dozens of broad-leaved helleborines. Their Scottish counterparts were still coming into bloom, but these individuals had long since finished flowering. Their ovaries were fat and green, as potently promising as ripe gooseberries. They had been present in New York for over a century, and their evident fecundity was mute testament to their rapid spread across the continent. Given the tenacity of the broad-leaved helleborines on the streets of Glasgow, it was tempting to wonder if it was the tough, adaptable Glaswegian strains of the orchid that had been inadvertently exported to the United States over a century ago.

Foreign plant species are rarely naturalised without consequences of some kind or another in the ecosystems in which they newly flourish. I was pleased to learn from Eric that evidence was mounting against broad-leaved helleborines in the United States. I could cherish them at home in Britain, but in the US their impact needed to be understood and, if appropriate, action taken to address them. I resolved that, one day, I would return to the United States to hunt for their many beautiful native orchids, but, for now, I stripped one of the Central Park helleborines of its ample ovaries. Each one contained some three thousand ripening seeds and, with an untroubled conscience while heedless New Yorkers sunbathed, rollerbladed and flirted with one another all around me, I dropped around thirty thousand potential new invaders into the nearest rubbish bin.

15

My lady's-tresses

Returning from my time spent in New York looking for a British orchid species that had made its home in North America, I now needed to look for another orchid that had crossed the Atlantic – a species common in North America, but one that is rare in Britain and Ireland. Putting the complexities of our helleborines behind me, it was time to hunt for Irish lady's-tresses.

Known as hooded lady's-tresses in North America, the Latin name *Spiranthes romanzoffiana* commemorates the prominent Russian politician Nikolai Petrovich Rumyantsev who, in the late eighteenth and early nineteenth centuries, was a notable patron of

Russian voyages of scientific exploration. While his political career stalled badly with Napoleon's invasion of Russia – Rumyantsev had advocated closer links with France and, after the invasion, the Russian Emperor Alexander I lost all confidence in him – his patronage ensured him a global legacy in which his name was attached to not only an American orchid but also *Papilio rumanzovia*, a large butterfly found in the Philippines.

Sadly, Rumyantsev did not live to see his name immortalised in an orchid. On hearing the news of Napoleon's invasion he suffered a stroke, causing the loss of his hearing and a gradual decline in his health. He died in 1826, two years before the orchid that was to bear his name was officially described by the German botanist and poet Adelbert von Chamisso. Chamisso had been the botanist on the *Rurik*, a scientific exploration ship financed by Rumyantsev during its voyage in 1815–18.

For the most part, *Spiranthes romanzoffiana* is an orchid that belongs where Chamisso originally discovered it – in the Aleutian Islands and on mainland North America. It is, however, also found at the very fringes of Western Europe, in north and west Ireland and in just a few locations in west Scotland. The first Irish record of the species dates to 1810, when it was found by a Mr Drummond in County Cork on the north side of Bantry Bay – an event not published until 1828, when it was noted by the preeminent British botanist Sir James Edward Smith, founding member and first president of the Linnean Society of London. The Linnean Society, the world's oldest active biological society, continues to this day to play a central role in the documentation of the world's flora and fauna – had Smith only formally described the orchid before Chamisso, the Latin, Linnaean binomial name might have been very different.

This, then, was an orchid with a particularly rich heritage, and was another orchid that I had never seen for myself before this summer. I had seen creeping lady's-tresses in the company of Peter Stronach in the Highlands some weeks previously and, upon hearing I planned to see Irish lady's-tresses on the Hebridean islands of Colonsay and Oronsay, Peter had eagerly asked to join me. Getting our timing right had been crucial, as Irish lady's-tresses vary their flowering time in response to weather conditions. While much of the published literature stated that they were to be readily found on Colonsay, I had spoken with Andy Knight, the RSPB manager of adjacent Oronsay, and he had cautioned that the best colony was on Oronsay, an island accessible for visitors only at low tide, at which point one can walk across the exposed, wide tidal strand the receding waters reveals.

My journey began at Peter's home near Aviemore. Here, in the garden of his small white-painted cottage, he proudly showed me the remains of the colony of creeping lady's-tresses that flourished beneath the pines that surrounded the house. Most had finished flowering, their blooms crisping russet or entirely spent, but a handful remained in fair condition, their white, hairy flowers luminous in the gloom cast by the trees above. I imprudently lay myself down on a soft cushion of moss and cast pine needles in order to compose a portrait on my camera. Peter, meanwhile, foraged for chanterelle mushrooms – these beautiful apricot-coloured fungi were prolific here and would accompany the slow-cooking lamb tagine that was currently suffusing the house with fragrant promise. It was only much later, after tagine and mushrooms washed down with red wine, that I found several deer ticks screwed tightly into my shins; while Peter had reaped a wild harvest, they had crawled, unfelt by me, into my clothing in search of a feast of their own.

The following morning we headed for Oban on the west coast of the Scottish mainland, passing through the Highlands to the port where we would catch a ferry to Colonsay. The skies above us were grey as we pulled away from land – the preceding week had been unsettled, with strong westerly winds scything off the Atlantic. Andy Knight had written from Oronsay to warn me that 'the tresses are flowering well, a little bruised from the weekend gale, though', and as if that were not warning enough, he had also mentioned the small matter of 'a dodgy neap tide'.

I did not like the sound of a dodgy neap tide, and even less so when Andy qualified that that this meant even less time on Oronsay than I had anticipated. Having never been there before, I had no idea how easy the orchids would be to find and, if I had learned one lesson so far this summer, it was that I could not afford to be complacent where orchids were concerned. We would have perhaps as little as four hours on Oronsay before the tide turned, rendering impossible a crossing on foot back to Colonsay. Andy had mentioned that, weather permitting, he could get us across to Colonsay in his small boat, but this kind offer, though intended to be reassuring, was in fact anything but, as it spawned a fresh bout of fears of the consequences of being stranded overnight on Oronsay by a combination of neap tide and bad weather, missing the ferry back to the mainland, and then my subsequent flight home to Shetland.

Colonsay is described as the 'Jewel of the Hebrides' – a description that, having been bowled over by North Uist's spectacular machair, and chastened by Rum's austere landscape and weather, I had reserved judgement upon. Having landed on Colonsay I soon realised that the title was well chosen. The island is a rich tapestry woven of myriad threads of habitat – farmland, woodland and moorland jostle for space on an island ten miles long by two miles wide, framed by seabird-jostled cliffs, sandy beaches and flower-rich machair.

The landscape is studded with signs of human activity reaching back as far as seven thousand years ago – excavations of shell-mounds, midden heaps dating to the Mesolithic period, have unearthed barbed bones and antler points created by skilled ancient human hands. Known as *sheeans* locally, in later years the mounds were reputed to be fairy knowes, the homes of supernatural beings. Bronze Age field systems and settlements remain visible in the land to this day, as do subsequent Iron Age forts, signs of more unsettled and less pastoral activity. Place names of Norse origin can be found on the island, evidence of later immigration and settlement, while both Colonsay and Oronsay boast evidence of early Christian activity on the islands.

How long the object of my attention, the Irish lady's-tresses, had been flourishing on Colonsay and Oronsay is a matter of much less certainty. The first ever Scottish examples were discovered on Colonsay at Uragaig in 1930, and thereafter, the island gained a reputation as a place in which the orchids might be found, particularly on old lazy beds – lazy beds being the local name for the old ridge and furrow cultivation method prevalent in much of Ireland and Scotland until the nineteenth century. This reputation was somewhat misleading, as the orchids prefer poorer, less well-drained ground, happiest where low nutrient soil is permanently damp or saturated. How long they had gone unnoticed on Colonsay or Oronsay one could not say – indeed, how long they have been on this side of the Atlantic as a whole is pure conjecture.

Nobody knows how they came to be here. One hypothesis is that they are relicts, survivors of the last glacial period – while others suggest they are more recent natural colonists, brought to our shores either as seed carried across the Atlantic by the prevailing westerly winds or inadvertently brought as seed or viable fragments of root or rhizome by migratory wildfowl. Their origins are a mystery, but their beauty is irrefutable. Unlike our other native *Spiranthes* orchid, autumn lady's-tresses, they have three rather than two rows of white flowers spiralling up their stems, while each individual flower is a sculptured masterpiece with much longer lips than either creeping or autumn lady's-tresses, lending them a lascivious, suggestive quality.

We drove across Colonsay to where the single-track road ends and the tidal channel that separates Colonsay from Oronsay begins. As the tide recedes it leaves a passable silver strand of sand and mud across which, in a suitable vehicle, one can drive – there is, tide and weather permitting, a Royal Mail delivery to Oronsay – though we, erring on the side of caution, had opted to leave Peter's car on Colonsay and cross on foot. We arrived before the peak of low tide, hoping to cross a little earlier than the 10 o'clock Andy had indicated and, thereby, maximise our time on Oronsay. As far as we could tell from Colonsay's shore, the sea had, more or less, retreated enough for us to set out. We marched quickly out onto the exposed strand, peaty brown water making tabby stripes of the wet silver wave ripples the receding water had in its wake. The sand was hard beneath our feet and, with ringed plovers nervously scuttling ahead of us, fluting alarm calls at our temerity in invading their world, we made good progress towards Oronsay, interrupted only by my pausing to pick up cowrie shells from the sand; since childhood I have been unable to resist these delicate flesh-pink and white shells with their sharp ridges and alluring curves.

The island lay low on the horizon before us. Tyre marks carved into the sand revealed where vehicles habitually crossed and these guided our passage across the strand. A sanctuary cross once stood midway in the channel; any fugitive from Colonsay who reached the cross was said to be immune from punishment if he stayed on Oronsay for a year and a day. I considered the prospect with pleasure. I was fleeing nothing, but with a love of island life in my bones, this sort of challenge had always appealed deeply to me. Perhaps being stranded here overnight, for all the inconvenience, was not such a bad prospect after all.

Within a hundred yards of Oronsay we came across what was left of the falling tide, mounting anticipation driving us to risk wet feet. From the strand a rough bladderwrack-strewn track ran along the shore, in places blasted through spurs of protruding rock, leading up onto the island itself. As we walked uphill and onto Oronsay, my eyes already sought our target, though I had no idea where on the island we might find it. We had a rendezvous to keep with Andy, and I trusted all would be well.

The metalled track that comprises Oronsay's road network runs to the sole inhabited buildings on the island, a small complex that incorporates a large, sprawling farmhouse and the remains of the Oronsay priory, founded by Augustinians in the early fourteenth century. The gregarious chatter of a family of choughs was drowned out by the persistent calls of a territorial and magnificently incongruous male peacock. The RSPB have managed Oronsay as a reserve since 1996 in a farming partnership with the island's owner, predominantly to conserve populations of chough and corncrake, but with a careful eye to the other biodiversity of the island, orchids included. The peacock belonged to the owner, while Andy, as the RSPB's manager for the island, tended to a flock of sheep and a small herd of cattle that were carefully deployed to graze the island for the maximum conservation benefit.

Andy had been checking upon his livestock before he returned to the farmhouse shortly after our arrival. A genial, friendly man, he wasted no time in offering to show us the Irish lady's-tresses.

'They're just over there – only a field away.'

We walked with him towards the shore, through a gateway into a field studded with wildflowers. Two choughs flew up at our approach, an eddy of black wings rising from the meadow like charred paper off a bonfire.

'They're the pair that breeds behind the house,' said Andy, indicating a crag nearby. 'But these are what you're here for.'

Pointing at the ground at his feet, Andy showed us our first Irish lady's-tresses.

'They're not in bad condition, considering the weather last weekend. A lot of them got badly burned.'

As Andy wandered away in search of further, pristine examples of his charges, I knelt on the wet ground to take a closer look at this, the scarcest of our native *Spiranthes* orchids. Images of this plant did them scant justice – though no flower spike was particularly tall, the actual flowers themselves were exquisite. Arranged in a dense triple spiral, on each individual flower silvery white petals and sepals formed a long, bulbous bonnet from which a creamy lip protruded downwards, hanging like the tongue of a panting dog. Apple-green stripes ran up the lip and into the recesses within. Each flower had the chaste beauty and promise of a bride and, better yet, she bore a subtle perfume too – the flowers carried a faint but distinctive aroma of vanilla.

Such beauty came at a price for her admirers – clouds of biting midges boiled up from the grass, powerfully attracted to the attendant orchid hunters. I was familiar with these tiny insects, for they occur in Shetland too, but there I rarely found them bothersome, as it is a rare day that the wind drops sufficiently for them to venture above grass level. What I had never experienced were midges of such voracity and in such numbers – they swarmed about my head, settling on any bare skin they could find. They were in my ears, my nostrils and my eyes, and my hands were coated with them. Each one was minute, little more than a millimetre in length, but their bite had the sweet pain of the prick of a needle, and itched powerfully for hours afterwards.

This made simply enjoying the Irish lady's-tresses, let alone composing pleasing photographs, decidedly difficult. We swiped, swatted and wiped our faces, but the midges were insatiable and innumerable. For every one I smeared into oblivion many more came to take the place of the fallen. Peter, following Andy to search for more orchids while I attempted to frame a flower in my camera, whirled like a dervish, his hands blurring about his head. I was learning first-hand why the west-coast midges are so infamous amongst visitors to Scotland – and appreciated wryly why Scots take such an obscure pride in them. They had tenacity and an impact that projected way beyond their size, a fine metaphor for Scotland itself. While some Singaporean bank notes sport colourful illustrations of orchids, their national flower, the Royal Bank of Scotland £5 note features, for the keen-eyed, a midge – a blackly humorous touch I struggled to appreciate as my bites began to swell. With these and the deer ticks of the previous day, I was paying in blood for my lady's-tresses this weekend.

Walking was, I found, the best way to avoid or at least minimise the attentions of the indefatigable midges. I counted over seventy flower spikes in all before admitting defeat and gratefully accepting Andy's offer of sanctuary and a coffee in the farmhouse kitchen. As we left the field, a ringtail hen harrier began to quarter the ground behind us – the second notable raptor of the day, as we had watched a hunting golden eagle over the moorland of Colonsay earlier in the morning, both vivid examples of how birds of prey can thrive when unfettered by illegal persecution at the hands of man. While driving through the Highlands we had discussed the low population densities of both eagles and harriers in Scotland, and Peter was visibly agitated as he described the extent of wildlife crime committed by unknown perpetrators on his very doorstep in the Cairngorm National Park.

'They've even destroyed heronries,' he confided. 'Any animal that competes for something that can be fished for or shot at is fair game. But it's impossible to prove anything unless people are caught in the act. And that almost never happens.'

Sitting in Andy's kitchen, we discussed his work on Oronsay. His love of the land and the wildlife that he cared for was as inspiring as our conversation about wildlife crime had been depressing.

Here was somebody who not only cared deeply but had devoted his working life to making a positive difference.

'I worked on Orkney for the RSPB for years,' he reflected, 'but the job changed. In time I found myself responsible for people, not habitats – I'd become a manager of people and paperwork, not birds or the land. We decided that it was time for a change. This job on Oronsay came up, so I went for it. Of course, it's not for everyone, living here, but we're happy for now. It's not for ever, of course. It's hard physical work, running this place, but as long as I'm fit and able, I'll keep doing it.'

I completely understood the feeling of pride Andy obviously felt for what he did. I felt exactly the same at home in Shetland on my small croft. Responsible for a mere seven acres of land, I took enormous satisfaction from seeing wading birds breed successfully in my fields – including, lately, whimbrels – a nationally scarce and declining British bird. Andy, meanwhile, was responsible for so much more, from the glossy black, red-billed choughs that bred within a stone's throw of his island home to the rare orchids nearby, and more besides. Part of me envied him – his was the life I had inchoately yearned for as an adolescent, my ill-formed dreams being snuffed out by parents who insisted I get 'a proper job'.

Andy took us halfway back across the strand to Colonsay in his Land Rover, saving us time and wet feet as the tide began to turn. We walked back to Peter's car along the shore, exploring the machair and looking for vagrant American wading birds that might, just possibly, have been blown across the Atlantic in the gales that had preceded our arrival. We found none, but the machair itself was blazing with colour – flowers of all colours lit up the turf like fireworks: acid-pink common centaury, deep-violet autumn gentians, pearlescent blooms of grass-of-Parnassus, and everywhere countless eyebrights. While Peter searched the shoreline for birds, I ricocheted from plant to plant, intoxicated with the variety before me. I hoped I might some more Irish lady's-tresses before we left the island, though this drier machair habitat was surely not right for them.

We stopped at a likely loch-side field halfway down the island as we drove back to the ferry terminal to catch our ferry back to Oban. This, Andy had told us, once supported a reasonable population of orchids, though he had not seen any there yet this year. This was entirely typical behaviour for Irish lady's-tresses – they are renowned amongst orchid hunters for their habit of dying out suddenly and without obvious reason, colonies contracting as rapidly as they flourished in the first instance. This particular meadow seemed a little overgrown compared to Andy's carefully managed pasture, but enjoyed a reputation amongst visiting botanists as the *locus mirabilis* for Irish lady's-tresses on Colonsay. I had been given details of it by two separate botanists before our visit.

Peter and I walked systematic transects back and forth across the field, but to no immediate avail. It seemed as if we would have to be content with our Oronsay flowers until, on the verge of giving up, I spotted a familiar white spike in the grass some way off – and, sure enough, we had one final Irish lady's-tresses to enjoy. Unlike on Oronsay, where one flowering plant was invariably accompanied by half a dozen more within a close orbit, here we could find no further plants, flowering or non-flowering. It seemed as if this lonely orchid was the site's last gasp where the species was concerned.

With Irish lady's-tresses now safely seen, there were just two orchid species left to find before the conclusion of my quest. One I hardly dared to think about – I had been concentrating hard on the logistics involved in seeing all the species that went before, and had tried not to worry about the improbability of seeing, let alone finding for myself, a ghost orchid this year. That challenge was now drawing uncomfortably closer and I could not avoid fretting about the complexities involved, for the last regularly flowering orchid species I needed to see would pose no problems whatsoever. Autumn lady's-tresses is, by some margin, the commonest of the two *Spiranthes* orchids found in Britain.

Not so long ago there was a third *Spiranthes*, found only in a handful of sites in the New Forest. Summer lady's-tresses was an orchid at the very most northerly extremity of its range in Hampshire, being found in suitably boggy locations throughout Western Europe. As close to us as France it remains locally common, but since the early 1950s it has been lost to us in Britain. First recorded in the New Forest in 1840, old accounts of it recall years in which the flower spikes were so numerous the surface of the bog in which it occurred was smothered white, so densely packed together were the flowering plants. Botanist Ernest Marquand recalled in 1901, 'I once saw half an acre of bog perfectly white with these flowers, but the following year only a few spikes of bloom appeared.'

I read these accounts with the pain of unrequited love – the species declined catastrophically in the twentieth century, a loss driven primarily by changes in land management that fundamentally altered the nature of the sites at which the orchid had once thrived. Forestry work and drainage were the principal culprits, though with hindsight it is likely that overeager and thoughtless botanists may also have contributed to the orchid's demise. In the nineteenth and early twentieth centuries summer lady's-tresses were all too frequently collected to star in herbaria, where they remained as baleful dry, pressed relics for the botanists who had loved them too much for the plants' own good. By the end of the 1950s, summer lady's-tresses had been lost altogether from the British flora.

From time to time since, rumours have surfaced that summer lady's-tresses have either been rediscovered or even reintroduced into the New Forest by unknown, rogue orchid enthusiasts. I was not sure how I felt about this, were such a rumour to prove to be true – on the whole, botanists tend to take a dim view of deliberately introduced plants although, in the case of the sawfly orchid in Dorset, I was still troubled by the unquestioning presumption of innocence adopted by some of the botanical establishment. There is, however, a growing movement elsewhere amongst conservationists to reintroduce species where they have been lost, to right the wrongs of the past using suitable stock from similar populations elsewhere in Europe. Whether this is good ecology or a salve to our collective conscience is questionable. Maybe it is both.

Certainly in some instances such reintroductions are at worst benign and, at best, hugely beneficial to our countryside. Who can fail to delight in the sight of large blue butterflies on the wing once again in abundance, nor feel their heart soar at the sight of red kites gyring above our woodlands with their long, forked russet tails twisting and turning ceaselessly? Beavers once again swim in some of our rivers, and will help to improve not only the habitats in which they occur, but also those rivers' abilities to cope with excessive water running off the land as climate change wreaks havoc with our weather. These are all good things – so would it really be so very bad if someone reintroduced a beautiful, delicate white-flowered orchid where once it thrived?

On balance, I felt that I would welcome the news that summer lady's-tresses were, once more, flowering in a secluded New Forest bog. Sadly that news was not forthcoming this year, but, by way of ample consolation, I still had the imminent flowering of autumn lady's-tresses to look forward to. They are found widely across England, Ireland and Wales, albeit with a southerly and coastal bias. Always an endearing habit in an orchid, they are prone to popping up unbidden in suitable habitat – I saw my first ones growing in a suburban front lawn in Kent in 1993. Victor Summerhayes, the botanist in charge of the orchid herbarium at the Royal Botanical Gardens at Kew and author of the magnificent orchid monograph *Wild Orchids of Britain*, recalled them flowering in Somerset on a grass tennis court, near the net, where the mower's blades had spared the vegetation.

In Dorset, autumn lady's-tresses may be found flowering within yards of the grave of Mary Shelley, who was buried in the churchyard of St Peter's in Bournemouth, as her son and daughter-in-law considered the graveyard at St Pancras to be 'dreadful'. When Shelley's box desk was opened after her death, her son found she had wrapped the ashes of her late husband, Percy Bysshe Shelley, along with the remains of his heart, in a silk parcel contained within a page of his elegiac masterpiece *Adonais*, cherished alongside locks of her dead children's hair. As the master of Gothic Romanticism, she would surely have appreciated nature's gesture in this regard, these spiralling, ghostly white orchids rising annually at her graveside, echoing her memory of her lost children.

I had chosen to see what would, possibly, be the last orchid species of my quest at the very furthest point in Britain at which it might be seen. Having sought orchids in the far north on desolate Unst in Shetland, I was now bound for the subtropical surroundings of the Isles of Scilly, twenty-eight miles off the coast of Cornwall, to see my first autumn lady's-tresses of the year. I had visited the islands many times before, but always in the late autumn, in the hope of seeing rare, displaced vagrant birds.

In the 1980s and 1990s the islands had enjoyed their heyday, years during which thousands of the very keenest birders flooded to the islands during October, an olive-green-clad army touting binoculars, telescopes and CB radios. When news broke of a newly found rarity, the CBs would crackle into life, a local grapevine that predated the immediacy of mobile phones, and the birders would begin running, streaming along the narrow lanes of St Mary's, the main island, hastening either to where the bird had last been seen or to the pier in Hugh Town, from where they could catch a boat to the adjacent island in question. The birders still migrate to Scilly every autumn, but their numbers have diminished greatly. Shetland is the new Scilly nowadays and mobile phones have replaced the CB radios, but the impetus to see rare birds remains undiminished.

All of my previous visits to Scilly had been to birdwatch during the frenetic days of past Octobers. Arriving on the pier in Penzance from which I would board the *Scillonian*, the ferry that serves the islands from Cornwall, I found myself in very different company from that on former visits. Gone was the tense focus and competitive camaraderie I had once known – instead an almost carnival atmosphere pervaded the queue waiting to board the boat. Birders back then were almost exclusively male – but my travel companions today were a mixture of all ages, genders and backgrounds. Children bounced with excitement alongside retired couples, dogs strained on their leads, and a small party of young Londoners loudly marvelled that the *Scillonian*'s onboard café served flat white coffees.

I took myself outside onto the deck to spend the crossing sitting in the warm sunshine looking for shearwaters and cetaceans. My hopes of seeing a Cory's or great shearwater were not to be realised, but I was pleased to find both common and bottlenose dolphins feeding actively near the boat as we moved along the Cornish coast.

'What are you looking at?'

A small girl, maybe seven or eight years old, was intrigued by my binoculars. I explained that there were dolphins nearby, and presently she saw them, before running off to find her brother and parents to share the exciting news. Word spread quickly around the deck, and I found myself joined by a small crowd of would-be cetacean watchers. My stock rose a little further when, passing the small village of Porthgwarra on our right-hand side, I found a glossy black minke whale surfacing languorously between us and the prominence of Gwennap Head.

Numbers thinned on deck after we passed Land's End and began crossing the open water between Cornwall and Scilly. The *Scillonian* enjoyed a dim reputation amongst birders back in the day for her uncomfortable progress in choppy water, a consequence of her shallow draft. She did not so much cleave the waves as wallow through them with a rubber duck's grace and stability. This had not changed and, as her peculiar motion began to make itself felt, first one or two and soon many of those on deck sought the sanctuary of the passenger lounge. Having earned my spurs using a ferry daily in Shetland and leading wildlife tours at sea, I knew better – I stayed in the open air and kept my eyes fixed on the horizon. I might not be seeing any shearwaters, but neither did I feel seasick.

Upon arriving at the pier on St Mary's I left my companions to explore the shops and eateries of Hugh Town. I knew where I was going, though not specifically the whereabouts of my quarry – I had heard that autumn lady's-tresses were numerous 'around the walls of the Garrison'. Built in the aftermath of the doomed Spanish Armada, this walled enclosure sits atop the Hugh, the headland overlooking Hugh Town on one side and the open-water approaches to the harbour on the other. At the heart of the fortifications is the Star Castle, an eight-pointed granite fortification, flanked by a thick granite curtain wall that, over the centuries, came to encircle the headland. Walking up the short, steep lane to the gateway leading into the complex, I was struck by the lushness of the vegetation in the gardens that lined the way – greenery and flowers spilled over their garden walls in waves of abundance. Scilly enjoys an enviably mild subtropical climate, warmed by the benevolent Gulf Stream.

I began to walk anticlockwise around the Hugh and, not sure where I ought to find my orchids, my progress was slow. Looking wistfully north over the azure water, I could see the island of Tresco, home to the famed Abbey Gardens. Created by Augustus Smith, the gardens feature a panoply of exotic, tender plants from around the world. Smith was, by all accounts, a remarkable man who transformed the fortunes of Scilly in the middle of the nineteenth century at a time when the islanders had few prospects, little employment or education and, for the most part, scratched a subsistence lifestyle from the land and sea. The Reverend George Smith, writing in 1818, said of the islands' inhabitants, 'What strength could they have from limpets and dried leaves off the hedge, which they mix with hot water?'

Augustus Smith acquired the lease of the islands from the Duchy of Cornwall in 1834, and set about a programme of radical investment and reform. He built schools on Scilly's five principal islands, instituting compulsory education decades before it became the norm on the British mainland. By investing heavily in infrastructure improvements, he created employment where there had been little hitherto. His botanical works were as transformative as his social reform. On Tresco, where he built his home, one of his first acts was to have a granite wall built enclosing what would be his gardens, and the seeds of gorse scattered about the perimeters, hoping to create windbreaks. In time he augmented this with a tree-planting scheme – trees were almost entirely absent from the island – and with shelter belts created from elm, oak, poplar, sycamore and, latterly Monterey cypress and pine, Smith created the sheltered haven that would allow his subtropical garden to flourish.

I only had time enough for a day trip so, with the autumn lady's-tresses my priority, I could not make my long-anticipated pilgrimage to the Abbey Gardens on Tresco. Access from St Mary's is via one of the islands' several small inter-island boats or, if local legend was to be believed, via a four-mile natural tunnel that runs from a deep cave on St Mary's known as the Piper's Hole to a cave of the same name on Tresco. Rumour had it that a dog, released into the cave at the Tresco end, emerged from the cave on St Mary's with most of its fur missing, testament to how narrow the sub-sea passage must have become in places.

Safely still above ground on St Mary's, I stopped my idle sightseeing and subterranean daydreaming, and concentrated upon the task at hand. A pair of Dutch hikers sped past me, clearly a little perturbed by my slow progress and plant-hunting stoop.

'Have you lost something?' one asked. I explained that I was looking for wildflowers, and one species of orchid in particular.

'There are no orchids here!' he replied cheerfully. I dearly hoped he was wrong, but as time passed and I found nothing I began to wonder if, in fact, he might be right after all. Large areas of bracken had been cleared on the sides of the headland, and my imagination began to fear the worst. Perhaps the two Dutchmen harboured a historically dim view of the islands – during the English Civil War the Isles of Scilly had been a staunchly royalist stronghold and a base from which royalist privateers preyed on passing shipping. The Dutch endured heavy losses from privateers operating from Scilly, prompting Admiral Maarten Harpertszoon Tromp to demand reparations from the islands for lost ships and goods. His request, unsurprisingly, went unanswered and in 1651 Holland was reputed to have declared war on the Isles of Scilly – a state of war that existed until 1986 when peace was finally declared after Roy Duncan, the leader of the Isles of Scilly Council and Jonkheer Huydecoper, the Dutch ambassador in London, signed a peace treaty. With no shots having been fired in the intervening years, this remarkably bloodless affair came to be known as the 335 Years' War.

While this notional state of war existed, the Garrison fortifications continued to be enhanced and developed, with the construction of several strategically placed bastions and batteries about the curtain wall's perimeter. It was just after one of the largest of the latter, the Woolpack Battery, that from the seaward side of the curtain wall I caught a glimpse of an intriguing twisted white flower head high above me on the lip of the wall. My heart began to quicken with the now familiar rush of adrenaline each new orchid engendered. I knew I should retrace my steps and approach from the higher, landward side of the wall, but where was the adventure in that? Leaving my camera on the path, I set about climbing the wall, a relatively easy ascent, as the large granite blocks from which it was formed provided ample foot and handholds. All the same, as I neared the top and my prize, I was keenly aware that a fall, though unlikely to be fatal, was bound to break some bones. I began to feel a little foolish, but then there it was; inches from my face was a small patch of a dozen autumn lady's-tresses, only a few centimetres high, growing from the short, stunted grass that topped the wall. All thoughts of my personal safety were forgotten. I had done it! Here was possibly the last species of orchid I would see this year.

I joined the orchids on the top of the wall, and lay nose to nose with my first autumn lady's-tresses of 2016. While no individual autumn lady's-tresses plant is ever a giant to threaten the likes of a towering broad-leaved helleborine or a trunk-stemmed lady orchid, these particular plants were especially diminutive examples of their kind. I hoped I would find further, larger plants nearby and, with my camera retrieved from beneath the wall, I continued walking back towards Hugh Town. Between the Woolpack Battery and its easterly sister, the Morning Point Battery, my hopes were amply rewarded. Growing both on the walls and within them on the short turf of several bastions I found further, and much larger, orchids in their very prime. With the sun beating down on me, I lay amongst them, watching bumblebees chart erratic courses from plant to plant.

Autumn lady's-tresses have an ingenious method of ensuring that cross-pollination occurs. Each flower opens slowly, over a period of a day. At the beginning of this process a visiting bumblebee can only inadvertently remove the pollinia from the flower in question, but cannot deposit them on the same flower's stigma. A more advanced flower, with a more widely spread lip and open column, allows the bee to probe the flower a little more deeply – at which point the bee-borne pollinia can rub against the flower's stigma. The pollinia are brittle and break off in small fragments, which stick to the receptive stigma. In this way older flowers are always pollinated with the pollinia from younger flowers. More usefully still, the flowers on an individual autumn lady's-tresses flower spike open one after another from the bottom of the spike heading upwards – and bumblebees habitually work their way up a flower spike from base to top. As this means that a nectar-questing bee will always visit older flowers before younger ones on an individual orchid, it is almost impossible for the bee to fertilise that plant with pollinia from itself.

The bumblebees of St Mary's proved to be wonderfully busy and obliging. While I lay amongst the orchids, a succession of white-tailed bumblebees made their way around the flowers. I began to feel drowsy, lulled by the soporific sound of their buzzing flight, the warmth of the sun on my neck, and the aftermath of orchid euphoria. It was hard to keep my eyes open, but I feared that sleep, if allowed to overtake me, might cost me catching the *Scillonian* in a few short hours' time. I fought the impulse by concentrating on taking photos of the diligent bumblebees as they unwittingly pollinated the orchids.

Walking back towards Hugh Town, I came to where my circuit of the Garrison had begun, at the gatehouse. A small bastion, replete with cannon, overlooked the bustling harbour and compact town at my feet. I paused to take in the view, my mind now veering towards the promise of a cold beer and perhaps an ice cream, too. With the orchids safely found, I could afford to let myself be every bit as much a tourist as those I had shared a boat with earlier that morning. The ice cream, naturally, would be vanilla-flavoured…

A familiar shape caught my eye – there, on the grassy area that topped the bastion's walls, were three more autumn lady's-tresses. Had I only worked my way clockwise around the walls, I would have found my orchids within ten minutes of making landfall on St Mary's. As I walked to the cool depths of the Mermaid Inn, I reflected that today's experience had been exactly what I had always hoped this summer would prove to be – not so much about simply seeing the orchids as expeditiously as possible but, rather, about the manner in which I saw them. I'd hoped to immerse myself in the places in which they grew, the history of those places, and the people past and present who shared the landscape and the flowers with me. Armed with accurate directions and a little luck, anyone might emulate the numerical achievement of seeing all of Britain and Ireland's orchid species in one summer, but how hollow that would have been without appreciating the flowers in the context of where one had found them.

16

Hunting ghosts, chasing shadows

With the spiralling, twisting forms of autumn lady's-tresses safely seen across the south-west of England, there remained only one orchid left to see before my quest would have reached its conclusion. Just one species, but of all the orchids I had set out to find in the colourful maelstrom that had been my orchid summer, I had always known that this would be the most challenging of all.

Never was an orchid so aptly named as this final species – ghost orchids are ephemeral, fleeting creatures that haunt dark woodland places and orchid hunters alike. They are the very rarest of our native orchid flora, and decades can pass between sightings.

Amongst botanists they are considered legendarily difficult to find, notorious for their fickle habits – they are quite capable of flowering beneath the leaf litter through which they otherwise tentatively raise their pallid heads and, when they do emerge, they are frequently consumed by slugs and snails, often before the flowers have had a chance to set seed.

Lacking chlorophyll, those emergent flower spikes are a wraith-like apparition, the few drooping flowers hanging downwards like dripping church candle wax, faintly washed with ivory and pale pink. They are variously described as having a scent like fermenting bananas or, more appositely given their corpse-like pallor, as possessing a foetid aroma. There is something of the churchyard about them, something slightly unwholesome and yet, simultaneously, strangely compelling.

The very first British specimen was discovered in Herefordshire in late July 1854 by Mrs Anderton Smith, beside a footpath in a heavily wooded area on the banks of Sapey Brook. Mrs Smith was walking to visit her brother-in-law and, when she stumbled across this unknown flowering plant, she picked it and posted it to William Crotch in Taunton. Crotch, a clergyman and master of Taunton Grammar School, was also unable to put a name to this strange plant, so forwarded the specimen to Hewett Watson, one of the more colourful botanists in British history.

Watson was infamously cantankerous and eccentric, but possessed of an acute and questing intellect, qualities that collided in 1856 when he declined a personal invitation to discuss evolutionary theory with Charles Darwin and Joseph Hooker, complaining that he was too busy and did not wish to travel to meet them. Darwin, nonetheless, graciously acknowledged Watson in *On the Origin of Species* as a vital source of scientific information.

Watson returned Mrs Smith's mystery orchid to Crotch in Taunton, ascribing it correctly as *Epipogium aphyllum*. Meanwhile in Herefordshire, Mrs Smith's husband, the Reverend W. Smith, had returned to Sapey Brook to search diligently where his wife had found the mystery flower. On 23 August 1854, in an area that had been recently cleared of trees, he found a 'considerable mass' of the same type of orchid. The area in which the plant was found was, apparently, being heavily churned by horses moving timber, so Reverend Smith decided to dig up the orchid and plant it in his garden. This transplanted orchid was doomed to die shortly after this rude treatment, but not before it had produced three further flower spikes.

Sapey Brook was searched for further ghost orchids in July 1862 and again in August 1896 by members of the Worcester Naturalists' Society, but no further plants were discovered there. In between these abortive searches the phantom had appeared again, once more to a lady strolling in the woods, but on this occasion in Shropshire. Upon finding the plant growing from the leaf litter in Bringewood Chase in 1876, Miss Lloyd picked it and took it to an artistically inclined companion, Mary Lewis, who painted it and, once the painting had been sent to Professor Cardale Babington at Cambridge, the identity of the orchid was determined.

A second example was said to have been discovered two years later in the same locality. Mary Lewis's painting, a luminous, delicate watercolour, is held in the Cambridge University Herbarium. A letter from Mary Lewis, dated January 1882, accompanies her watercolour. It sheds a little more light on the circumstances of the discoveries of ghost orchids in Bringewood Chase – circumstances that have uncomfortable echoes of the Sapey Brook plants of 1854:

Dear Sir,
    Owing to an outbreak of typhoid fever in Ludlow just after I had the pleasure of meeting you (one case – a bad one – next door to us) I was unable to have a good hunt for the *Epipogium* last August.
    Neither of the two finders have a dried specimen – Miss Lloyd's was thrown away by mistake. Miss Peele tried to get it to grow in 'their' garden – of course unsuccessfully.

A pattern was developing for British records of the elusive ghost orchid – predominantly found by women and, no matter what the gender of the finder, inevitably either picked or, worse still, dug up entirely. Perhaps we should be thankful that the members of the

Worcester Naturalists' Society were unsuccessful in their searches of Sapey Brook.

In early September 1892 Dr George Claridge Druce set out purposefully to find a ghost orchid for himself. His original plan was to search Sapey Brook but, in a fortunate twist of circumstances for him, though not so much for the orchids, he changed his plans and went to Ludlow instead. There he met Miss Lloyd, finder of the 1876 ghost orchid in Bringewood Chase. She accompanied him to the woods and together they searched, unsuccessfully, for the orchid in the area in which she had first found it. Druce described what happened next in an article in the *Gardeners' Chronicle* of 1924:

> The next day, a renewed and arduous search was made, when at length, in quite a different part of the wood, in dense shade of Oaks on a level part of the steep, sloping wood facing northwards, a small, solitary flowering example was found which I had the pleasure of showing to Miss Lewis, and it is now one of the chief treasures of my Harbarium.
>
> Although many botanists, especially the lynx-eyed Mr Wedgewood, have repeatedly searched the wood, no other example has been found.

Once again, the discovery of a ghost orchid marked the occasion of its removal. Druce's account has an avaricious tone, and a note of one-upmanship – the lynx-eyed Mr Wedgewood was no match for Claridge Druce. Druce had ample cause to feel pleased with himself: in the years between his removal of the latest ghost orchid from Bringewood Chase and his writing in 1924 only one further plant had been found, near Ross-on-Wye in Herefordshire in 1910. However, what had prompted Druce to write his account in 1924 was the latest emergence of the phantom of the woods. In June of that year a schoolgirl, Miss Butler, had found and picked two flowering ghost orchids in Lambridge Woods, near Henley-on-Thames in Oxfordshire. A painting of one of these small, forlorn specimens was made by the local botanist and artist Miss Baumgartner, and forwarded to Druce in July, at which time he was holidaying in Jersey.

What Druce did next is a sign of the mania that orchids in general, and ghost orchids in particular inspire in botanists. He recalled,

> I at once hurried back in order to visit the locality. After two days' search I was at length rewarded by finding a specimen in flower, but past its best, and what was possibly the dried remains of a second plant.
>
> For obvious reasons I am not allowed to give the precise locality. I may add that the two examples discovered by the original finder withered and were not preserved, so that at present not more than four British specimens are known to exist.

Naturally, these specimens were taken by Druce and, once again, Druce strikes an acquisitive and triumphant note. He is plainly proud that his herbarium features something as rare and hard to come by as British specimens of the elusive ghost orchid – something his peers simply do not have. There are clear parallels with the contemporary activity of collecting birds' eggs, still prevalent at the time and, indeed, encouraged as a healthy and wholesome activity in which youngsters might engage. Egg collectors took particular pleasure not only in possessing examples of uncommon species, which their peers might not have in their own collections, but also in obtaining more and more specimens. One clutch was never enough. This attitude extended to botanists, too, so herbariums rarely featured solely one example of a species if more could be collected. Druce states that he is 'not allowed' to divulge the location in which he found these latest ghost orchids, but one is left with the distinct impression that he does not, in fact, want to share the location with his peers, for fear others might have a chance to diminish his personal triumph and satisfaction.

Two years later, on 28 May 1926, another Druce entered the ghost orchid story. Francis Druce, a keen botanist unrelated to Claridge Druce, received a telephone call from Alfred Wilmott at the British Museum. Wilmott had learned of the name of the wood in which the schoolgirl, Miss Butler, and Claridge Druce had found their ghost orchids. Better still, he was prepared to share this information with Francis Druce.

Francis Druce summoned two botanical companions, Elsie Knowling and Eleanor Vachell, to accompany him to Lambridge Wood. Armed with a map provided by Wilmott, the hunt was on. Eleanor Vachell's diary entry that day captures the excitement of the chase:

> Mr Wilmott had found out the name of the wood and was ready to give all information!!! Excitement knew no bounds.
> The little party searched diligently that part of the wood marked in the map lent by Mr Wilmott but without success, though they spread out widely in both directions … Completely baffled, the trio, at E.V.'s suggestion, returned to the town to search for the finder.[1]

Eleanor Vachell was a Welsh botanist who, blessed with a private income, spent her entire life striving to see every single known British native flowering plant. By the time of her death in 1948 it was understood that she had seen all but thirteen of the currently recognised species. Evidently Eleanor was a driven and extremely competent botanist – and, as events in Henley-on-Thames were to prove, she was also a determined and persuasive detective. The trio managed, circuitously, to locate the home of Miss Butler – the schoolgirl was there when they knocked at her door and, remarkably, she had company. Eleanor Vachell recalled:

> The girl too was at home and there in a vase was another flower of *Epipogium*! In vain did Mr [Francis] Druce plead with her to part with it but she was adamant! Before long however she had promised to show the place to which she had led Dr [Claridge] Druce and from which the two specimens had been gathered.
> Off again. This time straight to the right place, but there was nothing to be seen of *Epipogium*![2]

Five days later Eleanor Vachell returned to Lambridge Wood to search one more time, as her diary records, 'stealthily' for the ephemeral ghost orchid. On this occasion, the search was rather more intrusive, as she dug with her fingers in the leaf litter at the spot at which the orchid was said to have been picked, and discovered, just below the soil, the orchid's rhizome. She carefully covered it over once more and 'fled home triumphant'. A few days later she received a small parcel in the post with an excited and thankful letter from Francis Druce – he had visited the wood, armed with Vachell's latest information, and uncovered the orchid. The parcel contained some earth and, within it, a fragment of the ghost orchid's rhizome. Vachell divided the rhizome and sent some of it to Elsie Knowling. Now all three had a little bit of the orchid they could call their own. Once more the ghost had appeared and, in so doing, had been thoroughly exorcised by its admirers.

It should come as little surprise to learn that the next ghost orchid was, once again, found by a schoolgirl and summarily picked. Vera Smith was looking for butterfly and fly orchids in Great Bottom Wood in Oxfordshire with her father on 30 June 1931, just four miles away from Lambridge Wood. She did not recognise what she found growing in the midst of an old tree stump, so picked it for later identification.

Vera Smith (later Vera Paul) revisited the wood on several occasions in the years that followed. In 1933 and again in 1953 she found single ghost orchid flower spikes and then, in 1963, she found no fewer than five flower spikes, albeit ones already suffering badly from the attentions of the local slugs.

For a while, starting in the 1950s, it seemed as if the ghost orchid was no longer quite the elusive, slippery phantom it had once been perceived to be. Botanists could have been forgiven for thinking it had become much easier to see a ghost orchid in Britain. Vera Paul's five flower spikes in Great Bottom Wood in 1963 had been preceded by seven spikes discovered by Job Lousley in the contiguous Ovey's Wood in 1954, but more remarkable still had been the discovery of no fewer than twenty-five flower spikes beneath the beech trees of Pullingshill and Hollowhill Woods in Buckinghamshire in 1953 by Rex Graham.

The story of Britain's ghost orchids is beset with coincidences, and Rex Graham provides yet another, for he was the son of Elsie Knowling, who had searched Lambridge Wood for ghost orchids with Francis Druce and Eleanor Vachell. Graham found, at first, a mere thirteen flower spikes on 18 July 1953, but in subsequent weeks the remaining dozen were located. He described his finding 'Eppie' as 'just beginner's luck' – this was a typically modest claim from a gifted botanist who, amongst many other notable discoveries, went on to find the British mainland's first ever Irish lady's-tresses in Ardnamurchan a mere year after his discovery of these ghost orchids. His good fortune was to provide orchid hunters in the following three decades with the *locus mirabilis* for British ghost orchids but, with a certain dread inevitability, in 1953 it also provided a number of institutions and private herbaria with specimens to be pressed, dried and kept for posterity. Everyone, it seemed, wanted their slice of the cake – but few seemed to be considering the conservation of this rare flower.

The story of Graham's discovery received considerable press coverage at the time, spurred by his own announcement of the event in a letter to *The Times*. While precise details of the location of his find would, inevitably, leak out to become an open secret amongst botanists in years to come, at the time he was deliberately vague as to their whereabouts, saying, 'I can tell you only that the flowers were found under fairly heavy shade in a hilly wood in the south of England.'

When asked by one particularly prescient journalist if any of the orchids had been picked for preservation, Graham was equally evasive: 'I am not allowed to reveal even that. I am not being discourteous, but the utmost secrecy is imperative.'

Graham was being somewhat disingenuous – he would, surely, have known that specimens were in fact being taken for preservation in herbaria. In his correspondence with Max Walters, the curator of the Cambridge University Herbarium at the time, in which he modestly ascribes his find to beginner's luck, he confided, 'I have a spare specimen which I picked off the ground eaten through at the base by slugs. It's quite a nice one, and as soon as it is in the right condition I shall send it to you for inclusion at the C.U. herbarium.'

This specimen was one of three Graham took that year and, in the next few years, he collected more when he found them eaten off by rapacious and thoughtless slugs. In time he accumulated no fewer than four ghost orchids in his own herbarium, adding to the scrap of rhizome accrued by his mother.

Ghost orchids would be seen in these woods near Marlow in at least twenty-five of the subsequent thirty-four years, the last confirmed sighting being in 1987. On one memorable occasion during the 1970s one was even said to have been discovered growing out of a rotting, abandoned mattress lying in a ditch beside the road that bisects the woods. It was around this time that the site became an open secret amongst botanists, and towards the end of the orchids' tenure in the mid-1980s the numbers of annual visitors had escalated dramatically from the handful Rex Graham had entrusted with directions some thirty years previously. In 1986, the Nature Conservancy Council estimated that as many as a thousand people came to see a ghost orchid in that year alone.

An orchid as capricious as the ghost orchid would never allow itself to become so readily seen by all and sundry. After 1987 confirmed sightings from the woods dried up entirely; rumours of the orchids' flowering were just that, unsubstantiated rumours. Credible sightings were reported from the Chilterns, but without supporting photographs. Twenty-three years after the last confirmed sighting near Marlow, in 2009 wildflower charity Plantlife issued *The Ghost Orchid Declaration*. This sonorously titled publication began with a stark statement: 'With no sightings for 23 years, Ghost Orchids are the latest of the UK's native wild plants to have become extinct.'

The *Declaration*'s foreword was written by Plantlife's patron, HRH Prince Charles. His thoughts were both elegiac and a rallying call, mourning the passing of the ghost orchid; commending the practical approach taken by Plantlife; and urging us all to cherish, protect and conserve our wildflowers.

Plantlife had declared the ghost orchid extinct as a British species and, in its extinction, it had become the poster girl for a campaign to engage the public with the need to cherish and value our remaining flora. The ghost orchid was gone, but it was now emblematic of a greater cause than the loss of one orchid – it represented the loss of biodiversity in the British countryside as a whole.

It was deeply unfortunate, then, that the ghost orchid chose 2009 as the year in which it would once more deign to reveal itself in a British woodland. Unknown to Plantlife, only days before the publication of *The Ghost Orchid Declaration*, an amateur botanist had stumbled across a small, distinctive and keenly anticipated form in a secluded corner of a Herefordshire wood. Mark Jannink had approached finding a ghost orchid with a systematic rigour, identifying ten possible sites in the damp Welsh borders and visiting them regularly throughout the summer and autumn of 2009. His commendable patience and resilience finally paid off on 20 September when, in an ancient cart track running through Haugh Wood, he finally discovered what he had craved. Anyone who has sought an elusive, rare orchid would understand his heartfelt exclamation at the moment of discovery: 'Hello you! So there you are...'

With a magnificent irony only the ghost orchid could muster, it had risen from the grave even as it was being officially declared extinct. The location in Haugh Wood at which Mark had found this latest diminutive flower spike was where a ghost orchid had been found, quite by chance, in 1982 by Valerie Coombs. Happily, this plant was not only left well alone, being seen by just nine people, but was kept a closely guarded secret. A photograph of some of those fortunate observers looking at the orchid in 1982 is a perfect time capsule – the orchid itself is barely discernible, a tiny waif lost on the floor of the leafy sunken track. Of the four onlookers three are visible, and it is these worshippers at the ghost's altar who place the photograph at a moment in time – seated on the left of the gulley is a man in a flat cap, on the right of the gulley is a young blonde woman in a fetching burgundy Afghan coat, while in the background stands an older man in jacket and tie. All four are wearing mud-spattered wellington boots, alluding to the dampness of their surroundings. Somehow, boots aside, their wardrobe speaks of a time past – looking at this photograph I cannot imagine a current gathering of orchid hunters so attired.

With the relatively small number of ghost orchids found in England, opinions differ as to precisely what the optimal conditions are for their occurrence. Unhelpfully, they have been found beneath both beech and oak trees. They have been found growing in undisturbed leaf litter and recently churned ground alike – and even, of course, once on a fly-tipped mattress. What seems certain is that the phantom shuns the light; they are happiest where they have little competition from other plants on the forest floor, in other words, in dark places where their lack of chlorophyll is compensated by their ability to draw nutrients from mycorrhizal fungi in the soil – ghost orchids are fully mycotrophic. The conditions that preface actual flowering are less certain. Botanists have hypothesised that a wet British winter followed by a warm, damp spring and summer is ideal, though firm evidence for this conjecture remains as elusive as the orchids themselves.

Sean Cole, a birdwatcher and committed orchidophile, had devoted years to his personal quest to find a ghost orchid. We had been friends for a number of years and, were a ghost orchid to be found in the summer or autumn of 2016, I was confident Sean would hear about it and let me know. While ghost orchids have been found in Britain over a remarkably long flowering period, spanning late May to early October, the peak time for the emergence of flowering spikes appears to be August and September. I had primed friends, family, colleagues and correspondents: if news broke of a ghost orchid anywhere in Britain this summer, I would drop everything there and then, and make my way to the location immediately. History taught me that, on the odd occasions a ghost orchid actually flowered, it often fell prey to hungry slugs. I would race the molluscs to the prize.

Meanwhile, simply waiting for news was, of course, not enough. I planned actively to try to find a ghost orchid for myself. While the chances of actually doing so seemed vanishingly small, I could draw some small solace from two quarters – the weather, especially in Herefordshire, in the preceding months seemed propitious for a good emergence of fungi and, hopefully, an attendant ghost orchid; and, if Mark Jannink could set out to find a ghost orchid in 2009 and actually do so, perhaps I could too. I intended to spend as much time as possible searching in the woods this year.

I decided to focus my search in Herefordshire, partly because this was the location of the latest sighting, albeit one seven years previously, and partly because the lack of confirmed sightings from the Chilterns since 1987 suggested that something may have changed in the local environment there. Botanists had speculated that the woodlands in Buckinghamshire and Oxfordshire might have dried out somewhat, either as a consequence of climate change or water abstraction, or both.

The epicentre of my ghost orchid hunt would be Haugh Wood. A confidant, who asked to remain anonymous, had provided me with both a grid reference and a hand-drawn map of exactly where in the wood the 1982 and 2009 plants had been found. This would be my starting point, buried deep in the corrugated, tree-smothered Herefordshire landscape. I arrived early on a promising Tuesday morning in September. Sunlight streamed in diagonal golden bars through the canopy as I picked my cautious way into the heart of the wood. The pathway that led in from a narrow country lane was churned with glutinous, sticky mud. At first I tried to avoid the worst of it, but in time this became quite impossible – dense waves of brambles spilled onto the path while, on one side, the ground fell steeply away beneath me. There was no alternative but to plough on, the very substance of Haugh Wood sucking and dragging at my feet, impeding my progress. It felt as if the place itself sought to reject humankind.

The path finally broadened into a wider track – here paths branched off in several directions. I took a moment to orientate myself, rummaging in my camera bag for the precious hand-drawn map. The air smelt richly promising, a heady perfume of decay, damp leaves, forest soil and fallen wood. I made my way uphill, following the map's directions, close now to where the ghost had last been seen, so I walked slowly, sweeping the woodland floor before me with my gaze. It seemed inconceivable to me that the orchid seen here in 2009 and previously in 1982 could be just one plant, clinging on tenaciously all by itself. What would have been so special about that one spot in which it was found?

Surely there must be others too that had persisted, unseen, in the general area?

I found no ghosts, but plenty of fungi – the weather conditions in the preceding days had been perfect for an emergence of fruiting bodies on the woodland floor, as colourful as the wall of an old-fashioned sweet shop, and marvellously varied in shape and size. Parasols towered eight inches tall with wide brown caps shading the ground beneath. Orange corals rose delicate, tangerine branches while, nearby, the small Parma-violet toadstools of amethyst deceivers and the scarlet, white-spotted caps of fly agaric warned against casual browsing. More sinister fungi lurked nearby – I found at first a panther cap, and then many death caps scattered through the wood's darker, moister places. Closely related to the fly agaric, the latter lacked that mushroom's red warning colouration, having instead an innocuous plain olive cap, as shiny as if freshly varnished. Seen in profile each had a pendant, frilly ring around the white stipe, or stalk, just below the cap – the annulus, as ominous as the condensation ring of a mushroom cloud. They are deadly poisonous and invariably fatal when eaten, either by the unwary forager or the unwitting victim – death caps were implicated in the deaths of both the Roman Emperor Claudius in AD 54 and the Holy Roman Emperor Charles VI in 1740. I could not help but feel that it was somehow fitting that the ghost should flower in the Gothic company of such lethal fungal companions.

I tried to imagine what it would feel like if I were blessed with the beginner's luck that had so memorably aided Rex Graham in 1953 when he found his first ghost orchids. His initial reaction to his find was said to have been to hurry to the nearest pub to drink a pint of beer to calm himself down, before hastening back to the orchids for another look. I could well believe how excited he must have felt.

I had had the faintest taste of this when I stumbled across my first flowering orchid of the summer, the solitary sawfly orchid in Dorset back in late March. I had known it was there, but had still felt that soaring exultation and trembling excitement when I laid eyes upon it – and had been unable to tear myself away from it, leaving several times only to turn around to walk back and spend more time gazing upon this rarest and most improbable British orchid. Had there been a nearby pub, and had this been an entirely unexpected find … yes, if I was honest with myself, I would have needed a stiff drink too.

I found myself circling the sunken track in which the last ghost orchid had been seen, seven years previously. I tried to tell myself this was because I wanted to have that genuine sensation of surprise when I found my very own orchid rather than one that I hoped to find in a specific place, but realised that I was fooling myself – this reticence to look in the last place a ghost orchid had been seen was because I was scared. I was frightened it would not be there.

I knew this was irrational. The odds were stacked heavily against me, and I ought not to expect to find a ghost orchid where Mark Jannink last found one, but nevertheless, I was afraid that, after seeing all the other British and Irish orchids, now I would fail to see the last one at the place in which, perhaps, I might have the best chance of finding it. Recognising the reason for my reluctance made finally climbing down the bank of the track no easier, and I found myself shaking with a welter of emotions – fear, certainly, but excitement and hope too. Perhaps this was my moment, the point at the end of my orchid summer when fate would deliver in one momentous crescendo a tiny, ectoplasmically pale orchid rising from the leaves at my feet. I had told myself that I thought this was the year the ghost would flower again, and I had dared to hope that I would be the one to find it. Now I feared I had tempted fate.

My fears proved well founded, for a quick glance and then a much slower, more methodical search revealed no sign whatsoever of a ghost orchid. The sense that a ghost orchid was, somehow, present nearby was overwhelming, but the phantom itself was nowhere to be seen. The track itself was, in places at least, easy to search. Flanked on both sides by steep banks, it formed an enclosed and sheltered microclimate in the sloping sides of the wood. One bank was swathed with vegetation, while the other was barer. Here and there trees overhung the track, rendering passage along it impossible, while the floor of the track was smothered with fallen dead leaves from years past. Might a ghost orchid be emerging, unseen, beneath those leaves? I crouched low to change my perspective, hoping against hope that I might now see that waxy, white form pushing tremulously through the pale brown oak leaves.

Still nothing.

I felt a little sick. The realisation now sank in that, if I could not find a ghost orchid where the last British sighting had been made, I would need to look further afield. I would have to search places in which it had once been seen, maybe decades previously, and delve into woods where it had never been reported but looked like promising haunts. If I found nothing, I would come back to Haugh Wood again and again as the autumn passed by, to search harder and harder where the ghost's trail last petered out.

Hours after I had first entered Haugh Wood I emerged, dejected and spattered with mud, back at the road where I had begun. For the rest of the day I had enlisted help, in the form of the sharpest pair of orchid-hunting eyes I had encountered that year. Richard Bate, he of the colourful turn of phrase and ability to spot a stunted green-flowered helleborine at thirty metres range' in shimmering sunlight, was waiting for me at the roadside. To his immense credit he did not so much as flinch as I lowered my filthy form into his cherished Subaru and let him drive to the site of the very first British ghost orchid, in the valley that concealed the passage of Sapey Brook.

I have searched for hummingbirds and orchids in the improbably lush surroundings of the forests of South America, and can attest that the Amazonian basin would not have been ashamed to call what we found at Sapey Valley its own. A track of liquid red mud ran parallel with the wide, rushing brook itself in the valley bottom, overhung by lush tree growth vanishing into low white cloud that swathed the canopy. One side of the valley, where Mrs Anderton Smith had found a ghost orchid in 1854, was heavily wooded. Fallen trees, their trunks smothered with emerald moss, spanned the brook. The morning's sunshine in Haugh Wood was a distant memory, and in heavy, ceaseless rain we worked our way downstream, fording the brook where we could, following the track, and pressing uphill into the thick understorey. The area had been described to me as paradise but, soaked to the skin, torn by thorns, and plastered with mud, it felt like a humid green hell.

I now appreciated the serendipity that had surrounded Mrs Anderton Smith's discovery, as finding a ghost orchid in this habitat would require supernatural good fortune. Small wonder the Worcester Naturalists' Society were unsuccessful in their speculative searches for the phantom in the latter years of the nineteenth century – or that Richard and I, over 150 years after that very first discovery, could not find a ghost orchid there either.

Our day ended near to where it had begun, a little way from Haugh Wood. As daylight leached from the sky, we entered another Herefordshire woodland that had been recommended to me as a potential site for them, as it had a particularly rich fungal flora. Paget Wood felt decidedly creepy – what remained of the day outside the wood was almost entirely gone within, shaded by a dense, dripping canopy overhead. Some ghost orchid hunters suggest searching for their quarry at night, by torchlight, the theory being that they are more easily seen in low light as their pale forms stand out more readily to the human eye. We would put that hypothesis to the test here in what remained of this first day of ghost hunting.

The ruined remains of lime kilns and the steep-sided, dark sockets of medieval quarries beneath the trees ensured Paget Wood felt like a place abandoned by humankind. The recommendation that had brought us here was amply borne out by the many fungi we found glistening on the woodland floor – shaggy lion's manes, a kaleidoscope of corals, and yet more death caps growing poisonously through a scatter of crudely blown Victorian bottles half-buried in the leaf mould, like a forgotten rural apothecary. Every glimmer of white on the dark woodland floor set my pulse quickening, but invariably proved to be yet another fungal fruiting body.

It was soon too dark to continue without torches. Cold, wet and dispirited, we left the woods and headed for the warm sanctuary of the nearby Green Man pub. This, had history only repeated itself, would have been where I headed in Rex Graham's footsteps to drink a calming pint of beer before returning to my ghost orchid for a second look. Sitting in the bar, receiving curious and not wholly approving looks at my mud-slathered boots and trousers and torn, scarred hands, I ruminated on the orchid hunter's lot – my first day of ghost hunting had been arduous, hard-fought and all for naught.

That was the first day of my ghost orchid hunt, but it would not be the last before the autumn was over, for every week until the first hard frosts of the autumn in late October I took myself back to the woods. I returned to Haugh Wood on several occasions, like a detective returning to a crime scene hoping for some revelatory clue to present itself, but also casting my net further afield into Buckinghamshire, Oxfordshire and, speculatively, Gloucestershire too. I would not be alone – the annual search for a ghost orchid consumes many British orchidophiles; a small army of searchers, marshalled by Sean Cole under the banner of the Ghost Orchid Project, regularly check places where this most ephemeral of wildflowers has once been seen.

By December those fruitless searches were all fading memories, as spent as the leaves that had fallen in the woods I had haunted for weeks on end. I was left with the uncomfortable feeling that some of those leaves had settled on the remains of a ghost orchid that had flowered in some remote, dark corner of an English wood. Perhaps it flowered there regularly every year, unknown to everyone and, crucially, unseen by me this year. There was only one place left to go now if I was to see a ghost orchid in 2016 – my final orchid expedition of the year would take me to Cambridge.

Britain's very first ghost orchid, found and picked in 1854 by Mrs Anderton Smith in the paradise (or green hell) of Sapey Brook, exists to this day. Sent by Mrs Smith to Reverend William Crotch in Taunton for identification, the specimen eventually found its way into the herbarium of Charles Babington, chair of botany at the University of Cambridge and another contemporary of Charles Darwin. Many years previously, in 1829, the two men infamously squabbled over who should have the pick of a number of beetle specimens offered by a coleopteran dealer. After his death in 1895, Babington's herbarium and library were conserved by the university.

Mrs Smith's husband returned to the woods above Sapey Brook in the days following his wife's discovery, and removed a further 'considerable mass' of ghost orchids, which he planted in his garden. Of the few flower spikes this mass produced before their inevitable death, one was presented to the botanist Edwin Lees and, ultimately, was pressed, dried and conserved; it is now to be found in the Natural History Museum in London. This is, incorrectly, labelled as the original specimen found by Mrs Smith; however, as it came via Lees and not Crotch, the provenance of it is clearly that of one of the later specimens emanating from Reverend Smith himself, and not his wife. The specimen she found and sent to Reverend Crotch, the original specimen, is now to be found in the Cambridge University Herbarium, housed in the imposing Sainsbury Laboratory off Bateman Street.

On an icy morning in early December I walked to the barred security gates that secure the perimeter of the Sainsbury Laboratory, and pressed the intercom button to announce my arrival. This meeting had been arranged well in advance – one cannot simply turn up hoping to see the first ever English ghost orchid on a whim. As it happened, I discovered from Christine Bartram, chief technician and my host at the herbarium, I was the first visitor in over twelve years to come to see their ghost orchid in the flesh.

Christine met me in the Sainsbury Laboratory's reception area, a large atrium of tasteful glass, steel and stone. Another researcher, secateurs held casually in earth-stained hand, signed in for the herbarium at the same time as me – I felt slightly over-dressed. Christine was an effusive and friendly host – leading me into the heart of the herbarium, a windowless, brightly lit area in the bowels of the laboratory, she brought me to a work bench in the centre of the room. There, carefully laid out in preparation for my visit, was the Cambridge University Herbarium file for *Epipogium aphyllum*, the legendary ghost orchid.

'Here it is,' Christine announced cheerfully. 'Help yourself.'

She carefully opened the ghost orchid folder and, with no further ceremony, there it was before me – the first ever ghost orchid found on British soil. Mounted on a sheet of white paper, the specimen was remarkable for its history, rarity and significance but not, if I was honest with myself, for its physical beauty. The pressing and drying process, and the passage of time, had robbed the flower of the colour and form it had once enjoyed. Rather than a delicate pale confection of downturned lip and bulbous spur, and long, trailing sepals and petals, what sat before me resembled a squashed sultana peeled off a bus seat – this 162-year-old herbarium specimen was the ghost of a ghost orchid.

Christine was clearly aware that this flower was not looking at its best.

'We've got another one I can show you – it's much more recent and ought to be in much better condition. I can show you that one in a minute.'

Yet if my shaking hands were anything to go by, this original, very first ghost orchid still moved me deeply despite its rather sorry countenance. Seeing it revealed there before me felt, for an orchid hunter who had spent the last months of his life doing nothing but search for orchids of all shapes, sizes, colours and hues around the British Isles, like a moment of epiphany – this was it, the holiest and most elusive of all our orchids. This was no longer simply a dried plant specimen – it had assumed, for me, the potency of a fragment of the True Cross held inside a reliquary.

Turning the large pages of the file, Christine brought us to a page with a montage of newspaper clippings, a handwritten letter, and a carefully folded white sheet of paper bearing the details of another ghost orchid specimen. One of the cuttings contained an article from *The Times*, and a letter printed in the same edition, announcing the discovery by Rex Graham on 18 July 1953 of thirteen ghost orchids in Pullingshill and Hollowhill Woods. The handwritten letter alongside this was that sent by Rex Graham to Max Walters, the curator of the Cambridge University Herbarium, announcing that he had 'quite a nice' spare specimen he would send Walters for inclusion in the university herbarium. The data label on the folded sheet of paper above revealed that this contained that very flower – specimen number 666/1, collector R. A. Graham, species *Epipogium aphyllum*: 'This specimen was not cut, but was found eaten through at the base by slugs.'

'This should be a much better example to show you,' Christine said, reverently unfolding the paper that contained this precious orchid, almost one hundred years fresher than the specimen we had just seen. The paper was folded in such a way that the contents could not slip out, so it took Christine a few moments carefully to unlock the folds and safely reveal what was inside.

The shock was palpable on Christine's face and in her voice, too, when the final fold revealed that there was nothing inside the envelope.

'Oh! That's not right!' she exclaimed. 'It's gone. Somebody must have taken it … it couldn't have fallen out, that's quite impossible. But nobody's been here to see this file in all the time I've been here. It must have been taken years ago…'

I was disappointed but, somehow, not in the least bit surprised. Such slippery behaviour was wholly in keeping with everything I now knew about the ghost orchid, the most elusive and capricious of our native orchids. Christine was visibly mortified to find that one of her two ghost orchid specimens was missing; I, meanwhile, was relieved I had at least seen the very first one of all and felt wryly amused that an orchid, infamous for being snatched from the wild no sooner had it been found, appeared to have been spirited away once more. This was truly ghostly behaviour, befitting the orchid's reputation.

What remained to be seen in the file were further historical arch-ive materials relating to past ghost orchids. I felt as if I'd been trans-ported back in time, reading the letters of Mary Lewis, the artistic friend of Miss Lloyd, finder of the 1876 Shropshire flower. Lewis's beautiful watercolour of a ghost orchid flower spike bearing four flowers, rising from a delicate bed of moss, sits next to her two letters. The sentiments in the later of these letters struck a chord with me and, I suspected, with many other thwarted ghost orchid hunters past and present – in it Lewis describes *Epipogium* as 'that ignominious wretched little flower'!

Most touching of all, personally, were two large black-and-white photographs of single ghost orchid spikes rising delicately above a sea of surrounding leaf litter. Taken on 31 July 1953 'within 100 miles of London', it was not the deliberate vagueness surrounding the location of these, Rex Graham's ghost orchids, that struck me when I turned the page to reveal these portraits. It was, instead, the photographer's name – J. E. Raven. This was the same John Raven in whose botanical footsteps I had walked on Rum months previously.

I realised now that, while I might not have found a living, flow-ering ghost orchid this year, my search for one and my final pil-grimage to Cambridge in order to see Britain's first ever example had brought me back into the orbit of a number of orchid hunters from the past who had been absent, late companions for me on my orchid-hunting excursions throughout the year. The ghost orchid had brought us all together at the end: not only John Raven, scholarly don, plant hunter and amateur detective; but also Francis Druce, commemorated as subspecies *frances-drucei* in the Latin name of the Hebridean (Pugsley's) marsh orchids I had seen on North Uist; Alfred Wilmott, keeper of the British Herbarium and keen Hebridean orchid hunter; and Job Edward Lousley, original finder of the military orchids I had wandered amongst in Buckinghamshire's Homefield Wood. All had, at some point, been involved in the ghost orchid's story in the past century. Finding John Raven's photographs here in the Cambridge University Herbarium was not entirely unsurprising, for he was, after all, a don at the university, but this felt like a sign, a friendly nod from the past from one ghost hunter to another. I had tried, and I had failed, but there was no shame in that.

My year now had finished as it began – with a dried, pressed orchid specimen. The first orchid I had laid eyes upon in 2016 had been the desiccated remains of an early purple orchid, the one that I had picked on a family walk in Somerset and pressed between two sheets of newspaper in the early 1980s as a young boy. It resides inside the cover of my childhood *Observer's Book of Wildflowers* and, on New Year's Day this year, I had opened that book and touched that dried orchid flower, wishing myself good fortune and happy hunting in the months to come.

For the most part, I had superstitiously to conclude that this orchidaceous token from my past had proven itself extraordinarily potent – until I came up against the ghost orchid, I had seen all of Britain and Ireland's orchid species in the course of the glorious, unfolding flowering season. More than that, I had seen the very rarest and the most contentious species to be found on our shores, and I had been fortunate to encounter a kaleidoscope of orchid subspecies, variant forms and hybrids.

It felt strangely fitting that, even though I had not managed to find a ghost orchid in the wild, I had come full circle from my first orchid to Britain's first ghost orchid. Both still exist, preserved lovingly by their respective custodians. My early purple orchid specimen has none of the national significance of that vintage ghost orchid, yet, to me, it represents something very special in itself. Without that orchid I would not have found myself walking through some of Britain and Ireland's most extraordinary places in the past year.

Were it not for that flower, I would not have found myself standing in the cool, sterile surroundings of the Cambridge University Herbarium mere inches from a ghost orchid, nor enjoyed the company of inspiring and dedicated naturalists who shared my passion for this remarkable family of flowers. I realised now that this quest had never been merely about the numbers of orchids seen – it had, instead, been an exploration of my past, our collective present, and a glimpse into the future for our orchids and the countryside upon which they depend.

Epilogue

I never kept count of how many species of orchid I was seeing in the course of my orchid summer. If my exploration of our orchid flora taught me anything, it was that what actually constitutes a species is a mutable, shifting thing. Orchids don't like to be pinned down and categorised – their readiness to throw up radical variations and to hybridise with one another suggests a family in flux, one that defies definition.

All the same, I had set out to see all the currently accepted species that occur in Britain and Ireland. According to the latest field guide available to me at the time, Simon Harrap's *Orchids of Britain and Ireland*, that meant I had a target of fifty-two regularly occurring species, one of which – the Hebridean marsh orchid – is not universally accepted as a valid species on the basis of the latest published genetic analysis. Harrap prefers to regard it as a valid species for now but, in the interests of scientific accuracy, I preferred to view my target as fifty-one species.

Harrap includes four additional species that have occurred in Britain in the relatively recent past. Two of these – summer lady's-tresses and small-flowered tongue orchid – appear to be extinct, the latter a brief colonist on the cliffs of Cornwall. One species, greater tongue orchid, was recorded once on Guernsey in 1992, but not since, with a further report from South Devon in more recent years now viewed with some scepticism by botanists. The last of the four additional species is the sawfly orchid first seen in Dorset in

2014, which would, if we assume it to be wild, bring my target to fifty-two species.

In the end, I saw fifty of the fifty-one regularly occurring species in Britain and Ireland. I failed, in the end, to find a living example of a ghost orchid, and I spent a day looking, fruitlessly, for the long-lost small-flowered tongue orchid too. I did, however, see the contentious sawfly orchid and, additionally, both Hebridean marsh orchid and the two naturalised orchids that occur at Wakehurst in West Sussex, greater tongue orchid and loose-flowered orchid. The latter I also saw in the Channel Islands though, like Harrap, I prefer not to include this as biogeographically part of Britain and Ireland.

Including the sawfly orchid, I saw fifty-one of the fifty-two possible species available in Britain and Ireland or, if you prefer to include the two naturalised species, fifty-three of the possible fifty-four species (or fifty-four of the possible fifty-five if Hebridean marsh orchid becomes, once again, a widely accepted valid species in its own right).

Confusing, isn't it? Matters are cloudier still if one follows the standard European orchid text book, Pierre Delforge's *Orchids of Europe, North Africa and the Middle East*. Delforge is an exuberant advocate of the principle that more is more. What Harrap defines as subspecies of our native orchids, Delforge elevates to full species status. Early marsh orchid, for example, becomes no fewer than five individual species occurring in Britain and Ireland. Conversely, Delforge lumps our three native fragrant orchids into one species. If I followed Delforge, and included the two naturalised species, my thoroughness in seeking out subspecies meant I saw fifty-seven out of fifty-eight possible species.

(What doesn't change is that seeing a live British ghost orchid specimen remains a dearly held wish...)

As I said, orchids are confusing, and it was never about the numbers. If I leave you with one concluding thought, it must be that you make an effort to see at least some of our native orchid flora, whatever they may be. They are beautiful, wonderful, mesmerising plants that don't care if they're a species or not, but they need you and me to care about them, regardless. Their conservation depends on us all.

Acknowledgements

My orchid summer would never have germinated, let alone blossomed as magnificently as it did without the assistance, cooperation and guidance of a small army of fellow naturalists who variously provided accurate site details, a wealth of anecdotes and, above all, good company and encouragement on my travels: Jamie Armstrong; Christine Bartram; Richard Bate; Professor Richard Bateman; Heather Blenkinsop; Mike Chalk; Alix Chidley-Uttley; David Clements; Steve Coates; Sean Cole; Julia Corden; Lindsey Death; David Fairhurst; Neil Forbes; Emilia Fox; Emma Franks; Katie Frith; Heather Furse; Steve Gale; Alfie Gay; Caroline Gibson; Chris Gladman; Mark Golley; Peter Greenwood; John Hamilton; Lois Harbron; Tom Hart-Dyke; Paul Harvey; Grant Hazlehurst; Victoria Hillman; Paul Holt; Ian Howarth; Sally Huband; Judd Hunt; Tim Jenkins; Steph Johnson; Brian Jones; Andy Knight; Jim and Dawn Langiewicz; James Lowen; Louise Marsh; John Martin; Richard Mason; Susanne Masters; Dr Eric Morgan; Douglas Peacock; Jeff Picksley; Mike Powell; John Richards; Ian Robinson; Brendan Sayers; Julie Schiebold; Mark Sewell; Snoopy; David Steere; Katey Stephen; Dr Helen Steward; Peter Stronach; Steve Tandy; Chris Thorogood; Mike Waller; Robin Walls; David West and Bryan Yorke.

To you all, to those who preferred to stay nameless in the orchid world's shadows, and to anyone I have carelessly omitted, my sincere thanks – I really couldn't have done the tale of our native orchid flora justice without you.

Many of the flowers I enjoyed seeing flourish thanks to the benevolence and care of those who manage the land on which they grow, not least on the nature reserves managed by the RSPB and the Wildlife Trusts. I wholeheartedly urge anyone who cares for the flora and fauna of the British Isles to support these organisations – they really need our help if they are to continue their good work. Meanwhile, if you find yourself becoming in thrall to our native orchids, please consider joining the Hardy Orchid Society and the Botanical Society of Britain and Ireland (BSBI) – both organisations will feed your addiction with regular orchid fixes in their respective journals.

How I came to find myself writing *Orchid Summer* is a wonderful story in and of itself – I'm deeply indebted to all those who populated the string of happy accidents and coincidences that took my germ of an idea and allowed it to flourish: Dr Jonathan Wills, captain of MV *Dunter III*; Tessa David, and my tremendous agent at Peters, Fraser & Dunlop, Tim Bates; and, at Bloomsbury, my excellent editor Michael Fishwick and his team of gifted botanical helpers – Marigold Atkey, Sarah Ruddick, Jasmine Horsey and Holly Ovenden. If any of them had not played their part, my dream could not have come true. I am grateful to them all.

Above all, my heartfelt thanks go to Roberta Fulford – her patience and support was boundless during the months of my prolonged absences from home, and her company made my time in New York the start of the very best adventure of all.

To you all, may your summers be long, sun-kissed and bursting with orchids.

Jon
www.jondunn.com
www.orchid-summer.com
@dunnjons

Species list

Taxonomic list of the orchids seen:

Lady's Slipper, *Cypripedium calceolus*
White Helleborine, *Cephalanthera damasonium*
Sword-leaved Helleborine, *Cephalanthera longifolia*
Red Helleborine, *Cephalanthera rubra*
Marsh Helleborine, *Epipactis palustris*
Dark-red Helleborine, *Epipactis atrorubens*
Violet Helleborine, *Epipactis purpurata*
Broad-leaved Helleborine, *Epipactis helleborine*
Narrow-lipped Helleborine, *Epipactis leptochila*
Dune Helleborine, *Epipactis dunensis*
Lindisfarne Helleborine, *Epipactis sancta*
Green-flowered Helleborine, *Epipactis phyllanthes*
Common Twayblade, *Neottia ovata*
Lesser Twayblade, *Neottia cordata*
Bird's-nest Orchid, *Neottia nidus-avis*
Fen Orchid, *Liparis loeselii*
Bog Orchid, *Hammarbya paludosa*
Coralroot, *Corallorhiza trifida*
Autumn Lady's-tresses, *Spiranthes spiralis*
Irish Lady's-tresses, *Spiranthes romanzoffiana*
Creeping Lady's-tresses, *Goodyera repens*
Musk Orchid, *Herminium monorchis*

Greater Butterfly Orchid, *Platanthera chlorantha*
Lesser Butterfly Orchid, *Platanthera bifolia*
Small White Orchid, *Pseudorchis albida*
Chalk Fragrant Orchid, *Gymnadenia conopsea*
Marsh Fragrant Orchid, *Gymnadenia densiflora*
Heath Fragrant Orchid, *Gymandenia borealis*
Frog Orchid, *Dactylorhiza viridis*
Common Spotted Orchid, *Dactylorhiza fuchsii*
Heath Spotted Orchid, *Dactylorhiza maculata*
Early Marsh Orchid, *Dactylorhiza incarnata*
Southern Marsh Orchid, *Dactylorhiza praetermissa*
Northern Marsh Orchid, *Dactylorhiza purpurella*
Pugsley's Marsh Orchid, *Dactylorhiza traunsteinerioides*
Irish Marsh Orchid, *Dactylorhiza kerryensis*
Early Purple Orchid, *Orchis mascula*
Lady Orchid, *Orchis purpurea*
Military Orchid, *Orchis militaris*
Monkey Orchid, *Orchis simia*
Man Orchid, *Orchis athropophora*
Burnt Orchid, *Neotinea ustulata*
Dense-flowered Orchid, *Neotinea maculata*
Pyramidal Orchid, *Anacamptis pyramidalis*
Green-winged Orchid, *Anacamptis morio*
Lizard Orchid, *Himantoglossum hircinum*
Fly Orchid, *Ophrys insectifera*
Early Spider Orchid, *Ophrys sphegodes*
Bee Orchid, *Ophrys apifera*
Late Spider Orchid, *Ophrys fuciflora*
Loose-flowered Orchid, *Anacamptis laxiflora*
Greater Tongue, Orchid *Serapias lingua*
Sawfly Orchid, *Ophrys tenthredinifera*
(Ghost Orchid, *Epipogium aphyllum*)

Glossary

Simon Harrap

From *A Pocket Guide to the Orchids of Britain and Ireland*
(Bloomsbury, 2016), and reproduced here by kind permission
of the author.

achlorophyllose Lacking the green pigment chlorophyll and therefore unable to photosynthesise.

adventitious Buds and roots that appear in abnormal places on the stem.

ancient woodland Woodland that has maintained a more or less continuous cover of trees, probably for thousands of years.

annular Ring-shaped.

anther The pollen-bearing, male reproductive organ. In most orchids, the pollen is grouped into two pollinia.

anther cap In some orchids, such as the helleborines *Epipactis*, the anther lies on top of the column and is hinged or stalked. It may be contrastingly coloured.

anthocyanins Group of pigments that produce purple or reddish colours.

asymbiotic When a symbiotic fungus is absent.

autogamy Self-pollination with pollen from the same flower (see self-pollinate).

back-cross Cross between a hybrid and one of its parent species.

base-rich Soil with a high concentration of calcium or magnesium and a pH above 7.0.

bog Plant community on wet, acidic peat.

bosses Irregular swellings.

bract Structure at the base of a flower stalk, varying in size and shape, but often leaf-like.

bulbils Tiny, round growths, e.g. along the rim of the leaf of bog orchid, which can separate and are capable of developing into a new plant.

bursicle The pouch-like structure on the column of some orchids that contains and protects the viscidium (q.v.).

calcareous Rich in calcium carbonate, e.g. chalk, limestone or sea shells.

Caledonian woodland Ancient pine woodland, a relic of the 'Forest of Caledon' that supposedly once covered Scotland.

capsule The dry seed pod of an orchid.

carapace Hardened shell.

caudicle The stalk present in some orchids that attaches the pollinium to the viscidium (q.v.).

cilia Minute, thickened or fleshy hair-like structures.

ciliate With cilia projecting from the margin.

chlorophyll A green pigment, important in photosynthesis, found in discrete organelles (chloroplasts) in the cells of plants, usually in the leaves.

cleistogamy Self-pollination in bud, after which the bud may remain closed or may open.

clinandrium Depression on the top of the column, below the anther and behind the stigmatic zone, in which the pollinia lie.

clone Individual of identical genetic make-up to its 'parent' that results from asexual, vegetative reproduction.

column Specialist structure characteristic of orchid flowers in which the stamens and stigmas are fused together.

crenate With scalloped margins.

'Critically Endangered' Facing an extremely high risk of extinction in the wild in the immediate future.

cross-pollinate Pollination in which pollen from one flower fertilises another; usually taken to mean a flower on a different plant.

'Date Deficient' There is inadequate information on distribution and/or population status to make an assessment of the risk of extinction. More information is required and future research may show that a threat category is appropriate.

decurved Curved downwards.

deflexed Bent sharply downwards.

deltoid Shaped like the Greek letter 'delta', i.e. triangular.

diploid Having two matching sets of chromosomes. This is the normal state for plant cells (see tetraploid).

ectomycorrhizal Association of a fungus with the roots of a plant where the fungus forms a layer on the outside of the roots.

'Endangered' Facing a very high risk of extinction in the wild.

endomycorrhizal Association of a fungus with the roots of a plant in which the fungus penetrates the tissue of the root.

epichile Outer portion of the lip, often heart-shaped, in those orchid genera where the lip is divided into two (e.g. *Epipactis, Cephalanthera, Serapias*).

epidermis 'Skin' or surface layers.

epiphyte Plant growing on the surface of another plant without receiving nutrition from it.

esker Glacial debris, often sands and gravels.

eutrophication Enriched with plant nutrients, often leading to a luxuriant and eventually stifling growth of vegetation.

fen Plant community on alkaline, neutral or very slightly acidic soil.

filiform Thread-like.

flexuous Wavy.

geitonogamy Fertilised by pollen from another flower on the same plant.

glandular hair Short hair tipped with a small spherical gland containing oil or resin.

half-life A measure of the life expectancy of the orchid after its first appearance above ground, marking the point at which 50% of the population that emerged in any given year has died.

herbarium (plural: **herbaria**) A collection of dried and pressed plant material.

hooded Formed into a concave shape resembling a monk's cowl.

hybrid Plant originating from the fertilisation of one species by another.

hybrid swarm Population in which the barriers between two species have largely or completely broken down. Hybridisation is commonplace and random, producing a population that forms a continuous range of intermediates between the two parent species.

hybrid vigour When the first generation of hybrids between two species are exceptionally large and robust.

hyperchromic Intensely coloured, with an excessive amount of pigmentation.

hyperresupinate When the ovary and/or flower stalk twist through 360° to position the lip at the top of the flower, e.g. bog orchid.

hypha (plural: **hyphae**) Fine, thread-like structures that make up the body of a fungus.

hypochile Inner portion of the lip, often cup-shaped, in those orchid genera where the lip is divided in two (e.g. *Epipactis, Cephalanthera, Serapias*).

intergeneric hybrid A hybrid whose parents are in two different genera.

lanceolate Narrowly oval, tapering to a more or less pointed tip.

lax Loose, not dense.

lip Highly modified third petal of an orchid; also known as the labellum.

lough Irish term for loch.

machair Sandy, lime-rich soil with a species-rich sward of short grasses and herbs. The machair is confined to the coasts of W Ireland and W Scotland.

meadow Grassy field from which livestock are excluded for at least part of the year so that it can be cut for hay.

monocarpic Flowering once and then dying.

mutualism An intimate relationship between two or more organisms from which all derive benefits.

mycorhizome Early stages in the development of the underground rhizome in which the seedling is nourished entirely by fungi.

mycorrhiza Association of a fungus with the roots of a plant in which the fungus may form a layer on the outside of the roots (ectomycorrhizal, q.v.) or penetrate the tissue of the root (endomycorrhizal, q.v.).

mycelium The mass of branching filaments that make up the body of a fungus.

mycotrophic Acquiring nutrition from fungi.

'Nationally Scarce' Occurring in 16–100 hectads (10km x 10km squares) in Great Britain.

'Nationally Rare' Occurring in 15 or fewer hectads (10km x 10km squares) in Great Britain.

native Growing in an area where it was not introduced, either accidentally or deliberately, by humans.

non-sheathing leaf A leaf with its base clasping the stem but not completely encircling it.

NNR National Nature Reserve.

ovary Female reproductive organ that contains the ovules.

ovule Organ inside the ovary that contains the embryo sac, which in turn contains the egg.

pH Measure of acidity.

parasitic Organism that lives on or at the expense of other organisms.

pasture Grassland that is grazed for some of all of the year but not cut.

petals Inner row of 'perianth segments', one of which is modified to form the lip.

papilla (plural: ***papillae***) Small, nipple-like projection.

pendant Hanging downwards.

peloton A coil-like structure formed by fungi inside the cells of an orchid.

pheromone Chemical secreted by an animal, especially an insect, that influences the behaviour or development of others of the same species.

photosynthesis Production of food by green plants. In the presence of chlorophyll and light energy from the sun, carbon dioxide and water are converted into carbohydrates and oxygen.

phototropic Acquiring nutrition through the process of photosynthesis.

pollen Single-celled spores containing the male gametes.

pollinium (plural: ***pollinia***) Regularly shaped mass of individual pollen grains that is transported as a single unit during pollination; the pollinia are often divided in two.

propagules Various vegetative portions of a plant such as a bud or other offshoots that aid in dispersal and from which a new individual may develop.

protocorm Initial stage of development for every orchid formed by a cluster of cells.

pseudobulb Swollen or thickened portion of stem, covered in the leaf bases. It fulfils the same storage function as a bulb or tuber; found in fen and bog orchids and common in tropical species.

pseudocopulation Attempts by an insect to copulate with an insect-mimicking flower.

pseudopollen Structures in a flower that imitate pollen in order to attract insects, e.g. in the *Cephalanthera* helleborines.

reflexed Bent back or down.

resupinate When the ovary and/or pedicel twist through 180° to position the lip at the bottom of the flower.

reticulation Marked with a network of veins.

rhizoid Hair-like structure on the surface of a protocorm or mycorhizome that facilitates the entrance of fungi (i.e. a root hair).

rhizome Underground stem that lasts for more than one year from which roots and growth buds emerge; also a horizontal stem, either growing along the surface or underground.

rostellum A projection from the column that often functions to separate the pollinia from the stigma and thus prevents self-pollination (the rostellum is actually a modified sterile third stigma). The rostellum may exude a viscidium (q.v.).

runner Horizontal stem that grows along or just below the surface of the soil.

saprophytic Plants, fungi, etc. that feed on dead organic matter.

scale leaf A leaf that is reduced to a small scale.

secondary woodland Woodland in which the continuity of tree cover has been broken for a substantial period of time.

self-pollinate Pollination of a flower by pollen taken from the same plant; usually used in the context of autogamy, where pollination is by pollen from the same flower, but sometimes also geitonogamy, where the pollen comes from another flower on the same plant.

sepal Outer row of 'perianth segments' that form the protective covering of the bud. In orchids they are either green or brightly coloured and form a conspicuous part of the flower.

sheathing leaf Main leaf on an orchid with a base that completely encircles the stem.

sinus Indentation between two lobes on the lip, used especially when describing the flowers of marsh orchids and spotted orchids in the genus *Dactylorhiza*.

speculum Pattern on the lip, often with a metallic lustre or shine, in the bee and spider orchids, genus *Ophrys*.

spur Sac-like extension of the base of the lip, which contains nectar in some species of orchid.

stamens Male reproductive organs of a flowering plant.

staminode Sterile stamen that forms a prominent shield-shaped structure within the flower of lady's slipper.

stigma Receptive surface of the female reproductive organs to which the pollen grains adhere.

stolon A horizontal stem, either growing along the surface or underground, not necessarily forming a new plant at the tip.

symbiosis An intimate relationship between two or more organisms; formerly used for a relationship where all participants derive benefits (mutualism, q.v.). but now used in a broader sense to include parasitism.

sympodial Pattern of growth in which the tip of the stem or rhizome either terminates in a flower spike or dies each year. Growth continues from buds formed at the base of the old stem.

synsepal Structure formed when the two lateral sepals are joined for almost their entire length, found in lady's slipper.

tetrads Groups of four pollen grains originating from a single 'mother' cell.

tetraploid Having four sets of chromosomes (see diploid).

tubers Swollen underground roots or stems, functioning as storage organs.

tubary An area where peat or turf is cut for fuel.

turlough Irish term, used for a seasonal lake on limestone in which the water level may fall dramatically during the summer.

vice-county Divisions of Britain and Ireland based on the nineteenth-century county boundaries that are used for biological recording; larger counties, such as Norfolk and Yorkshire, are divided up into smaller units.

viscidium (plural **viscidia**) Detachable sticky exudation from the rostellum that attaches the pollinia (sometimes via a short stalk, the caudicle) to a visiting insect.

'Vulnerable' Considered to be facing a high risk of extinction in the wild.

WCS Schedule 8 Wildlife & Countryside Act Schedule 8, which lists all the wild plants that are specially protected, making it illegal to damage or destroy them in any way (including removing flowers or leaves, or even seed).

Notes

CHAPTER 5

1 'Ireland with Emily', from *Collected Poems* by John Betjeman © 1955, 1958, 1962, 1964, 1968, 1970, 1979, 1981, 1982, 2001. Reproduced by permission of John Murray, an imprint of Hodder and Stoughton Ltd.

CHAPTER 7

1 T. Hey in *The Dalesman*, 1949.
2 *The Naturalist*, 1976.
3 Svante Malmgren, www.lidaforsgarden.com/orchids
4 Ibid.

CHAPTER 11

1 *The Botanist – The Botanical Diary of Eleanor Vachell (1879–1948)*, Eleanor Vachell. © National Museum of Wales, 2005.
2 *The Intelligence of Flowers*, Maurice Maeterlinck. SUNY Press, 2007.
3 Vachell, op. cit.
4 *The Orchid Trilogy*, Jocelyn Brooke (copyright © Jocelyn Brooke). Reproduced by permission of A. M. Heath & Co Ltd.

CHAPTER 13

1 'In Praise of Limestone', from *Collected Poems* by W. H. Auden © 1948, 1944. Faber & Faber, London.
2 'The Birkdale Nightingale', Jean Sprackland. Reproduced by permission of David Godwin Associates Ltd.

CHAPTER 16

1 Vachell, op. cit.
2 Vachell, op. cit.

Index

Wallace, Alfred Russel 40–2, 45
Waller, Mike 269–70
Walls, Robin 19, 22–4
Walters, Max 318, 329
Warburg, Edmund 105
Warner, Sylvia Townsend 28, 35
wasp orchids 79–80
Watson, Herbert 312
Webster, R.E. 20
Wedgewood, Mr 314
weed helleborines 287–9
weevils (*Stethobaris ovata*) 288
West, David 22
western marsh orchids 118–19
Whalsay 184–5, 189–91
Wharry, Olive 144
whimbrels 299
'white angels' 164
white helleborines 161
White, Gilbert 160, 168–9
whitethroats 29
Wilberforce, Bishop Samuel 41, 59
wild boars 221–2
wild thyme 203

Wildlife Trusts 252
Wilks, Hector 55–6
willow tits 197
willow warblers 169
Wilmott, Alfred 105, 108,
    315–16, 331
women, and orchids 144–5
wood rein orchids 164
wood warblers 169
woodcock orchids 21–3
woodlarks 167
Woolf, Virginia 168
Worcester Naturalists' Society
    313–14, 326
'wraith of the woods' 54
Wye Downs 70–2

Yell 185
Yorke, Bryan 251–4, 275–7
Yorkshire Naturalist Union 132, 134
Yorkshire Post 132
Young, Donald 258

Zugunruhe 225

A Note on the Author

Jon Dunn is a natural-history writer, photographer and tour leader based in Shetland, who travels worldwide searching for memorable wildlife encounters. A childhood exploring the water meadows and abandoned orchards of the Somerset Levels and the droves and ancient woods of Dorset's Blackmoor Vale spurred a lifelong passion for all things natural history. His Shetland home features otters on his doorstep, and summer evenings watching porpoises from the kitchen window. Once stalked by a mountain lion in Mexico's Sierra Madre Occidental, he generally prefers experiencing wildlife on his own terms and not as part of the food chain.

A Note on the Type

The text of this book is set Adobe Garamond. It is one of several versions of Garamond based on the designs of Claude Garamond. It is thought that Garamond based his font on Bembo, cut in 1495 by Francesco Griffo in collaboration with the Italian printer Aldus Manutius. Garamond types were first used in books printed in Paris around 1532. Many of the present-day versions of this type are based on the *Typi Academiae* of Jean Jannon cut in Sedan in 1615.

Claude Garamond was born in Paris in 1480. He learned how to cut type from his father and by the age of fifteen he was able to fashion steel punches the size of a pica with great precision. At the age of sixty he was commissioned by King Francis I to design a Greek alphabet, and for this he was given the honourable title of royal type founder. He died in 1561.